D1732312

PAUL FRIJTERS | GIGI FOSTER | MICHAEL BAKER

THE
GREAT
COVID
PANIC

WHAT HAPPENED,
WHY, AND WHAT TO DO NEXT

The Great Covid Panic:

What Happened, Why, And What To Do Next

by Paul Frijters, Gigi Foster, and Michael Baker

Copyright © 2021 by the Brownstone Institute,

Creative Common Attribution International 4.0.

ISBN: 9781630692773

PAUL FRIJTERS | GIGI FOSTER | MICHAEL BAKER

THE GREAT COVID PANIC

WHAT HAPPENED, WHY, AND WHAT TO DO NEXT

BROWNSTONE
INSTITUTE

CONTENTS

INTRODUCTION

The year 2020 was above all a year when billions of people were very afraid of something they could not see.

Will I die if I leave the house and catch the virus? Have I brought it inside? What if my children play outside? Will they catch it?

The neighbour is coughing — he should not be allowed out of his house.

That woman is looking strange — I wonder if she has it. She'd better keep her mask on.

It's windy today — someone told me it floats for days on the breeze so I'd better not go out.

Other people are scared too. I clear my throat in the supermarket line and everyone turns to look at me. A couple of them glare at me. I know what they're thinking.

The fearful wanted desperately to hear there was a solution – something to make the fear stop. They were drawn to anything that offered escape from the oppressive anxiety pounding in their heads. Spending vast sums from the government purse and withholding the joys of millions started to seem like sensible ideas when they came with the promise of alleviating the fear.

The elderly need to be locked away for their own good? Yep, no problem.

The neighbour committed suicide because she was lonely? Well, too bad, but at least she didn't infect us and let's hope no one else moves in soon.

Kids shouldn't go to school? Of course not, kids are vulnerable and need to be protected from germs.

We need to buy 100 million tests? Yes, definitely, and more if we need them, whatever the price.

The teenagers are partying? They should all go to prison for having fun when there's a deadly virus going around. Same with the crowds at the beaches. Arrest them all so the rest of us can be safe.

All those months of obsession crowded out attention, care, and concern for so much else. The fearful were the perfect victims for those with cooler heads who recognised that this was a unique opportunity to seize power and wealth for themselves. The paralysis of the fearful led in the end to heartless neglect, social disintegration, widespread theft, and totalitarian control.

The human costs were vast. Children depressed about their worth in life, told that their slightest expression of love and joy could kill their grandparents. Whole populations unhealthier, too afraid to exercise outside or actually prevented from doing so by government edict. Hospitals closed to normal caregiving and surgical procedures cancelled. Mass starvation in poor nations that cost the lives of millions and plunged millions more into misery, caused not by a virus but by active government policies. Hundreds of millions lost their jobs, life roles, freedom to travel and motivation to rise in the morning.

It could be said that in the first three months of 2020, billions of people on the planet turned their backs on life, living instead in a kind of twilight zone weakly illuminated by the vague hope of a vaccine. Many became zombie conformers, stuck in their homes and gradually losing their humanity.

In these pages we explain what happened, and carefully consider how to avoid a repeat next time — because of course there will be a next time and a next time after that. Only a fool believes that the memory of his own experience will protect future generations. Alas, new generations will be just like ours, subject to their own new terrors. Fresh-faced viruses and other threats will emerge that ambitious leaders will be willing to exploit to amass more power. Humanity has to learn to weather these coming fears without falling victim to the opportunism of the powerful.

In this book, the personal dramas of the Great Panic's individual protagonists are embedded in the narrative of a grand global story. The personal dramas tell stories of fear, hope, sacrifice, arrogance, greed and lust for power. The grand story considers the economy, the social system, science, politics and alternative scenarios for the end game and what comes next.

Little can be achieved by thinking about Covid as a public health problem created by bats and solved by vaccines. If we really want to understand it as an historical phenomenon, to understand how we humans reacted to it in the way we did and to learn something useful for the future, we need to fit together many pieces of a puzzle. Some of the pieces repose in the heart, while some are in the mind. Some are at a micro level, some are macro. Some are good and some are unspeakably evil. This book aims to make sense of it all, to make these disparate strands coherent so we see clearly what happened and deduce what must be done to avoid a similar tragedy in future.

The book is organised as follows. We begin with Phase 1, The Great Fear (approximately January-March 2020) by introducing the three representative characters who are defined by their response to the virus: Jane the conformer, James the decider and Jasmine the doubter. Jane and Jasmine will reappear periodically throughout the book to voice their personal experiences in each of the three major phases of the pandemic — the Great Fear, the Illusion of

Control and the End Games. James, meanwhile, will be a constant presence throughout the book. In his many guises he was the one with the power to stop the madness but instead kept it going for his own interests.

In Chapter 2, we give the reader a quick primer on viruses, how the human body responds to them and how we test for them. We explore the problems — rife during the pandemic — with statistical measures of virus severity, and how they can be misused to hoodwink and scare the public.

Then, in Chapter 3, we fold the knowledge of the first two chapters into the storyline of the Great Fear itself, showing how the extreme social distancing measures and other interventions practiced during the pandemic were destined, except in rare instances, to fail, and fail at great cost to humanity.

Phase 2, the Illusion of Control (approximately April-December 2020), begins in Chapter 4 with the voices of Jane and Jasmine again, revealing their contrasting experiences of the events that unfolded. There is a certain arbitrariness to using the end of 2020 as the cut-off point for the Illusion of Control because sadly, in many countries, that phase is still very much in full swing. However, it was around that time that new vaccines brought the hope of a return to normal life, enabling some governments to prepare the groundwork for walking back their interventions. Chapter 5 quantifies the sheer scale of the disaster caused by those misguided government interventions, while Chapter 6 shows how parts of the scientific establishment were complicit in the tragedy.

Chapter 7 lifts the lid on the crowd psychology behind the Great Covid Panic and its historical antecedents. Chapter 8 shows how modern political and economic structures made it possible for authoritarian governments and the barons of modern capitalism to ruthlessly exploit populations.

Then comes Phase 3, The End Games (January 2021-), where we again ask Jane and Jasmine to voice their experiences. In this phase, much of the world still clings tenaciously to its Covid obsession, just as the beneficiaries of the pandemic cling to their newfound wealth and power. In Chapters 10 and 11 we draw out lessons, provide alternative scenarios about what comes next, and offer our ideas on how similar mistakes can be avoided next time.

So with warnings to the faint of heart, we start by inviting the reader to relive the overwhelming force of the Panic as it hit and tightened its grip on the world at the start of 2020.

PHASE I

THE GREAT FEAR
(JANUARY-MARCH 2020)

THE EXPERIENCES OF JANE, JAMES, AND JASMINE DURING THE GREAT FEAR

JANE'S EXPERIENCE

Jane is a normal human being who scares easily and seeks security in compliance with rules. She expects her government to look after her in times of emergency and will do her best to protect her family and friends from trouble when she can.

There are Janes in all walks of life. She represents women and men from across the occupational spectrum: manual labourers, office workers, computer scientists, nurses, teachers, farmers, housewives, househusbands, taxi drivers, journalists, policemen. She represents people of all ages, races and cultural backgrounds.

In mid-February 2020, Jane first heard about a new virus from China that the World Health Organisation had, on the 11th of the month, officially designated as SARS-CoV-2, causing a disease called 'Covid-19'.[1]

She had never heard of this virus and this disease before, but it was presented to her on the TV and in social media as extremely dangerous. She saw ambulances speeding through the streets of Wuhan and Rome. She watched with horror scenes of dying patients, unconscious and strapped to

---

1 For simplicity and consistency, the virus is referred to as 'Covid' everywhere in this book.

ventilators. She heard that people who fell ill were immobilised for weeks and couldn't even lift their fingers. That the virus attacked the young and the old, the fit and the sedentary. That you could acquire it by getting too close to other people, touching your own face, or touching surfaces others had touched – even just using the same door handle that someone else had used to enter a building. She heard that some people who were infected might not even know it and could walk around infecting dozens of others. The jogger who just ran past her on the street could be the cause of her death or the deaths of her family members.

Fear gripped her as media coverage of the virus became more saturated, as story was heaped upon story, rumour followed rumour and the headlines became more shrill. Still, throughout February she managed to control her anxiety enough to keep going about her normal business. Her government was putting out some soothing messages. Health officials said it wasn't yet clear how deadly the virus was, and it probably wouldn't be so bad where she lived anyway. People around her were still living their lives as they always had.

On February 24, the UK government's reassuring messaging was exemplified by the BBC, which ran a story under the headline: 'Covid: UK "well prepared" to deal with cases, says government'.[2] In the same week and halfway across the world, Australia's government was expressing similar confidence. A February 22 headline in The Australian read: '"Virus Has Been Contained in Australia": Minister'.[3] Meanwhile, the President of the United States was not just confident but downright upbeat, tweeting on February 25: 'The coronavirus is very much under control in the USA. We are in contact with everyone and all relevant countries. CDC & World Health have been

---

2 https://www.bbc.com/news/uk-prepared
3 Wuth (2020).

working hard and very smart. Stock Market starting to look very good to me!'.[4]

Jane tried to be reassured by these stories, but nevertheless felt increasing unease as each day passed. If everything was under control, then why was the media so saturated with news about this one topic?

The news extended beyond the severity of the virus itself to its possible effects on the economy. Businesses warned of disrupted supply chains. In the UK, Australia and the US, she heard that her favourite brands were expecting shortages because factories in China had closed and container ship operators were cancelling voyages from Asia. Clothing chains were worrying aloud about running out of inventory. Even Apple was warning about shortages of iPhones.

Worse still, in her local area, people had begun panic buying. She saw on the news pictures of supermarkets in Melbourne and Sydney where customers were brawling in the aisles over toilet paper and stores had to limit sales to one pack per customer. In Hong Kong, three armed men held up a delivery truck and took off with 600 rolls.[5] Reports of customer fights, stockpiling and empty shelves were in all her newspapers. Crazy things that Jane had never heard of happening before seemed now to be happening everywhere.[6]

---

4 Qiu & Bouchard (2020), https://www.nytimes.com/2020/03/05/us/politics/trump-coronavirus-fact-check.html

5 https://www.bbc.com/news/world-asia-china-51527043

6 Knoll (2020), https://www.nytimes.com/2020/03/13/nyregion/coronavirus-panic-buying.html

The panic buying in some places was not to secure a huge stash of toilet rolls or tampons but to acquire protective gear like face masks. TV news showed anxious lines of people stretching around the block waiting to buy masks at inflated prices. Some governments were moved to issue warnings of heavy punishments for hoarding and overcharging. These warnings didn't seem to matter because the crazy stories kept coming. Pharmacy chains ran out of face masks and hand sanitiser was selling for multiples of its normal price.[7] Jane had heard of scalpers for concert tickets, but never for face masks or hand sanitiser.

And if things were under control, why was the stock market crashing? The Covid stories had infected the financial columns too and bleak news from stock markets often made the front pages. Jane had never really been interested in the stock market and had certainly never paid much attention to its daily ups and downs, but the media coverage was so intense that even she couldn't block it out. She found out in spite of herself, for example, that between February 19 and March 23 — just 33 days — the S&P 500 in America lost a third of its value.[8] She didn't really understand what that meant except that it was scaring a hell of a lot of people.

Increasingly, images flooded the newspapers she read, the websites she started following obsessively and the social media reports shared by Jane's friends and family. Facebook, TikTok, Instagram, Reddit, Twitter, you name it: they were all confirming that the virus was real, that it was deadly, that anyone could get it and spread it, and that it was either coming or was already here. The news told her that a heap of scientists had written to the government telling it to follow the example of China and lock down the whole population to prevent huge numbers of deaths.

It wasn't just the medical scientists who were talking this way. The professional economists and others were chiming in too. On March 4, Warwick McKibbon, an economist at the Australian National University, said his model showed the virus could kill as many as 100,000 people in Australia and 68 million worldwide.[9] Jane didn't stop to think about why an economist would know so much about the future course of an epidemic and how many it

---

7 Sakkal & Fowler (2020), https://www.theage.com.au/national/victoria/hand-sanitiser-price-doubles-face-mask-shortage-amid-coronavirus-panic-20200203-p53xfm.html

8 The S&P 500 closed at 2237 on 23 March, 2020, down 34% from its closing value of 3386 on 19 February.

9 Kehoe, J. (2020), https://www.afr.com/policy/economy/virus-could-kill-up-to-100-000-australians-20200303-p546a0

would kill, much less why an economist was in the business of actually modelling it anyway, but the guy was from a top university and was being quoted in respectable media sources so she figured he must know what he was talking about.

Yes, Jane thought, we need to close the borders, lock down and stay safe inside. First though, she joined the panicked mobs at the supermarket where she bought massive quantities of food, toilet paper, hand sanitiser and other necessities. She made clear to everyone in public that she expected the government to protect them all by locking down, and in her heart she hoped furiously that the virus would not catch her or her loved ones.

Let's relive the feelings experienced by real-life Janes, to give a visceral sense of Jane's Great Fear.

BOB PEPPERSTOCK'S STORY

Bob's story is based on that of a real person living in Vietnam.

I'm a New Zealand-born journalist and entrepreneur domiciled in Ho Chi Minh City, Vietnam, where I run a company specialising in English-language communications.

I will admit to you from the outset that I'm terrified of Covid. I mean, lock me up if you have to. I've now seen what it's done to people and I absolutely cannot accept the arguments of those who say Covid should be treated more like an ordinary flu. If I got it, I would not survive it. I am convinced of that, even though I'm only 55 and have no preexisting medical conditions that I know of. How do I know it would kill me? I can't say, just a strong feeling. Even if I am not going to die from it I still don't want to get the damn thing.

Our first case of Covid in Vietnam was diagnosed on January 23 in the north of the country, and even though Saigon where I am is in the south, it gave me the chills, because I knew it was on its way down here.

Vietnam can respond to Covid more easily than in other countries because it's a Communist state and has kind of what I'd call a 'surveillance and snitching' culture. So ordinary people are encouraged and empowered to report anything suspicious to the authorities, who can react quickly. In the case of Covid the government can lock down the hotspots and move the infected and their close contacts to quarantine camps where they are detained in isolation from the rest of the community. This is what happened in March 2020 and by the end of the month more than 100,000 were in camps.

Was I comfortable with this? Coming from a Western democratic culture, of course this was new to me. I was really afraid of being woken up at 5 o'clock in the morning KGB-style and taken away to a camp, not because I had Covid but because I had been in the wrong place at the wrong time. And if I did go to a camp then I thought my chances of getting Covid would be about 100%. The camps were awful. I heard stories. People were crammed together and the food was shit.

Still, it's a good thing that the government was acting decisively. I saw the pictures on TV of what was happening in America and the cavalier attitude of the government there, and I was happy Vietnam took the virus seriously.

SUSAN FORRESTER'S STORY

Susan's story is based on that of a real person, a semi-retired nurse in Philadelphia, PA in the USA.

What a horrible epidemic. There aren't too many of us in the extended family who haven't been affected in some way by illness, a job loss, eviction, or plans going off the rails.

The number of infections went up very quickly and on the last day of March we had almost 250 new cases in Philadelphia. The county we live in, Montgomery, had the highest number of cases in the city.

The governor of Pennsylvania and the local politicians in Philadelphia were pretty quick to react. They stopped flights coming in from Italy, canceled a lot of gatherings and closed the schools. They were also pretty good with their messaging. By March 23 we were already under a stay-at-home order.

I stopped working and my husband Mitchell, who is a programmer with a financial services firm, worked mostly from home. So we were sheltering in place pretty much from the beginning of the epidemic here and that was fine with me.

My greatest worry at the time was my daughter Jennifer, who was 16 weeks' pregnant with her second child and living in the New York area where the epidemic was getting really out of hand. Her husband Jay is a doctor and was assigned to work in the White Plains Hospital directly with Covid patients. I was very anxious that he would be infected and sure enough he was. A lot of other personnel on that floor were infected too. He was very sick for a week but then he got better quickly. He's a young, strong guy.

It was impossible not to be on edge all the time. I drove up to White Plains twice before the end of March to babysit. Jennifer was working from home but even so she was exhausted just about all the time. It wasn't just the physical exhaustion but the emotional toll as well.

My cousin Jim in Maryland also got pretty sick with Covid, high fevers and the rest of it, and he recovered more slowly than Jay did. He might have gotten Covid from Mark, his oldest son, who was overseas when the virus broke out and seems to have brought it home with him. Mark and his mom both got light cases. They did the sensible thing and sent their younger son away while they were sick.

We're feeling blessed because we got through it without catching the virus even though we still had to make trips outside to Costco occasionally. The grocery stock-ups were a lot bigger than they had been before. Mitchell was coming home with the back of the SUV packed almost to the roof. We're also ordering in Chinese a couple of times a week. We enjoyed eating out and that's something we missed.

If you were to ask me how the president handled the whole thing, I'd have to say he wasn't the best person we could have had in charge of a pandemic. He just completely got off on the wrong tone with his messaging.

People in America listen to their president when there is a crisis. I've sung in choirs all my life and I think the president needs to be like a choir conductor, making sure everyone knows which note to hit. That's exactly what Obama did during Ebola, he had this way of calming people down and making them feel he was in control, while Cuomo and Christie were jumping up and down in panic.

WILLIAM WILKERSON'S STORY

William's story is based on that of a real person.

I was born in Australia but I established myself as a career economist in the US. My American colleagues prefer to call me a 'policy wonk' rather than an economist. This makes me sound a little dull, like Monty Python's accountant, the one who has a secret yearning to be a lion tamer.

I went to graduate school in England, got an economics PhD and secured an assistant professorship position at an American West Coast university. From there, I built connections with influential people in my home country of Australia, accepting a variety of affiliate positions at Australian universities and think tanks.

By early 2020 when Covid hit, I was pretty well known in Australian policy circles. I was a bit naughty about calling myself a 'professor' when engaging with the media, since really my academic rank is a 'lecturer' in Australian parlance, but it was a harmless little fib that gave my messages more weight.

I found myself part of a group that espoused what was essentially the road already being taken by the politicians: to immediately close borders, get the kids out of schools, get everyone working from home, close down all venues where people were entertained such as restaurants, shopping malls, pubs and clubs, and suspend lots of other normal activities. By the end of March, federal and state governments in Australia were already busy locking down the economy, just as the Chinese had done.

I just want to add that in April I was to assist my group of like-minded economists in drafting and securing signatures for an open letter arguing the case that saving lives from Covid was tantamount to saving the economy. We rejected the arguments of a handful of maverick economists who were questioning lockdowns, and argued instead that in order to restore the economy to health as quickly as possible the strictest measures were needed to control the virus first.

On social media I spent the following few months on the offensive, flaying contrarian economists mercilessly. We stuck to social media rather than direct engagement. Our opponents challenged us to open debates but I wasn't up for that. It might have been bad for my career.

JAMES' EXPERIENCE

In an emergency, James likes to think he keeps his head cool and figures out what should be done.

James was close to or actually in government, and part of the group advising and deciding on key steps in the crisis that affected large numbers of people. There were Jameses at high-level positions in government ministries, company boardrooms, fortuitously positioned start-up firms, government service departments, political groups and universities. Hundreds of people in every country were Jameses — the leaders of the main political parties, elected officials at all levels of government, senior civil servants, pharmaceutical company executives, editors of state media, scientific advisors, coordinators of emergency response teams, health service managers and chiefs of police.

James heard of the new virus from the media, like nearly everyone else. His role in decision-making meant that he couldn't remain on the sidelines and watch. He had to act. And to make his actions sensible he was expected to understand the complexities of science. Sometimes he succeeded in grasping the difference between, say, case fatality rates and infection fatality rates, but often he struggled to see connections. For example, he might have had problems seeing how suppressed replication numbers relate to herd immunity. Or he might have struggled to understand the whole possibility space when evaluating whether or not implementing a track-and-trace regime for all infections was realistic.

What he understood very clearly though was that he would get blamed if people died from this virus on his watch. So, while he had a private professional opinion, he was aware of the huge potential threat to his career of being seen not to have acted or to have done the wrong thing. James had to cover his ass, and he didn't have much time to do it.

It soon became clear to James that doing nothing or doing very little would constitute enough of a 'wrong thing' to have him portrayed on national media not just as delinquent or incompetent, but as a murderer. Whatever needed to be done, it had to be significant, highly visible and presented with great confidence. It had to have scientific backing. Locking down the whole population seemed to be an option that could check all the boxes. Plus, the Chinese seemed to have done it successfully so if it worked there, he reasoned, then why not here?

So James became an advocate of lockdowns, though at first reluctantly, since most of the advice emanating from previous government and scientific inquiries about what to do in a health crisis favoured focussing on those most at risk from a disease rather than incarcerating the whole population. Still, the waves of petitions, media reports and clamourings from all sides convinced James that indeed something big had to be done. Lockdowns were big.

He started forming committees, planning contingencies, running models, producing reports, issuing guidelines and writing media releases. As the whole machinery of state clanked into action for the purpose of shutting its own society down, he increasingly felt that he was doing his bit to protect his country from catastrophe.

The UK provides a good illustration of how quickly James was out of the gate. As early as February 10, 2020, the UK government's Department of Health was brandishing its new Health Protections (Coronavirus) Regulations, which gave NHS staff dealing with suspected Covid cases 'strengthened powers' to keep individuals in isolation if medical professionals believed they posed 'a reasonable risk' of being infected.[10] This meant that someone suspected by an NHS staff person of being a Covid case could not simply discharge herself from a hospital against medical advice, as she could do if, say, she had just had surgery.

After a month of escalating rhetoric, the UK government took another step and banned mass gatherings on March 14. On March 18 it announced that all children had to be kept home from school, except for those whose parents had jobs deemed by the government to be important. On March 23 it closed businesses and implemented a three-week 'stay-at-home' order. These steps were deemed to require the police to have special powers to enforce and issue fines, which were duly granted on March 26.

How did all of this happen in just 12 days? Of the Jameses behind these decisions, arguably none was more important than Neil Ferguson, an epidemiologist at Imperial College London, and member of the scientific panel advising the UK government.[11] Ferguson had already attained some notoriety during previous epidemics owing to his penchant for modelling the transmission of infections and then talking up the most extreme estimates of possible deaths.[12]

---

10 Health Protection (Coronavirus) Regulations 2020, https://www.legislation.gov.uk/uksi/2020/129/contents/made

11 This panel was the Scientific Advisory Group for Emergencies (SAGE).

12 For example, in 2009, Ferguson's over-the-top range of estimates for the case fatality rate of swine flu resulted in a worst-case prediction of 65,000 deaths in the UK. Only 457 people died. Earlier, in 2001, his modelling on the foot and mouth outbreak resulted in the mass culling of more than 6 million farm animals and a loss to the UK economy of millions of pounds. Experts later said that Ferguson's model was seriously flawed and much of the culling had been unnecessary.

Despite his dodgy track record as a modeller and his reputation as a scare-monger, there was no way Ferguson and his colleagues were going to let a good virus go to waste. The computers modelling Covid at Imperial College hummed tirelessly through the early months of 2020, culminating in a famous report released on March 16 that predicted 510,000 deaths in the UK, 2.2 million in the US and 40 million worldwide unless governments took radical action. The number of severe cases, according to Ferguson's models, would be of such magnitude that the supply of ICU or critical care beds would be overwhelmed.[13] The only way to prevent this, he said, was to quickly employ suppression strategies, which amounted to a total lockdown of the country.

A huge worldwide media blitz ensued, and within days Ferguson's name was everywhere. By March 23, a week after the release of the Imperial College report and with almost no serious attempt at senior levels of government to question its projections or its recommendations, the UK was put to sleep.

The breakneck speed of the capitulation in the UK was by no means unique. On March 19, Governor Gavin Newsom of California became the first US governor to issue a statewide stay-at-home order. For getting out ahead of the rest of the country by locking down his state's 40 million inhab-itants, Newsom earned widespread admiration for decisiveness that could be parlayed into political support. His snap decision was made in response to frightening pictures coming in from Italy and New York, and to California's own data showing a rapid rise of case rates. Something drastic had to be done, and in the opinion of Newsom's public health guru, a paediatrician named Mark Ghaly, a stay-at-home order was the only game in town.

The problem for Newsom and Ghaly though was that California is home to a lot of smart people likely to baulk at giving up their freedoms without a blockbuster of a reason. Newsom obliged with one. He realised that to make

---

13 Imperial College COVID-19 Response Team (2020).

the public receptive to being imprisoned he had to frighten the crap out of everyone, which he accomplished by publicly releasing a letter he'd written to the president mentioning the prediction that 56% of California's population would be infected over the ensuing eight weeks.

At the other side of the world, Australia was in a similar condition of panic by the middle of March. In particular, Victoria — Australia's second-most populous state — was to provide a stunning illustration of how leaders, fed a daily diet of 'science' by health bureaucrats, held the public in thrall, acquired dictatorial powers and used them to turn the screws on their populations as the year went on.

In Victoria, the opportunity for a quick power grab fell initially to the Premier, Dan Andrews, who relied for his advice on Covid countermeasures on Brett Sutton, a general practitioner with no PhD and an unflattering field record.

The shortcomings of Sutton's CV mattered little when it came to wielding authority over Victoria's 6.7 million citizens. Sutton kicked off the Covid season in earnest on Sunday, March 15 by advising people in an article he wrote for Melbourne's *Herald Sun* newspaper to keep on hand a supply of essential items. 'You don't need too much, just a two-week supply of food and a 60-day supply of prescription medication.' This caused a run on supermarkets and pharmacies and the images of panic buying went viral around the world.[14] It also earned Sutton a rebuke from grocery retailers and pharmacies.

The next day Sutton tried to project calm by coming out against school closures, a position he reversed a week later by closing every school in the state. They didn't reopen again for all students until June 9.

The public was too frightened and distracted even to suspect that Sutton might be incompetent, and he was already warming to his role as scaremonger-in-chief. Speaking to the media with Health Minister Jenny Mikakos on March 24, he solemnly informed the assembled gathering that

---

14 Sutton (2020).

the department's models indicated thousands of Victorians could die from the virus, which would only be contained if people diligently followed the government's social distancing directives. The pair were only able to report the worst-case scenario for deaths: alternative estimates were conveniently not to hand.[15] By the end of the month, Victoria, along with the rest of Australia and thousands of other regions worldwide, was buttoned up and locked down.

Among the first concrete actions James took in most countries was to give orders to quarantine incoming passengers from overseas, which he was easily able to extend later to shutting them out altogether. Border restrictions were an important first step. Not only did blocking the borders eliminate the potential for the virus to be imported from outside the country, but they could also be politically useful. In a number of countries where weariness with tourism and xenophobia had already been mounting before Covid, the virus provided a popular excuse for putting a summary end to foreign arrivals.

Thailand, one of the world's most heavily visited countries, provided a spectacular example of how those with the most to lose from closing their borders were among the quickest to do so, under James's watch. Throughout February and March, the Thai government implemented increasingly stringent screening procedures at its international gateways, which many of the intended targets — including Thai nationals returning home from jobs abroad — used ingenious methods to avoid. Screening, and then forced quarantining, were followed by a complete ban on all incoming flights on April 4. At a stroke, the government deleted about 10% of the country's GDP, all in the name of 'protecting the people'.

If opinion polls are anything to go by, most Thais applauded, although there is reason to believe that many were not aware of how important the tourist dollars were until they finished up on food lines after their own employers

---

15 Smith (2020).

went out of business. Within a few months of the border closures there was massive unemployment and by mid-2021 ordinary Thais were crying uncle, but by then it was far too late: the economy lay in ruins and the food lines stretched for whole city blocks.[16] James, already the 'strong man' in most Southeast Asian countries, had discovered in Covid the perfect excuse to secure his grip and get his enemies off the street.[17] By striking early, he was catching people at their most vulnerable.

'Protecting his country' was even the catch cry of the most opportunistic Jameses in the business community, those who have a special knack for seeing and seizing a moment, who know it may be fleeting and that speed is essential before the window of opportunity slams shut. These entrepreneurial Jameses were in plentiful supply during the Great Fear.

James swooped in as panicked governments relaxed regulations and suspended normal due diligence in a desperate bid to acquire the medical wherewithal they thought they needed to fight the pandemic. Conditions became perfect for cronyism, corruption, counterfeiting and outright theft.

The Food and Drug Administration (FDA) in the US was just one of the national agencies that successively relaxed its certification standard for imported personal protective equipment (PPE), enabling a whole cottage industry to spring up consisting of middlemen with no prior connection to the healthcare industry importing supplies of PPE.[18] Most of this was merchandise that they found through the assistance of their own intermediaries and connections around the world. A lot of it was counterfeit. A lot of it was

---

16 The absurdly low official figures for unemployment in Thailand are partly attributable to their exclusion of workers in the 'informal' economy, which is responsible for as much as 50% of GDP. https://www.bangkokpost.com/business/2120831/q1-jobless-rate-at-12-year-high-amid-virus-outbreaks

17 Although most countries in Southeast Asia with the exception of Myanmar, Laos and Vietnam have multiple parties, elections, parliaments and other trappings of democracy, power is effectively concentrated in one party led by a 'strong man' of James' character. With the arrival of Covid, James had little difficulty tightening his grip.

18 https://www.fda.gov/media/136403/download. See also: https://www.porterwright.com/media/importing-masks-and-respirators-from-overseas-during-covid-19-under-fdas-relaxed-rules/

legitimately branded goods produced by reputable companies like 3M and Honeywell that had been mysteriously diverted outside normal distribution channels. Much of it was sitting in warehouses in China and various far-flung parts of the world.[19]

Many governments created optimal conditions for corruption by simply dropping their normal competitive bidding processes and handing out contracts to well-connected businessmen, without transparency or oversight. This practice, which flourished throughout 2020 and into 2021, was as much a global pandemic as the virus itself. It resulted in the siphoning of billions of dollars' worth of government contract money to the friends and family members of government officials.[20]

The shenanigans knew no geographic bounds. It went on in developed countries and developing ones, in large countries and small ones. In regions like South America, Central Asia and Eastern Europe, where corruption was already recognised as a particularly big problem before the pandemic, Covid presented itself to James as an extra-special payday.[21]

The beauty of it all was that James didn't always even have to supply the right merchandise. In Slovenia for example, Joc Pečečnik, a gambling mogul and one of the country's wealthiest men, had wasted no time positioning himself in front of the government's fire hose of PPE cash. He was one of several well-connected beneficiaries of an abrupt suspension of Slovenia's

---

19 The free-for-all market for PPE has been investigated and documented in many sources. See, for example, Tanfani & Horwitz (2020), https://www.reuters.com/article/us-health-coronavirus-masks-specialrepor-idUSKBN21I32E; McSwane (2020), https://www.propublica.org/article/the-secret-absurd-world-of-coronavirus-mask-traders-and-middlemen-trying-to-get-rich-off-government-money; and Salman et al. (2020), https://www.usatoday.com/in-depth/news/investigations/2020/07/23/covid-ppe-face-mask-shortage-draws-new-companies-us-contracts/5459884002/

20 See, for example, Transparency International (2020), https://images.transparencycdn.org/images/COVID-19-Documented-corruption-and-malfeasance-cases.pdf; Almonte & Bates (2020), https://www.corporatecomplianceinsights.com/corruption-coronavirus-latin-america-covid/; and Collins et al. (2020), https://www.thetimes.co.uk/article/tory-backers-net-180m-ppe-deals-xwd5kmnqr

21 Montenegro Almonte & Bates (2020), https://www.corporatecomplianceinsights.com/corruption-coronavirus-latin-america-covid/

strict competitive government procurement system in March 2020.[22]

Pečečnik's contract was for about €25 million to supply masks, gloves, goggles and protective clothing, even though he had no previous experience in the healthcare sector. He did, however, 'know people' in China who could provide the gear. When a consignment of masks and gowns arrived, Pečečnik reportedly bragged that the goods had been stolen. Worse, despite labelling that indicated the merchandise consisted of the required FFP2 masks, it turned out that Pečečnik's packages contained only ordinary surgical masks. The government decided to accept the merchandise anyway.[23]

Pečečnik's multi-million-euro piece of the action was not the only one in Slovenia that week. His contract was worth only 35% of the total that the government awarded. Another businessman with no link to the healthcare industry but with strong political connections was Miran Blatnik, CEO of a company called XAN-MAX that sells mangosteen juice. His contract was secured after a good word from the prime minister's wife.[24]

Sometimes, entrepreneurial James was so eager to gorge himself on the taxpayer's cash being tossed out that he overstepped and had to be reined in to spare government James' blushes. In the US, a company called Blue Flame Medical that had been incorporated in Delaware on March 23 by a couple of Republican fundraisers with no connection to the healthcare industry, won contracts from both California and Maryland to supply masks. On March 26, just three days after the company was formed, California's treasury wired US$456.9 million into Blue Flame's just-opened bank account

22 Delić & Zwitter (2020), https://www.occrp.org/en/coronavirus/opaque-coronavirus-procurement-deal-hands-millions-to-slovenian-gambling-mogul

23 Motoh (2020), https://china-cee.eu/2020/05/06/slovenia-social-briefing-purchases-of-medical-equipment-related-corruption-suspicions-and-the-public-response/; Delić (2020), https://www.theballot.world/articles/where-a-media-crisis-and-a-health-crisis-collide

24 https://www.total-slovenia-news.com/politics/6171-ministry-cancels-controversial-ventilator-delivery-contract-with-geneplanet

as a 75% down payment for 100 million masks. Hours later, it recalled the money and the masks never came. Maryland also subsequently cancelled its contract with Blue Flame without the order being filled. The company was placed under investigation by the US Justice Department.[25]

So while politicians, their public health advisors and others in the right place at the right time made a grab for power, the final days of March also saw a rush to the public feed trough, where opportunistic businessmen used taxpayer funds to enrich themselves.

This practice was to snowball during the Illusion of Control phase, as we shall see.

JASMINE'S EXPERIENCE

Jasmine was always an independent thinker, unmoved by fear and highly self-reliant. She was in the habit of making up her own mind about things and was naturally suspicious of believing something when others insisted that it had to be so. On many previous occasions, she had thought that nearly everyone else was wrong and she was right. She felt that way about religion, about politics, and even about most of what passed for science.

There were not that many Jasmines in January-March 2020, but in every walk of life there were a few. She was some of the top scientists, civil servants, politicians and business leaders. She was represented in a few housewives, househusbands, garbage collectors, police officers, salon owners, tradesmen and truck drivers. Some Jasmines were experts in their fields, while others simply had their own independent worldview that wasn't easily shaken by fear.

Like Jane and James, Jasmine heard of the new virus from the media.

25 Hamburger & Eilperin (2020), https://www.washingtonpost.com/politics/justice-department-investigates-blue-flame-medical-after-claims-it-failed-to-provide-masks-ventilators-to-maryland-california/2020/05/06/e30b5224-8fa1-11ea-9e23-6914ee410a5f_story.html; Rosenhall (2020), https://calmatters.org/health/coronavirus/2020/05/california-mask-deal-blue-flame-collapsed-republican-vendor-maryland-porter-gula-thomas/

She couldn't see what the fuss was about. New dangerous viruses and bacteria came and went like the seasons. She knew each season there were new flu viruses and she knew that humans lived in a veritable soup of viruses and bacteria. Looking at the early statistics, she saw that nearly all victims who died were old and had other health problems. Besides, there was not an overwhelming number of them. Although there had been relatively low numbers of deaths in Wuhan, Singapore, Japan and the other places where this new virus had first appeared, she wondered why so many people seemed to think this was a huge threat. Of course, if there was a sensible and practical way to avoid unnecessary deaths and suffering, great, but this was not the plague and should not be treated as such.

To her great surprise and horror, most of her colleagues and friends, even including those she respected greatly and considered extremely intelligent and broad-minded, became obsessed and fearful about this new virus. Daily they would send her media stories or new scientific papers on what a terrible threat this virus was. Most of them she dismissed after a cursory reading and some after a more thorough examination. She was perplexed by their warnings of doom and came to the conclusion that she was witnessing the onset of mass hysteria. She spoke out against it, telling colleagues, family and friends not to get so carried away.

To her amazement, her own government steamrolled the country into a lockdown, which she knew would at best postpone infections while doing huge damage to everyone. Moreover, she learned this was now done in the name of 'following the science' or 'protecting the health services', and that it was being declared immoral not to follow the new rules and regulations. She had to pinch herself a few times, asking others she knew if they thought either she or the world had gone mad. After double-checking what she could, she decided it was the latter. While many Jasmines did not openly speak out, and some veered off toward conspiracy theories, others in all walks of life resolved to do their bit to try to prevent a disaster.

Consider three real-life examples of Jasmine's experiences.

NEIL'S STORY

I am 21 years old, studying physics and music at Boston University. It is customary nowadays that when a news item sufficiently large to make it into public consciousness emerges, it is accompanied (in millennial circles) by memes. I happen to love memes, so in February 2020 as I went about my business at the university in Boston, I laughed as people joked about how someone in China ate a bat, and how 2020 was shaping up to be the worst year since 1939. Little did I know how bad things were to become. In one month the Coronavirus went from a casual conversation topic to such a serious health concern that Boston University closed its dormitories and sent everyone home to learn online. There was a stay-at-home order in Boston and new rules enforcing public masking and social distancing.

My family lives in Sydney, Australia, so when I came back I completed the latter half of my semester online, at night. Because of the time zone difference between Boston and Sydney, which throughout the year varies between 14 and 16 hours, my average daily routine consisted of classes from 11pm to 3am. My attitude changed. I was no longer learning — I was trying not to fail. My university was kind enough to give us a credit/no credit option instead of the normal letter grades. It is to my mind one of the only responsible policy decisions they have made in this period.

I have since come to realize that you can get attached to a place or a lifestyle in much the same way as a person. So when I was pulled away from my life in university, it was in some ways similar to being forcibly separated from someone you love. Of course, I also love my friends whom I left behind. This has no doubt contributed to the frequent periods of intense anger and frustration I have experienced which are manageable only with long runs and a copious supply of unripped paper. But I am also angry at *people* in an abstract sense (and some individuals too) for the nonsense they've absorbed and regurgitated, motivated in large part by fear.

Even before many of the facts about Covid were known, it was obvious that fear tactics were being employed by media channels to agitate people. I imagine this was a phenomenally successful strategy for selling news. People who in normal times would complain at the unreliability of the media and the systemic bias of our leadership were suddenly willing to give themselves wholeheartedly to the narrative being presented by those organizations. I was fortunate or unfortunate enough (I have not yet decided which) to have been presented with a different story: that lockdowns do more damage than they help prevent. It was a viewpoint which would become increasingly obvious to me as the pandemic progressed, particularly in Australia where in the first several months there were fewer total deaths from Covid than there were daily deaths from other causes (must have been the lockdowns, right? Ha ha.). But it is not a viewpoint that has been adopted by our governments or, I'm sorry to say, most of my friends. As I will explain later, this has been a cause of major conflict for me.

CARMEN'S STORY

I am a 22-year-old student of sociology at the University of Amsterdam. The first time I heard about Corona was somewhere early in January 2020. A friend mentioned a new virus in China. My first reaction was – well, this sounds a lot like the swine Flu, Ebola or Hong Kong flu … everyone reacts very scared but not many people will die, and no one will think much about it.

My second encounter with Corona was at the end of January, when several of my classmates asked for the exams to be postponed because they had 'Corona-like' symptoms. The response of my professor was that the same number of people were sick this year as there were every year in January and that if you were sick you had to sit either the exam or the retake just like every other student. At the time I thought these students were just using the news about a new virus to get out of an exam, something that I understood and even respected in a way, being a student myself.

In February I went on a ski trip in the south of France with a few fellow students, after which I was quite sick for a week or two – I assumed that this was the result of cold weather, little sleep and après ski. A few weeks afterwards, when infections started to rise in France and Italy, my flatmates and fellow students started to ask questions like "Where exactly did you go skiing again?"

At the beginning of March I celebrated carnaval in Eindhoven and then a week later news that Corona was spreading in the Netherlands absolutely exploded. At the same time, my friends, flatmates, co-students and professors talked about the lockdown in China. "They're locking people in their homes, they closed everything – we would never do that, it's completely ridiculous and undemocratic!"

Across multiple people in my immediate circle who got infected with Corona, the worst symptoms any of them had were reported by a girl who was sick in bed for two weeks and had lower stamina afterwards. The same girl's grandmother, a woman of 82 who had just been in the hospital for a serious kidney operation, contracted Corona and had a slight cough for two weeks.

Of course, you also hear about the people who were 'absolutely fine' and suddenly dropped dead, but for the most part it seemed that the people dying of Corona only had a few years left anyway. I made the mistake of saying something to that effect to a fellow student, who proceeded to shout at me that I 'only cared about myself' and that I was 'heartless.' Trying to explain how horrible the lockdown was for the health and security of others made no difference, and I was subsequently told that I should 'shut up about the economy, some things are more important.'

What angered me the most about the lockdown was the level of hypocrisy that I witnessed, day in and day out. From someone who berated me for not following social distancing rules after she had a party with 17 people, to the acquaintance who called the police on a group of students barbecuing outside even though she had hugged a number of people she didn't live with the week before, I felt like people only followed the rules when it was convenient. That was the worst – people were constantly shaming each other for not following the lockdown restrictions and claiming how much better they were for following them.

JIAXUAN ZHANG'S STORY

Jiaxuan Zhang is an imagined member of the research team of Sunetra
Gupta, who is a professor of theoretical epidemiology at Oxford University.
I'm perplexed by what happened in the UK in March 2020. As a member of
an epidemiological research team at one of the world's best universities (I'm
currently working on my doctoral thesis), I find it difficult to fathom, actually
I'm angry, that there was so much resistance among decision makers at the
highest levels, including the prime minister, to accept that the science around
Covid was still unsettled at the time and that to do something as radical and
potentially destructive as a lockdown was surely jumping the gun.

Or maybe they did accept it but they believed the absolute worst-case
scenario was the only one that was politically feasible to act on.

So there we were by the 25th of the month with the dire numbers that the
Imperial College team put out there — 510,000 deaths in the UK and an
overwhelmed hospital system — already seemingly biblical in their authority.
I think Sunetra felt, and I agreed, that it was really important to push for a
careful assessment of alternative possibilities.

It wasn't just lives that were at stake because of Covid. My team was very
much aware of the negative impact that a lockdown would have on common
working people and particularly on those who were in lower socioeconomic
groups. It seemed to us that the potential for hardship was just massive. No
one seemed to be focused on that. There was just this blind belief, this panic,
to take the most radical action to save people from Covid.

We had a model at Oxford that fitted the data and was telling us that the
outcomes in terms of serious illness and mortality from Covid could be a lot
better than what the Imperial people were suggesting. There was a strong
possibility that the virus had already been circulating in the UK since about
mid-January and that many more people had already been exposed and
infected than assumed in the Imperial model.

If that was correct, then the pressure on the hospital system going forward would be a lot less than the Imperial model indicated. It meant that a suppression strategy was probably not warranted and that targeted mitigation, which would have much less impact on normal human activity, was the way to go. But we needed to test a lot more people for antibodies, and quickly, to find out if we were right.

Disappointingly, the media blew it all up into a conflict between granny killers — that was Sunetra — and humanitarians. Science went out the window, and it has stayed there ever since.

REFLECTIONS ON THE GREAT FEAR

Take time out for a moment from the emotional maelstrom of the Great Panic that took hold in January-March 2020. Put the fear and the momentous events of those three months to one side. Let us step back and take our time to analyse what happened, and what might have happened if we had held our nerve.

In this chapter we consider the most important things that a rational person of the time would like to have known. We explore what fear is and what it does to people, and how this might cause them to react in particular ways to a new health threat about which little is known but which seems to be both easy to catch and deadly.

We explore what viruses are, how we acquire them, and how the human body destroys the ones it doesn't want around. We consider what the smart response to a new virus would be at each level of government, and gauge the capacity of the social system to cope with different strategies.

SOWING FEAR: THE LOCKDOWN MARKETING STRATEGY

Fear is an emotion everyone experiences. In mammals, fear's home is the amygdala in the limbic system and, evolutionarily speaking, it is a very old part of the brain. Its function is to alert the animal to a threat to life or something else of value, such as offspring, territory or mating rights.

One of the important rules about how fear works is that the fearful individual focuses obsessively on the feared object. There is a good evolutionary reason for this: when in danger it is important not to get distracted by other things and to focus 100 percent on the threat and how it can be extinguished. Politicians, businessmen and others in the right place at the right time can exploit this by promising fearful people a solution and then robbing them when they are not looking. Such robberies need not be confined to money — much more darkly, they can be stealing things that are harder won and harder to win back, like personal freedoms and human rights.

Another important rule about fear is that fearful individuals are not usually very good at weighing probabilities objectively. A person's perception of the importance of a threat is directly related to the number of incoming messages about it that she receives. Dangers with an infinitesimally small likelihood, like an asteroid hitting the earth, can be perceived as imminent by a person under continuous bombardment with images of an asteroid hitting the earth.

Incompetence at measuring the seriousness of a threat other than by the number of related messages that arrive also means that the objects people fear are somewhat random and highly socially determined. Fear comes in social waves, like fashion trends. Simply by talking about what they fear and incessantly sharing images about those things, people spread their own private fears to those they know. The nature of fear as a contagious social wave is juiced by imagery, because images of things to fear are easier than verbal expressions to disseminate and understand.

The Great Panic illustrated both the tendency of those in power to use fear to extend their control, and the social wave nature of fear itself. Images of sick patients created a panic inside China. Images of Chinese people being dragged away for the supposed safety of others went viral, giving the entire world an image of how authorities needed to react to the threat. Day after day, TV audiences were pelted with images of immobilised patients being wheeled into hospital emergency rooms. The message was, 'This is what becomes of you if you don't do what the government demands'.

Governments, we now know, deliberately created images to amplify danger, such as when UK health authorities used 'panic posters' on many street corners with pictures of struggling hospital patients wearing ventilator masks and carrying captions that would invoke shame, guilt and general stress, like 'look him in the eyes and tell him you always keep a safe distance.'[26]

---

26 https://timeforrecovery.org/fear/

Graphs depicting projections of large numbers of deaths, often based on worst-case scenarios, were presented to parliamentary committees to persuade legislators — as if they needed any persuading — to restrict their people's freedoms and subject them to greater government control. In May 2021, some of the UK scientists involved in those early fear campaigns apologised for being unethical and totalitarian.[27]

The public was also subjected daily to images of increasingly rumpled and bleary-eyed politicians behind microphones at their media conferences, shoulder to shoulder with their competitively rumpled and bleary-eyed health advisors, delivering ever-worsening news and using it to justify more severe directives to control people's behaviour.

Another fundamental tendency of fear is to make people eager to sacrifice something in order to defeat the perceived threat. Strange as it is to a rational mind, fearful people automatically presume that if they give up something important to them, then this action will help to reduce or remove the peril. For this reason, throughout human history, people have sacrificed the things most dear to them in order to avert a perceived threat.

The Aztec civilisation in Mexico, for example, believed that the sun god was in constant battle with darkness, and if darkness triumphed the world would end. To prevent that undesirable state of affairs, the sun god had to stay on the move, which the Aztecs had figured out required an energy output that could only be sated by a steady diet of their citizenry's blood and guts.

Prehistoric farmers sacrificed their children to 'buy' rain or a good harvest, believing that a satisfactory level of appeasement would avert starvation. Greeks, Romans, Vikings and Chinese sacrificed meat and other foods in exchange for luck in war, luck in love, or anything else they fancied.

This logic underpins the first part of the Politician's Syllogism: 'We must do

27 Raynor (2021), https://www.telegraph.co.uk/news/2021/05/14/scientists-admit-totalitarian-use-fear-control-behaviour-covid/

something.'[28] It is not truly rational to believe that every problem necessitates the doing of something, but to a fearful person the desire to have something done is overwhelming. Rationality would demand an analysis of what can actually be done about a threat, which has the potential to conclude that *nothing* can be done. One can fear a hurricane but logic does not dictate that something can be done to change its course. Yet to a person possessed by fear of the hurricane, that is unacceptable. Almost any scheme that purports to redirect the hurricane by offering up some kind of sacrifice will start to sound very appealing.

We saw this tendency repeatedly during the Great Panic. Together with other commentators, we recognised it as a classic religious response.[29]

Stopping children from going to school was something that could be done, so sacrificing the education of children and the productive time of their parents shifted, sometimes in the space of just a few days, from being something that no one thought was worthwhile into something that was 100 percent essential.

Taking everyone's temperature before letting them into a supermarket was another thing that could be done, so although it is intrusive and people have variable temperatures for all kinds of reasons that have nothing to do with an infectious illness, it moved from the 'no evidence that it helps' column to the 'obvious, compulsory and enforced' column, with little objection from those being subjected to it.

Similarly, travel restrictions, obsessive surface cleaning, testing, track-ing-and-tracing, restrictions on business operations, quarantining of individuals in hotels and purpose-built camps, separation between persons inside buildings, restrictions on exercise and many other directives started to sound necessary and obvious to the ears of whole populations, regardless of their logical or proven efficacy.

---

28 The Politician's Syllogism, or Politician's Fallacy, originated in the British sitcom, 'Yes, Prime Minister'. The full version: 'We must do something. This is something. Therefore we must do this.'

29 See, e.g., Foster (2021) and Alexander (2021).

In a further slap in the face to evidence-based policy making, when existing restrictions didn't work in controlling infections, governments automatically concluded that the restrictions weren't tight enough and doubled down on them, tightening controls and adding new ones. This behaviour was repeated over and over during 2020-21. The Covid god is an angry and rapacious one, and He seems to demand ever larger sacrifices.

For some of the less disruptive interventions, the WHO itself was a principal co-conspirator. In its 2019 guidelines on non-pharmaceutical public health measures during influenza pandemics, WHO recommended the use of face masks and surface- and object-cleaning even while admitting that there was no solid evidence of their effectiveness. There was, however, 'mechanistic plausibility for the potential effectiveness [of the measures]'.[30] In other words, 'we can think up a story of how it might help, so let's do it'. In this way, the pre-pandemic WHO guidelines killed two birds with one stone by recommending sacrifice *and* satisfying the second and third parts of the Politician's Syllogism ('This is something. Therefore we must do this.'). It even threw in a possible causal link between the sacrifice and the feared threat, as a bonus.

Scientists studying fear do not really know why humans have this innate belief that sacrifice will help avert a threat, but one possibility is that it is a leftover element of the 'lizard part' of our brain. Lizards drop their tails when pursued by a predator in order to distract that predator and escape. Perhaps this tendency is still a part of humanity, following the same basic logic: 'Let's give up something very important and hope it appeases whatever threatens us'.

There are other possible explanations for why humans have this reflexive sacrificial response to fear. Perhaps fearful people automatically follow whichever person has a plan and is actively doing something, because their own information is limited and they can reasonably expect that someone

---

30 World Health Organization (2019), p. 14.

taking methodical action knows more than they do about how to overcome the danger. This subservient behaviour becomes increasingly entrenched over time as the ones with the action plan recognise the magnitude of their power and repeatedly move to extend it.

This logic does not explain why people are drawn to sacrifice something of value but at least it might explain why they are prone to believing that 'Something must be done', since that adage is a simplified version of 'We must do whatever someone with a plan wants to be done'. A similar explanation for the appeal of the Politician's Syllogism is that doing something, anything, feels like taking control over the perceived threat, even if that control is purely symbolic.

Whatever the deeper reason, the tell-tale sign of the sacrificial reflex associated with human fear is disinterest among the fearful in the mechanism by which the sacrifice actually helps avert the danger. It is simply seen as axiomatic that the sacrifice helps. So, while many believe that face masks are to viruses what garden gates are to mosquitoes, people possessed by fear of infection are quite prone to believing that a face mask will prevent infection, because wearing one is doing something.

While locking down the elderly will accelerate the progress of degenerative diseases like dementia and increase the susceptibility of this already vulnerable group to other health problems, frightened people accept automatically that incarcerating them will save them from infection. While the repeated scrubbing of surfaces with chemical disinfectants is expensive, disruptive and environmentally damaging, this too is automatically assumed by the fearful to be a sacrifice worth making.

A fearful public will usually view information about how some measure will actually help to alleviate a threat as merely a bonus, not a requirement. The more painful the measure, the more likely they believe it will help – simply because it is more painful.

This ambivalence about the connection between a measure and its effectiveness makes it extremely difficult to question on scientific grounds a measure that has been successfully sold to the fearful as an appropriate sacrifice. It is nearly impossible to ask for scientific evidence or even suggest that there should be a rational discussion about it, and expect to be taken seriously. During the Great Fear and on through the Illusion of Control phase of the Covid era, anyone who didn't automatically go along with a new sacrifice for Covid was apt to be regarded as a dangerous heretic and quickly howled down by a baying public.

We saw this bullying repudiation of rational discourse time and again, in the twitterstorms against lockdown sceptics, in the millions of furious comments under news media articles, in the daily sermons of government officials and their health advisors, and in every other forum that could be co-opted by the crowd to express its disapproval of Those Who Dared to Differ.

Another key aspect of fear is how widely people vary in their susceptibility to different types of fear. This is partly a matter of learning and partly a matter of programming. Some people are innately very fearful beings, easily scared by many things and highly risk-averse, while others are truly afraid of very little.

Fear can also be learned. People who have had a very bad experience will fear a repeat, and become frightened by stimuli that remind them of that experience. Humans in this sense are just like Pavlov's dog.[31] We can be trained to experience fear of nudity, blood, zombies, social shame, particular foods, particular skin colours, sounds or smells. None of these things is feared by a newborn baby, but over time we humans learn to fear them as our carers and our experiences teach us that these things are associated with bad outcomes.

Fear can also be unlearned, but this takes effort and time. It requires that we confront and 'make our peace' with bad experiences, pain, loss, or the

---

31 Pavlov (1927).

death of a loved one. For example, we can consciously expose ourselves to feared stimuli, as in 'exposure therapy' to treat anxiety disorders. We can get into the habit of telling ourselves it is just not all that bad. We can learn to ridicule what we once feared, taking the edge off that fear. Some people find this easier to do than others, but in essence we can train ourselves to counter the feeling of fear and even to welcome things that once terrified us, including pain and death.

This learning and unlearning of fears is highly social, and thus something that can operate at the level of a whole society. Partly it is about general narratives: a society can choose a more relaxed narrative around death, or a more fearful one. One might say that societies can opt to become lions that are masters of their own story of death, or they can be sheep.

During the Great Panic of 2020, many countries adopted and nurtured new fears, while some displayed more lion-like behaviour and were reluctant to be drawn into the frenzy. Some US states such as South Dakota rejected the fear narrative, as did a small handful of countries including Taiwan and Japan, both of which avoided widespread lockdowns.[32] Belarus took a freewheeling approach, as did Tanzania, where the country's president, the late John Magufuli, made Covid an object of national ridicule by speaking to the media about how Covid testing had returned positive results for a goat and a papaya.[33]

There is hope in this malleability of fear. With conscious effort, societies can unlearn what they feared before. Ridiculing or otherwise confronting what was previously feared, and openly dismissing it, can slowly remove the fear. This is shown to be possible by the total disappearance of fears that transfixed whole populations in past centuries. Fear of vampires used to be ubiquitous in Eastern Europe but is now a distant memory. In other

---

32 Rocha (2020).

33https://news.sky.com/story/coronavirus-tanzania-testing-kits-questioned-after-goat-and-papaya-test-positive-11982864

regions, fears of voodoo, giants, dwarfs, dragons, basilisks, the devil and evil spirits were once rampant. What removed them was an active policy by the authorities to discredit those beliefs and to insist on a more scientific approach to understanding the world.

This offers hope to which we will return at the end of the book, when we draw lessons. If fear can be neutralised, the question becomes what kind of mechanisms our society can adopt to perform this neutralisation, and thereby prevent a wave of fear from overcoming our societal defences.

In all cases when populations become very afraid of something, some people work out how to benefit from those fears. In previous centuries, quacks sold amulets containing amber, jade and other gemstones, allegedly to ward off evil spirits and vampires. An English surgeon named Dale Ingram remarked that during the Bubonic plague outbreak in London in 1665, 'There was scarce a street in which some antidote was not sold, under some pompous title'.[34]

During the Great Panic, we saw the emergence of salesmen peddling all kinds of new treatments that offered hope of protecting us against infections. At the more primitive end of the continuum, these included African shamans selling magic water, but the inventory of remedies was modernised for the 21st century and also embraced far more lucrative industries. The Covid testing business was one example, protective equipment was another.

Whole industries either emerged or were greatly strengthened during the Great Panic and developed a vested interest in the fear being perpetuated indefinitely. Flourishing e-commerce businesses supplied people with the items they needed to remain bunkered at home for an unlimited period. Across the world, squadrons of sweaty individuals on two wheels, freshly empowered by governmental measures to throttle the 'normal' economy and promote techno-logical solutions, buzzed around cities making home deliveries of groceries,

---

34 Ingram (1755), p. 21.

prepared meals and other delights to keep stomachs full and arses wiped.

Both in fiction and in history, fear has been used by politicians to gain control over populations. In fiction, the aspiring dictator promises a solution for a threat over which the population obsesses. That proposed solution invariably involves more power for the aspiring dictator, which citizens notice too late to be able to avert or roll back.

This basic storyline occurs in George Orwell's *1984*, in which a society is controlled by the fear of competing superstates. This theme also shows up in the film *V for Vendetta*, wherein an elite rises to power through poisoning its own people, and of course in *Star Wars*, where the evil Palpatine becomes emperor during a war he created.

In real life, the use of fear to gain power has been observed many times. Hitler used fear of communists and Jewish bankers. The Emperor Augustus brought an end to the 400-year-old Roman republic and became supreme ruler by promising to stamp out lawlessness, property theft and political gridlock. The public were unfazed by the fact that Augustus had been an eager participant in the evils he vowed to eliminate. They just followed the promise of peace.

The industry of fear maintenance is central to the political economy of Covid, which we cover in depth in later pages. We will see how politicians grabbed more power while health and technology companies made fantastic profits by exploiting fearful populations that either looked away or made enormous sacrifices willingly so as to appease the object of their fear.

FRIENDS, ENEMIES OR BOARDERS? A PRIMER ON VIRUSES AND HOW WE CONTROL THEM

Before returning to the events of 2020, we now turn to what we really know about viruses and the steps humans have taken in the past, and can take now, to control them. We need to understand a little about virology, a little about immunology, and also something about the social system in which viruses spread — since natural limits to control of the social system carry implications for what can actually be done to control viruses.

WHAT A VIRUS IS, WHICH VIRUSES ARE OUR FRIENDS, AND HOW THEY MATTER

Viruses are bits of genetic code (DNA or RNA) encased in a layer of protein. They are infinitesimally small but come in a variety of shapes, some simple like rods or spheres, others more complicated with 'heads' and 'tails'.

There are four types of viruses: those that live with us in a mutually beneficial symbiotic way, those that are harmless to us, those that are part of us, and those that are our enemies.

Humans are not the only things that viruses prey on. There are far more bacteria in the world, in both number and total weight, than people. The vast majority of viruses present in natural environments, such as in a handful of sand or on the bark of a tree, prey on bacteria and are either harmless or beneficial to humans.

Viruses that keep bacteria in check are called bacteriophages, or just 'phages' for short. They enter bacterial cells, get those cells' machinery to replicate them, and eventually cause the host cells to explode, releasing thousands of phages that can likewise enter and destroy other bacterial cells.

This bacteria-killing ability of viruses has led to an increasing interest in so-called 'phage therapy' as an alternative to antibiotics, which have major drawbacks. Bacteria can become resistant to antibiotics, and antibiotics often kill the 'good' bacteria along with the 'bad'. Phages can circumvent both of these problems. They are species-specific, meaning that each kind of phage targets only one particular kind of bacteria, so phage therapy can skittle the bad guys and leave the good ones alone. Phages can also adapt quickly when the host bacterium tries to resist.

Biologists have recently found that mucus in the human gut is naturally loaded with bacteria-killing phages. Among other things, these little helpers protect us from the bacteria that digest our food and would poison us if they entered the bloodstream.[35]

Most of the useful viruses in our bodies get there through interaction with the outside world: they are not in our bodies from birth. It follows that we should not become so 'clean' as to lose contact with the viruses present in the natural environment, of which we need many to ensure our very survival.[36]

In addition to viruses that are helpful after being introduced from outside, some viruses are literally part of us. Some scientists now believe that approximately eight percent of the human genome consists of viral DNA that was imported into us by invading viruses. Some of these protect humans from illness, while others may have a more sinister design such as elevating the risk of cancer.[37]

Viruses are still blending with our bodies every day, a process that usually has bad outcomes but sometimes works in our favour. For example, medicines are being designed now that contain viruses 'programmed' to change the genetic code in particular cells of our bodies, usually to get rid of a genetic disease or to help our bodies produce desired chemicals. This process is called 'gene editing'.[38]

The bottom line is that viruses and humans go back a long way. There are good viruses and bad viruses, and unfortunately the latter type have given the whole lot a bad name. Most viruses are harmless to humans, preferring to focus on bacteria and plants. Some are part of the human body and do very useful work for us. They aren't all the villains they are often made out to be.

But what about the kind of virus that has bad intentions? Let's take a look at what makes the villainous virus tick.

---

35 Yong (2013).

36 Nuwer (2020).

37 Zimmer (2017).

38 Sample (2018).

IN THE SHOES OF AN ENEMY VIRUS

Viruses that are our enemies, including Covid, weaken their victims and can kill them without doing anything particularly good. They are the gate-crashers at the party who drink the beer, eat the food and pick fights with the legitimate guests.

But let's now stand in the shoes of this hoodlum for a moment and consider the world from its point of view. What makes for an evolutionarily successful enemy virus?

Consider a novel virus that makes it into a person, for example by jumping from bats or escaping from a lab, and finds the person poorly prepared for it with few existing cellular defences. This virus will be able to enter many cells freely and follow the normal viral *modus operandi* of transforming healthy cells into little factories for producing more of itself. This process is very rapid: a virus can produce a new generation of itself in less than 30 minutes.

After establishing a beachhead, some kinds of viruses are content to remain and multiply in the local area rather than spread around the body. This is the case with many respiratory tract infections, including the common cold. Other viruses, such as measles, go on a road show, travelling in the bloodstream and capillaries to attack distant parts of the body. Some less common but particularly nasty viruses, such as the one that causes rabies, use the nervous system.[39]

If a virus is too effective in overrunning the host's cells, the victim dies quickly because her body is left with too few functional cells to stay alive. The whole body is so busy producing more of the virus that it stops taking care of itself.

One might think this represents a triumph for the virus, but it's actually the very essence of a Pyrrhic victory, since a dead body can no longer circulate and infect other humans. Soon, the victim's corpse disintegrates along with its viral swarm. Evolutionarily speaking, it's the end of the road for that virus. For this reason, viruses that kill their hosts very quickly do not survive for

---

39 Baron et al. (1999).

long in the human population.

The more successful virus is one that does not kill the host. Its goal is simply evolutionary success, not putting its host to the sword. To flourish, it needs efficient ways of replicating itself. It is wholly dependent on its hosts to multiply and the longer a host remains alive producing more virus and sharing it around to other hosts, the more successful the virus is.

In fact, arguably the most evolutionarily successful virus would not even make its host ill enough to withdraw from social life. A human host who notices she is ill will take measures like staying in bed to avoid exerting herself too much. To a virus, this kind of protective response is almost as bad as the host's death because the infected body is not up and about infecting others.

It is better for the virus if a host not only continues walking around but also sheds a lot of the virus when exhaling, sneezing, coughing, perspiring, defecating or releasing other bodily fluids. The virus that hits the evolutionary jackpot is the one that spreads to other humans via the medium that runs the least interference: the air. A host can spread a virus via saliva, mucus and small moisture particles called aerosols that are produced when exhaling. The more forceful the breathing out, such as when singing, coughing or exercising, the more aerosols are produced. Covid is in this category and mainly spreads through the air into noses and lungs. It is very infectious and slow to cause notable symptoms.

How do our bodies deal with an intruder like this?

THE IMMUNE RESPONSE: HOW WE DEFEND OURSELVES AGAINST A VIRAL ATTACK

Our bodies' first line of defence against enemy viruses is the skin, which is normally impervious to them. The weak points are cuts, abrasions and areas of the body not covered in protective skin, including the eyes, ears, nose and other apertures. Once inside the gates, viruses can find exposed cells that grant them direct access to other parts of the body. The initial exposure is unavoidable because our bodies need these areas to be exposed for other reasons, such as to get oxygen, smell, hear, eat and get pregnant.

Covid is a virus that attacks the human respiratory system through the nose and mouth. There it homes in on, and binds to, exposed cells coated with an enzyme called ACE2. Covid's protein structure 'fits' with ACE2, and is able to invade the cells with the help of another enzyme, furin. It is a complicated process but one can think of the ACE2 and furin team as a kind of 'keyhole' into which covid fits to enter the cell.

Inside the host cell, Covid does what viruses do, which is to co-opt the cell's replication system into producing copies of itself. The copies are then shed outside the cell, ending up either in the mucus of the throat and nose from where they can hitch a ride on the next cough to another nose or mouth, or on the outside of other vulnerable cells and thus positioned for a second-tier invasion.

In a worst-case invasion, the virus first spreads from the upper to the lower respiratory tract, and may then enter other areas of the body. The victim may eventually die.

The lines of defence our bodies have are successful at eliminating a virus in over 99 percent of exposures. Neutralising defences take the form of antibodies, and more general defences exist of the sacrificial variety wherein cells suicide or are killed by other agents in the body when invaded. Either way, the body gets rid of the virus by breaking down the free-roaming viral cells or the infected host cells. These are then carried off in small fragments in the bloodstream to be used as building blocks elsewhere, or are processed for discharge by the liver or kidneys.

The neutralising team that the human body calls on to defeat its viral attackers is formidable.

When a virus first enters the body and invades healthy cells, peptide molecules from inside the infected cell are displayed on the cell's surface.[40] These are like tiny red flags signalling to nearby cells that they have an infection problem. Cells in the neighbourhood include roaming cells that are part of the immune system specialising in fighting invaders.

Our first internal line of defence against viruses like Covid is a type of white blood cell called a lymphocyte. Lymphocytes roam the body sniffing out, and then snuffing out, infections. There are three different kinds of lymphocytes, called T-cells, B-cells and natural killer ('NK') cells, each of which plays a distinct and crucial role. Working together, they are like the emergency crews that arrive on the scene of a house fire, putting out the blaze, rescuing the inhabitants and removing the debris.

These lymphocytes have receptors on their surfaces that can recognise the viral components of the peptides on infected cells and inform the decision about whether to proceed with killing them in service to the survival of the larger cell group, which is the human body.

A second line of defence against viruses is interferons, which are not cells but small proteins released by infected cells that inhibit the ability of viruses to replicate themselves once inside a new host cell. Their presence also acts as a red flag to other cells in their neighbourhood, warning them of the virus' presence and triggering the production of more 'red flags' on infected cells that can be recognised and destroyed by T-cells and NK-cells.

A third line of defence is large proteins called immunoglobulins, or antibodies, and this is where B-cells come into the picture. B-cells become activated when an invading virus or other infection becomes present in the body. Some B-cells will then transform into plasma that produces antibodies matching the specific pathogen. The B-cells are a little like scientists within the body, analysing the enemy and coming up with a countermove to neutralise

---

40 Peptides are small chains of amino acids. They are placed on the infected cell surface by resident molecules called 'class 1 major histocompatibility complex' (MHC class 1) proteins.

it by producing fit-for-purpose antibodies. These antibodies then bind to the invading pathogen before it gets a chance to infect more healthy cells. They either kill the pathogen directly ('phagocytosis'), or indirectly by making them an easier target for other lymphocytes ('agglutination').

Being pathogen-specific is a very handy feature of B-cells because after they have fought off the initial infection, they can 'remember' their specific target pathogen for a long time — in some diseases for a lifetime — and are capable of producing the necessary antibodies if the same invader is impertinent enough to try again.

Many particulars of this immune response are important for understanding why Covid outcomes have differed so much by age, season and country.

One important factor is that in a strong immune system, T-cells and NK-cells are able to clear infected cells efficiently, obviating the need for the body to trigger an antibody response. This holds for most healthy people everywhere, who consequently either don't ever notice they were infected with Covid or experience only minor symptoms. It is mainly in cases where Covid enters the bloodstream and becomes widespread in the body that people get very sick and antibody defences kick in. This is seen primarily in people with weakened immune systems.

The immune system does not respond adequately to Covid in about 20 percent of cases. We knew in February 2020 that the risk of death was heavily skewed towards the elderly, but only in about late March did it become clear just how skewed the risks were. Elderly patients with heart disease, coronary artery disease, hypertension, kidney disease and/or diabetes appeared to be at particular risk of developing severe symptoms. Such people have less efficient T-cells, NK-cells and even B-cells: their immune system is not as good at recognising enemies and quickly responding to a new threat.

In contrast, to those below 65 without a chronic illness, the risks of death from Covid infection are in the same ballpark as the risks encountered by driving a car. Among children and young adults the risks are even lower — less than the risk of drowning.

The quality of the immune system is higher in people who have a healthy lifestyle, are happy, and have a diet rich in nutrients that help their cells function well. This is where substances like zinc or vitamin D, which one gets from diet or exposure to sunshine, come in: such inputs are now thought by many doctors and scientists to be quite likely important in fighting off early-stage Covid infections, but not later-stage infections.[41] This has significant policy implications. It also offers the potential to mislead people for financial gain. Consider how this goes.

From a benevolent policy perspective, what matters is to keep people healthy by encouraging them to go outside and exercise a lot. The good policymaker would want to encourage behaviour that makes people happy, such as having an active social life, sleep, and sex, because a happier person has a better functioning immune system. A benevolent policy maker would also be encouraging people to eat a healthy diet with the right supplements, where needed.

What should one not do? One should not tell people to stay inside at home, out of the sun and with constraints on exercise. One should not tell people to stay away from other people, thereby becoming disconnected and lonely. One should not make healthy diets less prevalent through setting policy that increases anxiety and depression, whose victims find solace in drink and fast food. All of these things lead to weaker immune systems. Yet still, many countries, ironically at the behest of their public health 'scientists', put out official advice — 'stay home, save lives' — that was the opposite of smart. Worse, after a short time such 'advice' usually changed into mandates backed up by draconian fines.

The potential for abuse is also obvious. For example, suppose you want to

---

41 Swiss Policy Research (2021A), https://swprs.org/on-the-treatment-of-covid-19/

sell expensive treatments for Covid, like vaccines, and thus want to downplay the cheaper alternatives that prevent most mild infections from ever becoming a major problem. You can then deliberately talk up the situations in which a much cheaper substance doesn't work, conveniently not mentioning those situations in which it does. You might point out that for extremely ill patients in intensive care, giving people preventative medicines does not help, and then falsely claim that preventative medicines do not 'work' even though they may work to prevent rather than to treat. Such a ruse will eventually get found out, but you can enjoy another six to 12 months of profit in the meantime. As we will discuss below, this ruse was actually pulled, almost to the letter.

Then there is the issue of infectiousness. Just how airborne a virus is depends on the weather. In some types of weather, such as in the European and North American summers, the miniscule droplets containing Covid fall quickly to the ground. In winter, those same 'aerosols' float around for a long time, both indoors and outdoors, thus greatly increasing the infectiousness of the virus.

Not surprisingly, Covid waves were large in the Northern Hemisphere winter and early spring but died down in the summer. It is of course tempting for any government to claim that a viral wave dying down due to summer weather is doing so because of policy. That works when a population does not know better. And during the Great Fear the population didn't know better. The dangerous idea was implanted that government policies had worked and would work again in the future.

The memories stored in those T-cells and B-cells are also important. Since Covid has at least four close relations within the family of coronaviruses, different sub-populations had already been exposed to related viruses. These people carried T-cells and B-cells with what is termed 'cross-immunity', which greatly reduces the lethality of Covid and probably, equally importantly, leads to far fewer people shedding the virus and infecting others.

Cross-immunity may be a factor in the relatively low official death count in China and some of its neighbouring countries. Australia and New Zealand, which have large Chinese diasporas, may also have benefited. East Asia is the region where previous coronaviruses, including SARS, originated and roamed around most, giving the populations there a level of prior immunity.[42] In contrast, Latin American populations probably had relatively low exposure to these prior similar viruses, which may have been a reason they were more vulnerable to serious effects from Covid.

It is easy to overlook these factors in a political climate that does not permit or encourage an open, calm analysis and discussion of all relevant information. In a situation where governments are keen to claim it was their actions that led to 'positive' results, the authorities in China, California, the UK, Victoria and pretty much everywhere else will all claim they knew for sure it was their policies that led to the ebbing of Covid waves, rather than anything genuinely scientific. Of course, when the virus came back, those same governments were equally adamant that the blame rested on the shoulders of their own citizenry.

Sadly, the Janes in the world population, which is to say the overwhelming majority of people, fell for this sleight of hand every time. Jane not only gave governments carte blanche to repeat the same trickery, she often urged quicker action than even the authorities themselves were willing to commit to.

No one was really sure of the relative importance of various factors influencing the outcomes during April, May and June 2020. The avalanche of state propaganda simply owned the media space on this issue. Normal scientific discussions were extremely difficult as the public discourse was dominated by people wanting to curry favour with influential politicians.

The Greek dramatist Aeschylus has been credited with saying over 2,500 years ago that 'Truth is the first casualty of war', though in fact the actual

---

42 A medical study underway based on exactly this idea is announced in Souris et al. (2020) which found evidence of similar 'memory' in parts of Africa.

line came from US Senator Hiram Johnson in 1918.[43] In the 'fog of war' enveloping most of the world in these early Covid months, the incentives were overwhelming for politicians and scientists to claim that something very particular was the case. Rational, calm deliberations were almost impossible for any group, let alone for society as a whole.

THE PCR TEST: ITS USES AND ABUSES

Armed with an idea of the Covid disease trajectory, we now examine the ubiquitous polymerase chain reaction (PCR) test for the presence of Covid in an individual. This test essentially looks for distinctive bits of DNA typical of Covid. If someone has a lot of active Covid in their body, the PCR test will almost surely be positive, which is why so many authorities and companies insisted on a negative PCR test before people were allowed to travel or take part in events.

Yet the PCR test does not look for the whole virus, only specific bits of it, meaning it will also return a positive result for people whose immune systems have destroyed all the virus but who still have 'dead' fragments of it floating around in the tested area. This can be the case weeks after an infection.

Compounding the problem is that in order to pick up an early infection, one has to make the PCR test extremely sensitive so as to detect trace amounts of the virus. That comes with the high risk of finding a positive result when someone is not actually infected. According to some studies, this happens in about 1 in every 1,000 tests[44], which means that if a whole school of 1,000 pupils is tested every day, on average one will test positive each day even when no one is infected.

Finally, the PCR test was initially rather expensive — something like US$200 each in the first six months of 2020. This dropped to US$10 in 2021,

---

43 Aeschylus said something less modern and less damning to the lies of war, namely 'God is not averse to deceit in a just cause'. On the actual quote and the historical figures who said something very much like it, see https://quoteinvestigator.com/2020/04/11/casualty/ for an investigation.

44 E.g., Albendín-Iglesias et al. (2020).

which still means an unsustainably hefty bill for offices and schools with a thousand or more people being tested daily.

Consider these characteristics of the PCR test in the context of a politicised environment. If one wanted to claim there were more infections in a region, one would simply increase the number of tests conducted there and make those tests more sensitive, which would lead to more true infections being found and also to a huge glut of false positives and evidence of past infections. What results from this exercise are pretty graphs of increasing 'cases'. Not acknowledging false positives or the fact that the PCR test doesn't prove the existence of an active infection enables someone to make a lot of noise about the headline number, even creating a sense of crisis, when in fact there are many fewer actual infections.

Similarly, if one wanted to sell a lot of tests or simply wanted to appear 'responsible', one could make a big song and dance about how it is vital to screen out infected people 'for the safety of others'. A company selling tests would lobby politicians and the media to make its test compulsory for many things. Someone who wanted to appear responsible would insist on comprehensive testing, underplaying the costly consequences in terms of both money and mistakes.

MORE ON PREDICTING VIRAL SUCCESS OR FAILURE

Regional and situational variations in social habits have an influence on the spread and severity of Covid that almost no one would have been able to predict beforehand.

Consider differences in the lifestyles of those at elevated risk of real problems from Covid. In some parts of the world, older people may live alone but often go indoors with others and enjoy close contact, such as in bingo halls or at weekly family dinners.

In more traditional cultures, older people are continuously mingling with each other and with their extended family members throughout the day for a variety of reasons, such as buying and preparing food, cooking, manual labour, or just social chitchat. Extended families in such cultures also eat together on a daily basis, putting three or more generations in close proximity. In cold climates, this occurs indoors, while in hotter climates the interactions are outside.

The organisation of care for people with few years left also varies. Commonly in Western countries, large groups of elderly people reside inside the same nursing home, making it likely that everyone gets infected through shared indoor aerosols if just one person is ill. A 2021 Scottish study found that the larger the aged care home, the higher the proportion of Covid deaths, exactly as one would expect if it takes just one infected elderly person in such a setting to infect all the others.[45]

Elsewhere, the elderly may be in private homes, looked after by family or with some system of help-at-home that confers a significantly lower chance of being in proximity to another infected elderly person.

Whether in aged care facilities or in private homes, the living arrangements of the most vulnerable in a country cannot be changed at the drop of a hat.

There are also cultural differences around grooming habits, which can have their roots in religious practices. For example, in Southeast Asia, nasal rinsing is a normal practice. And then there are the variations in customs relating to shaking hands, touching the head, kissing, and so on. Even if everything else in two regions is identical, one might have far higher Covid infectiousness than the other purely for cultural reasons.

Then there is regional variation in diet. It has been suggested for example that the Japanese, who eat a lot of fish and have a diet high in vitamin D, are naturally more protected against Covid than other populations, such as Latin Americans.

Architectural and engineering designs also differ. In buildings where the

---

45 https://thecareruk.com/covid-death-rate-in-scottish-care-homes-higher-in-larger-homes/

air conditioning is 'parallel', with each room having a separate flow of air from outside, aerosols with Covid in one room are not pumped around the rest of the building. This is more typical of residential buildings. But where the air conditioning is 'circular', meaning the same air is shunted around from room to room, such as in office buildings, the infecting aerosols have far more opportunities to spread. This too is not something one can change quickly, making the virus automatically more infectious in some places than in others.

In some countries, like the US and the Netherlands, government scientists took a public position very early in the pandemic that aerosols were not important, and this wisdom fed into government actions. This made scientists reluctant to change horses when the evidence became compelling that aerosols were in fact Covid's favourite transportation mode. While reasonable observers had worked out by April 2020 that aerosols were the main way the virus spread, the WHO and many health authorities in Western countries openly derided that contention for almost a year.[46]

Many more 'left-field' aspects of Covid became important over time but could have been guessed by hardly anyone beforehand. Take, for example, the importance of pets and local wildlife. It turned out that dogs, cats, bats, mink, and other animals could be infected with Covid and some of these could be spreaders of the disease. This means regions with fewer pets and the 'right' wildlife could see far less spread via animals than regions with more pets and a lot of the 'wrong' wildlife. The latter regions would really have no hope of ever getting rid of the virus, even if every human were given a perfectly effective vaccine.

The importance of other animals can be seen in the only successful attempt we have ever made to eradicate a virus affecting humans. This is

---

46 Tufekci (2021), https://www.nytimes.com/2021/05/07/opinion/coronavirus-airborne-transmission.html

the case of the smallpox virus, which was exterminated decades ago.[47]

The eradication of smallpox was possible because of a unique set of circumstances. First, it does not circulate in other animals, and so it cannot jump back to us again from another species. Second, scientists developed a vaccine that was exceptionally effective in activating the immune system and keeping it activated over a long period: a vaccinated individual would never be able to contract the virus and spread it to others. Third, the vaccine was dirt-cheap to produce and easy to distribute and administer to everyone. Fourth, smallpox was so deadly that everyone wanted to cooperate in the mass immunisation of their own populations. If you contracted the virus, you had a one-in-three chance of dying from it, so motivation to vaccinate was high. And fifth, the symptomatology of smallpox was so particular that it was easy to spot people who had it.

The discovery that other animals shared Covid changed the calculus around what was possible and what was not in dealing with it. It made a repeat of the smallpox eradication success story impossible, and left only strategies that amounted to some form of learning to live with it.

Dozens more factors turned out to be important for both the spread of the disease and its lethality, ranging from the architecture of hospitals, to the age structure of society, to the difficulties of measuring the presence of antibodies, to the inevitable mutations in Covid that turned it into a recurring flu-like disease. We do not need to unpack that huge complexity here. The point is that a well-meaning person would want to consider these dozens of factors and discuss them calmly with others. Open-minded deliberation is essential to figure out the complex web that Covid has turned out to be.

Calm deliberation was off the menu, however, in a situation where both the media and scientific airwaves were saturated with claims by governments

---

47 The last reported case of smallpox occurred in 1977.
In 1980, the World Health Organization announced that the disease had been eradicated completely (National Institute of Allergy and Infectious Diseases 2014).

and their scientific advisors that they were confident — no, not just confident but *certain* — that their particular course of action was the only way. This subverted calm deliberation and made it politically almost impossible to change course even if the previous stance was looking suspect.

The desperate need by authorities and their advisors to be seen to have made the right call no matter what course of action they took undermined our ability to learn what was going on and consider appropriate responses. It is very difficult to publicly change your mind and backtrack on something once you make a pretence of certainty in the first instance. Covid politicians felt the need to exude utter and complete confidence in the measures they were taking, thereby making true deliberations impossible at the broader societal level going forward. This made their societies, our societies, slow learners and slow adapters.

Whenever politicians were challenged in their media appearances to justify a directive that seemed dubious they invariably responded with clichés. Vacuous assertions about 'following the science' and 'drawing on the best public health advice' were uttered robotically to justify anything and everything. When changes *were* made to the 'science' that in turn led to changes in the 'best public health advice', they were typically in one direction — toward greater stringency. Removing a particular measure might signal that the initial implementation of it was incompetent, while adding or strengthening existing measures was easy to badge as the result of a 'careful analysis of a growing body of evidence'. Marketed in this way, the new 'advice' could be made to look even more like the result of unimpeachable scientific analysis than before.

This 'fog of war' dynamic is extremely difficult to escape from once a population is in panic mode, which should make us wary of supposedly easy solutions to future problems. Any solution that relies on people 'just keeping calm' when others around them panic is not really much of a solution at all. Almost no country in the world managed that during the Great Panic, including the world's best-educated and best-run countries.

The challenge for us is figuring out how populations in the future can be steered clear of that mass panic in the first place. We discuss later our ideas for this, which involve using institutions to defuse the fear and to quickly organise deliberate counter-movements.

COVID'S PLACE AMONG HISTORY'S VIRUSES

Covid belongs to the family of coronaviruses that circulate widely in the human population, including those known as 229E, NL63, OC43 and HKU1.[48] Covid almost uniquely ticks the various boxes needed for successful replication among humans. Most of the people it infects are unaware of its presence for as long as one week, with only very minor symptoms. During this time the host could be actively transmitting it to others.[49] It is able to stay in the body for an unusually long time before the victim has either succumbed to it or has fought off the infection. Further, it is highly capable of infecting new hosts via the nose.

Have there been even more infectious diseases? Certainly. Smallpox, which killed off most native Americans, native Australians and several other populations when they first came into contact with it, was even more infectious. Not merely was smallpox spread in aerosols, but the smallpox virus stayed virulent and highly infectious when it was on the surface of many materials, including clothes, bedding, utensils, saddles and boats.

Evidence suggests that Covid does not transmit well from surfaces. This is because it does not have the features that would allow it to invade the cells in our gut. It may make it into our gut from tables or door handles, but there it gets broken down quite quickly without infecting us. It needs to get into the nose and lungs to start propagating itself, so small aerosol particles

---

48 Wu et al. (2020).

49 According to the WHO, the average duration between infection and symptoms is 5-6 days. Our present knowledge about asymptomatic transmission is exemplified by WHO (2020A) and Muller (2021).

hanging in the air are far superior to surfaces as a transmission vehicle.[50] This hasn't stopped governments from spending ridiculous sums of money on what has been called 'hygiene theater': the repeated and maniacal spraying, scrubbing and wiping of surfaces by people in hazmat outfits, with chemicals that are likely doing more harm than the virus to those they are supposed to protect.[51] Disinfectant has even been showered on villagers from drones.[52]

Have there been more deadly diseases than Covid? Plenty. Smallpox qualifies in that column too. Something like 99 percent of those never previously exposed to smallpox have died when infected. The plague, cholera,[53] typhus, yellow fever, trench foot, HIV, tuberculosis, SARS, MERS and hundreds of other diseases – not to mention diseases not directly caused by viruses or bacteria, such as heart disease – are more deadly to humans than Covid.

Table 1 shows the most notorious killer viruses in history, ranked by their case fatality rate (a.k.a. 'case fatality ratio' or 'CFR'), defined as the number of deaths divided by the number of confirmed 'serious' cases. This is the proportion of people with 'serious' symptoms who eventually die from the virus. Covid is a fair way down the list, on par with Hepatitis B and the Spanish Flu, both of which have killed a far greater number of people than Covid. In contrast, something like 90 percent of people who get Covid don't even notice they have it, and are therefore not a 'serious' case.

How dangerous was the Covid virus really for the 'average human', what was known about its virulence, and how could the various statistics describing its virulence be abused?

---

50 Ives & Mandavilli (2020), https://www.nytimes.com/2020/11/18/world/asia/covid-cleaning.html

51 This term appears to have originated in an article entitled 'Hygiene Theater is a Huge Waste of Time,' written by Derek Thompson for The *Atlantic* magazine in July 2020.

52 https://aseannow.com/topic/1218262-amazing-thailand-drones-spraying-alcohol-deployed-to-help-fight-covid-19/; Sagar (2020), https://opengovasia.com/how-drones-are-assisting-government-in-china-fight-covid-19/

53 The WHO reports annual cholera fatalities of 23,000-143,000 out of 1.4-4.0 million cases, implying a CFR of 0.5-11%: World Health Organization (2021), https://www.who.int/news-room/fact-sheets/detail/cholera

TABLE 1

Deadliest Viruses in Descending Order of Case Fatality Rate

Virus	Year discovered	Case Fatality Rate	Estimated Total Deaths	Source
Rabies	2300 B.C.	100%	59,000 annually	CDC
Ebolavirus	1976	65%	11,325 (2014-16 outbreak)	Nyakarahuka et al. (2016)
HIV	1981	43%	33 million	UNAIDS
Middle East Respiratory Syndrome (MERS)	2012	35%	858	WHO
Smallpox	10,000 B.C.	33%	300 million (20th century)	Our World in Data
Japanese Encephalitis	1871	25%	17,000 annually	WHO
Yellow Fever	1900	15%	30,000 annually	CDC
SARS	2003	10%	774	CDC
Dengue Haemorrhagic Fever	1943	5%	25,000 annually	World Mosquito Program
West Nile	1937	5%	2,384 (US only)	CNN
Lassa Fever	1969	3%	5,000 annually	CDC
Hepatitis B	1967	3%	600,000 annually	Hepatitis B Foundation
Spanish Flu	1918	3%	50 million	Taubenberger & Morens (2006)
Hantavirus Haemorrhagic Fever with Renal Syndrome (HFRS)	1931	3%	46,427 (China, 1950-2007)	Liang et al. (2018)
Covid-19	2019	2%	4.2 million (as of 31 July, 2021)	JHU Coronavirus Resource Center

NOTES:

(1) As of July 31, 2021, Covid-19 had killed 4.2 million people from a case pool of 197.0 million, giving a CFR of 2.1%.

(2) Marburg and Hantavirus Pulmonary Syndrome (HPS) both had higher CFRs than Covid-19 but killed very few people in total.

(3) The H2N2 'Asian flu' (1957-58), H3N2 'Hong Kong flu' (1968-69) and H1N1pdm09 'Swine flu' (2009-10) all had CFRs of less than 1%.

(4) Online data sources:

Rabies: https://www.cdc.gov/media/releases/2015/p0928-rabies.html

HIV: https://www.unaids.org/en/resources/fact-sheet

MERS: https://www.who.int/health-topics/middle-east-respiratory-syndrome-coronavirus-mers

Smallpox: https://ourworldindata.org/smallpox

Japanese encephalitis: https://www.who.int/news-room/fact-sheets/detail/japanese-encephalitis

Yellow fever: https://www.cdc.gov/globalhealth/newsroom/topics/yellowfever

SARS: https://www.cdc.gov/mmwr/preview/mmwrhtml/mm5249a2.htm

Dengue fever: https://www.worldmosquitoprogram.org/en/learn/mosquito-borne-diseases/dengue

West Nile virus: https://edition.cnn.com/2013/07/13/health/west-nile-virus-fast-facts/index.html

Lassa fever: https://www.cdc.gov/vhf/lassa/index.html

Hepatitis B: https://www.hepb.org/what-is-hepatitis-b/what-is-hepb/facts-and-figures/

Covid-19: https://coronavirus.jhu.edu/map.html

COVISTICS: THE STATISTICAL BOG OF VIRULENCE MEASURES

What is the likelihood that a random person exposed to Covid dies from it if health care is 'normal'? This is a natural question to ask if you want to know how scary Covid really is.

Right away we have a problem in answering it, however, because the definition for being 'exposed' sets a very low bar. Someone who has just inhaled some Covid aerosol on a street corner has been exposed, and may even test out as 'infected', but may merely have Covid sitting there in the nose. Someone whose lungs have ten different spots where the virus has invaded cells has clearly been exposed too, and is infected but certainly much less so than someone with 10,000 such spots. Different tests pick up different levels of 'infections', with no standard measurement referring to a standard definition.

There is also no obvious starting definition of what it means to 'have symptoms'. To a person who experiences breathing problems for other reasons, for example because she is a heavy smoker or lives in a city with serious air pollution, the presence of the virus may not yield perceptible symptoms. Meanwhile, for another who is unaccustomed to breathing problems, symptoms may declare themselves abundantly.

Apart from different degrees of infection and perceived symptoms, there are different illness trajectories depending on what a person does, what other health problems (such as obesity) she suffers from, and what support she has. Someone who is ill and has no one to help feed her will have to exert effort to prepare food and eat, making her more likely to succumb to the virus. Those living with little food, in cold places, and with other diseases around them will also have different experiences than those who are well-nourished and living among generally healthy people in a comfortable climate.

These nuances have long been recognised among public health professionals, but a large chunk of the general population remained unaware of them during the Great Fear because they had other things to worry about, such as how to manage their jobs and families. The lack of knowledge about these subtleties and the initial complexity of the official statistics made people extremely vulnerable to being misled.

To illustrate these difficulties, let's examine three of the most frequently cited statistics you will see regarding Covid: case fatality rates, infection fatality rates, and full-exposure population fatality rates.

The case fatality rate (CFR), mentioned earlier and reported in Table 1, is in a way the most accurate but also the least informative. The CFR is the ratio of the number of deaths from a specified condition to the number of confirmed cases. In the context of Covid it is, loosely speaking, the number of people who die with the virus in their body divided by the total pool of those who show up with Covid symptoms at the hospital and test positive.

This is a useful number for frontline hospital staff because they can share it with new patients who have tested positive. They can also use the information to organise their own resources in the hospital. For obvious reasons, the CFR is also the number that new patients themselves are particularly interested in. The main early estimate for the global CFR was around 3%, although that had slipped to just over 2% by mid-2021.

A significant problem with the CFR as an input to constructing a population-wide measurement of viral impact is that those who show up at the hospital are some of the worst affected. This selected group is also prone to have other health problems, making it difficult to ascertain exactly how dangerous the virus is for the general population and, to a lesser extent, whether the victims died because of the virus rather than merely with it.

The CFR is further muddied by the fact that some unknown but undoubtedly material number of people have died with the virus in their bodies but never went to hospital to have the diagnosis confirmed. If we want to know from a social standpoint how many years of quality life humanity collectively will lose by being infected with Covid, then the CFR is not particularly helpful.

History tells us that the first estimates of the CFR for a new disease are based on very vulnerable, small populations, and are therefore much higher than the later estimates derived from larger and more representative populations. In a sense, the disease picks off the 'low-hanging fruit' first, and this is the fruit that we first notice the virus tampering with. This offers an avenue to manipulate people. A high initial estimate based on a population of very old, frail people can easily be used to make the whole population believe that the same risk holds for everyone.

During the Great Fear, many media outlets continuously represented CFRs as if they captured the risk from Covid for the entire population. The World Health Organisation and government medical authorities should have vigorously countered those interpretations in the interests of keeping people calm. They did not, in large part because they preferred to raise rather than to lower the level of fear. Heightened public fear made it easier for governments to tighten control and easier for their police forces to maintain surveillance. Institutional integrity did not even enter into consideration.

A second widely used number that is meant in part to overcome the difficulties with the CFR is the infection fatality rate, or infection fatality ratio ('IFR'). This is the percentage of people infected by a disease who subsequently die of it. If one can determine using a test the number of people who have been infected with a particular microbe, and then work out how many of those died while still infected with it, then the IFR can be constructed as the ratio of the latter to the former.

The traditional user of this number is the general practitioner who can give the number to anyone who is worried about having received a positive test. However, like the CFR, the IFR too is highly problematic, because those who get tested are not random members of the public but people more likely to have symptoms or to be members of particular risk groups. Since the vast majority of people infected with Covid have been asymptomatic and hence had no idea they were infected, they were largely invisible in the early statistics on infections. Researchers therefore had to simply guess at the number of asymptomatic patients walking around.

Those infected for longer periods are much more likely to test positive than those infected at a very subdued level and for a short period of time, so once again the estimates of IFRs will be far too high in most studies. The main estimates for the IFR of Covid now range from 0.2% to 0.5%, where the latter number is based on a narrow conception of what counts as an infection: namely, a strong infection in a somewhat vulnerable person.

The third concept, which is of most interest but also the least amenable to measurement is the population total-exposure fatality rate. This is the percentage of the population that would die if everyone were to be exposed to the virus. In essence, this is the true 'let it rip' number, the Darth Vader of countless media commentaries on how many millions would die if the virus were to 'rip through' a whole population.

Given the huge number of factors that influence the spread and lethality of Covid, almost the only way to really get a handle on this number is to see how many people die in a population that looks a lot like the one you are interested in, and where you can reasonably suspect that virtually everyone got infected.

Such whole-country experiments don't really exist, but the closest substitute is to look at what happened in places like New York, or Manaus in Brazil, where it was likely nearly everybody got exposed to the virus. From these experiences we can reasonably estimate a population exposure fatality rate of 0.1%-0.4%, with a lot of variability across countries. Lower values in this range would hold for countries and regions with significant prior immunity, such as East Asia, while higher values are applicable to places like the Americas where prior immunity seems particularly low and there are many factors that Covid finds agreeable, such as poorly ventilated houses, obesity, and frequent hugging of the elderly.

The avoidance of hard-to-interpret data on whole countries, in preference to relying on 'published' CFR and IFR rates, resulted in predictions of fatalities that were simply in the clouds. The models of Neil Ferguson and his associates at Imperial College London are the poster children for this. Their models still used high-end IFR rates as stand-ins for fatality rates of a whole exposed population even as late as October 2020.[54]

When these models became dominant, the burden of proof reversed, with critics told in effect to 'prove that this published IFR rate does not measure the population exposure fatality rate.' That is how the scientific game came to be played, and all those who came to play it — editors, referees and scientific groups — thereby abandoned their normal scientific responsibilities.

THE CASE OF THE DIAMOND PRINCESS

A good example of how different people can draw different information from the same data, coming to wildly different storylines that are then presented to the general public, comes from the case of the Diamond Princess. The Diamond Princess was a cruise ship with just over 3,700 people on board,

---

54 Imperial College COVID-19 Response Team (2020B).

quarantined in the harbours of Japan while Covid was running its course inside with passengers confined to their quarters.

The ship had 1,045 crew members, 145 (14%) of whom became infected according to tests. However, none of them fell seriously ill or died, which suggested to scientists that the risk run by most of the population was small. Of the 2,666 passengers on board, 567 (21%) were found by a test to have been infected, and eight of these died before everyone was released. A total of 11 had died by the end of March 2020, approximately a full month after the ship had been totally evacuated. Of the total of 712 individuals found to have been infected as a result of the more than 3,000 tests that were run, 331 were asymptomatic.[55]

Consider how one can interpret this collection of data.

Some interpreted it to say that the IFR was 11/712, which is 1.5%. If one then simply assumes the same number would hold for entire populations, it means that 1.5% of those infected will die of Covid.

Others pointed out that the passengers on such a cruise ship are usually quite old and several will die in any given week, so they didn't want to count the three who died after the ship had been evacuated. They got to an IFR of 1.1%, which they still presumed to hold for the rest of the world.

Then there were those, like one of the authors in March 2020, who pointed out that in such a confined space as a cruise ship it was inevitable that nearly everyone had been exposed to the virus, and that there had to be a reason that some showed up in the tests as infected and others not.[56] The reason why tests did not pick up more infections was not clear at the time. We now suspect that prior immunity and particularly strong immune systems threw off the virus very quickly, so tests failed to pick up very minor previous

---

55 Statistica (2020), https://www.statista.com/statistics/1099517/japan-coronavirus-patients-diamond-princess/
56 Frijters (2020B), https://clubtroppo.com.au/2020/03/21/the-corona-dilemma/

infections. If one is prepared to accept that argument, it leads to an estimate of the population exposure fatality rate of 8/3711, or 0.2%.

However, even that number is likely to overstate the population exposure fatality rate in the wider world beyond a cruise ship. The median age of a cruise ship passenger is 65, which is more than twice the global population median age of 30.[57] Thus, even the 0.2% figure is higher than what one should expect for the general population in any country, with the caveat that the passengers on the Diamond Princess were probably relatively healthier older people if they were on a long cruise. Taking the age differential into account, it is not unreasonable to draw the conclusion from the Diamond Princess data that the population exposure fatality rate is well under 0.2%, and possibly as low as 0.1%.

The same data can be used to argue for a very high number, such as 1.5%, and a much lower one of around 0.1%. This range allows for a lot of room to manipulate a population that is not so used to reading statistics. Extrapolating these very different estimates to project eventual Covid deaths in the global population makes the difference between predicting 115 million deaths and eight million.

Because of the way science goes, it matters a lot which number is embedded first as a 'reasonable' number at top scientific journals. Whichever number gets its foot in the door first is the one that the editors of these journals will want to see used in subsequent analyses. They will send new papers and scientific contributions to those who published the first studies, which of course means that only papers using or finding similar numbers get accepted at the top journals. In this way, the ego and personal incentives of both editors and the first group of scientists to make it into the top journals line up to cement an initial number, no matter how wildly off it may be.

---

57 Alexander (n.d.), https://www.cruise1st.co.uk/blog/cruise-holidays/how-old-is-the-average-cruise-passenger/

Unfortunately for humanity, in the case of Covid, the initial numbers were vast overestimates of the numbers of most interest to the population.

PERSPECTIVES ON THE ROLE OF VIRUSES IN CAUSES OF DEATH

For quite a few centuries and in major cities, viruses and bacteria were the worst villains for bringing on the end, but in today's rich countries infectious diseases have been brought increasingly under control. What kills us off now in the developed world are mostly things like cancer, heart disease, strokes, diabetes, organ failure, autoimmune diseases, falls, embolisms and dementia (see Table 2). These all take place without the help of viruses and bacteria, and kill off close to 90% of people in the West. Only in poorer regions of the world and where circumstances are particularly favourable for the survival and transmission of viruses and bacteria are infectious diseases still the biggest killers.

TABLE 2

Leading Causes of Death in the US, 2017

Cause of Death	Number	Percent
Diseases of the heart	647,457	23%
Malignant neoplasms	599,108	21%
Unintentional injuries	169,936	6%
Chronic lower respiratory diseases	160,201	6%
Cerebrovascular diseases	146,383	5%
Alzheimer's disease	121,404	4%
Diabetes mellitus	83,564	3%
Influenza and pneumonia	55,672	2%
Nephritis, nephrotic syndrome and nephrosis	50,633	2%
Suicide	47,173	2%

Source: National Center for Health Statistics

Yet, while viruses and bacteria are increasingly incapable of engineering the final push to the grave, that is something of a hollow victory. In our final years we are so weak that a lot of things can kill us off. Cancer, heart attacks and strokes are just like infectious diseases in the sense that we would often be able to overcome them if we were stronger.

Keeping infectious diseases at bay on average buys humans only a few years more of life, depending on which particular disease might be lurking in a given setting.[58] For example, tuberculosis is more deadly the older you are: the death rate for those aged over 50 is more than five times higher than for those below 50.[59] In 2019, tuberculosis took 1.4 million lives worldwide according to the WHO, which is about 500,000 short of the number of people who succumbed to Covid in 2020. The difference is that unlike Covid, tuberculosis has been killing people for more than 5,000 years. About one in every four people on the planet is infected with the tuberculosis bacterium, although only 5-15% of those will ultimately fall ill. HIV, malnutrition, diabetes and smoking among the major risk factors for doing so.[60]

LOCKDOWNS, HUMAN LIFE AND VIRAL SPREAD

Lockdowns are strong restrictions on the movements of people. The most extreme lockdown possible is where everyone is told they literally cannot move at all, a situation only sustainable for a few hours until people start to die of thirst and need to go to the toilet. A mild lockdown is where humans are prevented from moving from one continent to another. The lockdowns of 2020-2021 were invariably in between these two extremes and differed by country.

In this book we use the word 'lockdown' generically to mean strong restrictions on the movements of people, and in particular on their ability to engage in normal activities (like entering shops or restaurants, or attending school)

---

58 HIV is an exception as it kills young people, but HIV today is highly treatable and hence deaths result more from not being able to afford medication than due to a failure to invent the medical treatment required for disease control.

59 The death rate for tuberculosis is 104.51 per 100,000 people above age 50, compared with 18.99 per 100,000 for those below age 50 (Richie & Roser 2019A).

60 World Health Organization (2020B),
https://www.who.int/news-room/fact-sheets/detail/tuberculosis

and to physically touch family and friends who live in different households.

When we look at data on lockdowns in different countries and over time, we use a particular measure of restrictions on movement, the Oxford Blavatnik Stringency Index,[61] that gives a daily severity level of restrictions for each country in the world since January 1st 2020. This stringency index combines information on nine government policies: school closures, workplace closures, cancellation of public events, restrictions on gatherings, closure of public transport, restrictions on internal travel, restrictions on foreign travel, and the presence of a Covid-cautioning public information campaign. The lowest value is 0 and the highest 100. We define a lockdown as what is indicated by a score above 70, corresponding to quite strong government limitations on the movement and social life of individuals. By this definition, from January 1st 2020 to August 1st 2021, the average world citizen spent about eight months in lockdown.

To evaluate lockdowns from a sociological and medical perspective, it is handy to start with a quick history of the basic coevolution of social life and viruses. From this will emerge the reasons for the social system being as it was in early 2020, and the resulting hard limits to restricting normal human activities.

For much of history, humans lived in fairly small groups of 20-100 people that interacted with other groups only infrequently, something we nowadays would call 'extreme social distancing'. It was an environment in which viruses targeting humans were in perpetual risk of dying out. If a virus emerges in a small hunter-gatherer population of 50 people and only gets a chance every few years to jump to other groups, then it would have to be able to survive in a host body for a very long time waiting for its opportunity. Normally, the virus either kills off the whole original group, or dies out as the humans within the group fight back, recover and neutralise it internally.*

It is also possible for a virus to be incompletely neutralised by its hosts.

61 Petherick et al. (2021), https://www.bsg.ox.ac.uk/research/research-projects/covid-19-government-response-tracker

The virus can keep circulating in a small group even if those originally infected clear the first infection. The virus could return, perhaps due to decaying efficacy of the antibodies. Herpes, responsible for cold sores, is like this. Still, few viruses can survive dormant in the human body. Instead they need to circulate by jumping from person to person in a never-ending cycle.

The only interaction between different human groups that was truly unavoidable in prehistoric times was the exchange of wives and husbands every few years in order to refresh the gene pools. That does not give a virus much to work with.

As a side note, the inevitability of infrequent mingling between groups throughout human history gave rise to two species of parasites that are much like viruses in how they spread and how they survive: head lice and pubic hair lice. These creatures, of which probably more than just a single variety of each exists, evolved with us, although it's not clear that they were ever much more than an annoyance. Afforded few opportunities to spread beyond a small group of hosts, lice evolved to capitalise upon a transmission route available in the one dimension of life where extra-familial social closeness was impossible to avoid: non-incestuous sex.

The viruses we regularly encountered in the hunter-gatherer period were those in the soil, in plants and in animals with which we interacted. The extreme social distancing of the hunter-gatherer period did not prevent humans from getting infected now and then by harmful viruses circulating in birds and other animals. But any virus 'lucky enough' to make it into a human and self-replicate inside that person had very little chance of jumping to other groups. They would have died out waiting for new hosts. There are likely to have been millions of unnamed viruses that humans contracted over the thousands of years of history that simply never spread beyond a small group of self-isolating people.

This situation changed dramatically when humans started to live in larger groups, when they started to live close to other animals, and particularly after cities arose around 10,000 years ago. Commerce among villages brought more frequent contact between groups. The domestication of animals brought a greater possibility that humans would contract their diseases, a process known as 'zoonotic' transmission.[62] Cities brought not only much more commerce but also the dense packing of many humans together, which made it easier for a virus to jump from host to host. Trade, conquest and colonisation mixed humanity even more and made circulation of viruses and bacteria even easier. In the last ten thousand years it was inevitable that humans acquired many viruses that have simply never decamped.

THE INTENT AND MECHANISMS OF LOCKDOWNS

Lockdowns — sometimes referred to as 'stay-at-home' or 'shelter-in-place' ('SIP') orders — come in a variety of flavours. The main idea of any lockdown is simple: if you can get people far enough apart from each other and force them to stay apart, they cannot infect each other. Whoever is already infected at the moment of halting all movement gets better or dies without infecting others.

There is an obviously true logic to this, and locking down whole cities has worked in past outbreaks of new diseases to prevent their spread to other cities. A famous example is the lockdown of whole neighbourhoods in Hong Kong during the SARS epidemic of 2003, when no one was allowed to travel out of their own small community. The lockdown response to Covid was essentially the same idea.

From a social perspective, lockdowns are like trying to get humans to act out a reprise of the hunter-gatherer period, isolated in small groups and interacting infrequently. The failures of lockdowns are all related to the impossibility of really trying to live that way again.

There were three fundamental problems with the Covid lockdowns in

---

62 A few viruses evolved inside us without originating from another animal. However, we can never be sure that a particular disease only originated within our own species because an animal from which we might have gotten it could well be extinct by now.

early 2020, two of which were widely realised before they happened, with the third coming as something of a surprise.

The first fundamental problem is that if a new virus is extremely widespread in the human population then there is no realistic chance of preventing it returning to a region in the future, unless that region fences itself off from the rest of humanity forever or acquires a 100% effective vaccine.

In early 2020 the experience with vaccines was that they took at least five years to develop and were rather ineffective in the case of coronaviruses anyway, so they seemed like a long shot. Therefore, at best lockdowns meant spreading waves of infections more over time, which is exactly what health authorities around the world said they were trying to accomplish in the first few months of the Great Fear. This made the lockdowns somewhat illogical to begin with: why spread an event over time at great cost?

The argument at the time was that smoothing a wave of infections meant hospital critical care facilities would not be 'overwhelmed' by the demand at any one time, and that hospitals could then process a larger caseload in total. However, it wasn't clear that hospitals were offering a superior treatment than could be offered at home or by community nurses, so the justification for a lockdown was perched precariously on the unarticulated blind belief that hospital treatment was useful.

Actually, it became clear over time that some of the treatments applied in intensive care (IC) units, such as ventilators that artificially push air into the lungs, were possibly harmful.[63] Researchers in Wuhan, for example, reported that 30 out of 37 critically ill Covid patients who were put on mechanical ventilators perished within a month. In a U.S. study of patients in Seattle, only one of the seven patients older than 70 who were connected to a ventilator survived. Just 36% of those younger than 70 came out alive. The supposed

---

63 E.g., Begley (2020), https://www.statnews.com/2020/04/08/doctors-say-ventilators-overused-for-covid-19/

benefits of hospital or IC treatments were simply oversold.

The second fundamental problem is the damage to social life, economic activity and population health that results from locking people down. Reducing exercise and social interaction ran counter to the general public health advice of decades. As we discuss later in more depth, it was generally known in government and public health circles that lockdowns would be extremely costly in many ways. That is the main reason guidelines for intervention against pandemics that Western governments had available in early 2020 did not include blanket lockdowns, although they advocated some very targeted social distancing measures in extreme circumstances.

The third problem was that the envisioned curbs on interaction were neither possible nor relevant to the spread and lethality of the disease. To see this, consider what governments were not able to do.

Think first of the limits to restricting the movements of healthy people. Governments liked to say that they were preventing people from mixing, but by forcing them into their homes they actually compelled them to mix more at home. After all, people live with others and often in large buildings with many others sharing the same air.

Also, people needed to eat. 'Essential services' like water and electricity needed to keep operating. People also had to go to shops, which required constant delivery and restocking just as before the outbreak. Many 'essential workers', including the police, health workers, and power plant engineers were still buzzing around as before.

While many healthy people no longer moved much out of their homes, others started travelling a lot more because they were delivering parcels or needed to work at the local shops. Large shops such as supermarkets were exactly the kind of indoor places where vulnerable people mix with others. Think of all those shop workers spending the whole day in the worst environment possible — indoors with many vulnerable people — and then returning home to infect others. Think also of cleaners and repairmen visiting their customers and thereby becoming potential super-spreaders. One could ban cleaners from going to houses, but one couldn't ban people like plumbers and electricians doing their rounds to ensure water and electricity was still working in homes. The highly integrated nature of modern economies made it impossible for people to live like hunter-gatherers.

Then think of the unhealthy people. Lockdowns essentially targeted the wrong people; namely, the healthy working population that hardly got sick from Covid and thus were also a small part of the story of infections. Those who were the likeliest both to get sick and to spread it to others were old people. They had pressing reasons to be in all the wrong places. Other illnesses forced them to get help in hospitals or at doctors' offices, or within their nursing homes. All three of these places in most Western countries are almost designed to be Covid distribution centres. They are large, indoors and mix together the easily-infected with the already-infected who are shedding masses of the virus. Moreover, having been shut inside their homes with little exercise and social interaction to improve their immune systems, the elderly became much more vulnerable over time because their health deteriorated.

Reducing the movements of healthy people was not going to move the needle in terms of stifling virus transmission among the truly vulnerable elements of the population. Worse, the logic of trying to keep movement limited meant there was almost no escape for governments from doing the wrong thing: once they and their health advisors had convinced the population that normal interactions were a serious risk, every move to 'open up' was seen as potential endangerment that could be exploited by political opponents.

There was also no escaping the imperative of having a lot of movement around the most vulnerable people because they had other health problems that would kill them if not attended to, and no realistic alternative places to house and help them other than large indoor places with many others.

Authorities did gradually become aware of this problem, but their reactions often made things worse. For example, it might sound logical to keep patients in hospital with Covid until they are fully healed so as not to send them back to nursing homes where they would infect hundreds of others. This mistake was made right at the start in many countries. Doing this in fact kept them longer in a hospital with many other patients and no realistic way to prevent them from sharing the same air. Also, it meant hospital beds were occupied that could have been allocated to patients with non-Covid-related illnesses, making more people vulnerable and leading to avoidable deaths from other health problems. Similar unintended consequences of actions often taken for understandable reasons abounded.[64]

One must stress that there is no 'easy optimal solution' for these kinds of problems. For the individual hospital manager there is often no realistic place to send patients other than back from whence they came, in this case the nursing home. Only via more radical choices, such as putting Covid patients in empty hotels with limited nursing staff around them could one avoid the two problems above, but that would then open the authorities to accusations of negligence. Only when there is much more tolerance for reasonable judgments without fear of blame can one avoid the trap that 'being seen to do the right thing' leads to the wrong thing being done.

The problem of infected animals is another instructive story of failure. During 2020 it became clear that bats, minks, dogs, tigers, ferrets, rats and many other animals with which humans regularly interact could also carry the virus. The fact that minks were able to infect humans was already documented,[65] but it's likely that many other ferret-type animals can infect humans

64 Many of these are discussed further in Frijters (2021B), https://clubtroppo.com.au/2021/02/03/covid-congestion-effects-why-are-lockdowns-so-deadly/

65 World Health Organization (2020C),
https://www.who.int/csr/don/03-december-2020-mink-associated-sars-cov2-denmark/en/

too. Wiping out all infected animals or vaccinating them is impossible: the history of trying to wipe out small, fast-breeding animals like minks and bats is a litany of failures.

This did not stop governments from trying. As recently as July 2020, the government of Spain ordered the culling of more than 90,000 mink at a farm in the north-eastern province of Aragón after it was discovered that 87% of them carried the virus. A mutated form of the virus then showed up in Danish mink three months later, leading the government there to order the country's entire population of mink to be culled. About 17 million of these animals were summarily placed on mink death row, waiting to be gassed with carbon monoxide. A wave of opposition to the moral and legal status of the government's extermination order gave the minks a temporary stay, but unfortunately from the minks' standpoint not for long, and they were duly executed.

Mink are farmed in Sweden, Finland, the Netherlands, Poland and the United States, and they are also found in the wild — nocturnal, shy, and living in little holes and crevices near water. Creatures like this in their millions, burrowed into holes and hiding in caves all around the world, simply cannot be eliminated. Nor can we vaccinate them. We thus cannot eliminate Covid either, not even if every human on the planet gets a perfect vaccine.[66]

Animals aside, governments weren't able to lock everything down as they had hoped because the necessities of life ensured that a lot of mixing continued, particularly by the wrong groups. Even well-intentioned governments had pretty much no chance of 'controlling' either the spread or the lethality of Covid once it became endemic in March 2020, but they could make matters worse with lockdowns that forced their populations to become

---

66 There have been numerous instances of invasive small species, such as rats, being successfully eliminated from islands. This was feasible because islands are relatively small and discrete areas where the watery perimeter forms a natural barrier to re-entry of a species once it has been removed. Eliminating species from mainlands, however, has been almost universally unsuccessful.

poorer, unhealthier, and more vulnerable to Covid itself. Lockdowns were a gigantic failure even on their own terms, as we will discuss later.

The smart thing to do would have been to encourage experimentation with different strategies around the world and even within regions of individual countries. More experiments would mean more to be learned from both the successes and the failures. Incredibly, governments and health scientists frequently did the opposite, which was to disparage the policies of others rather than encourage them and pay attention to the outcomes.

Think of some of the experiments that could have been tried in a more cooperative environment. As one example, suppose a regional government accepts the inevitability of a large wave of infections. It staffs the part of its health system in contact with the most vulnerable elderly with workers from other countries who had already recovered from the virus and were therefore probably immune.

Such a region could also try to achieve immunity in its own healthy population by openly encouraging healthy volunteers below age 60 to live normal lives, in the full knowledge that doing so brought a higher risk of infection. Once recovered, the now immune healthy people then could take over the care of the elderly and provide a larger pool of immune workers to share with other regions. You might call such a two-pronged experiment 'targeted protection and exposure'. It capitalises on the general idea of herd immunity, which is that if some fraction (like 80%) of a population acquires immunity to a disease then small waves of infections die out because the virus is not transmitted widely enough to survive, protecting the 20% who are not immune.

Many other experiments could have been tried in different regions and their outcomes shared. In the place of such cooperative experimentation was adversarial competition, with countries trying different things while constantly criticising all others who made alternative choices. Even when it was obvious that some success had been achieved with different approaches in other countries, the typical response of health experts in the West was to say, in effect, 'They have different circumstances and what they are doing will not work here'. This just made it harder to learn from each other in a calm, objective manner.

STORYLINE OF THE GREAT PANIC

The story started in China. On New Year's Day, 2020, the authorities closed the hotspot of a Covid outbreak, a traditional wet market called the Huanan Seafood Wholesale Market in the city of Wuhan. Three weeks later, on January 23, the whole city of Wuhan with its population of 11 million was quarantined, although by the time the lockdown came into effect five million residents had escaped by any means possible.[67] Those who remained were kept in their residential compounds like animals in a zoo. In Wuhan, the lockdown lasted 76 days.

By the end of the day on January 24, the quarantine had already been extended to 12 additional cities in Hubei province, sealing off about 50 million people. In the ensuing months, this example was followed elsewhere in China and then across most of Asia and the world. Only very few did nothing. By the end of March 2020, most of the world's population had succumbed to the Great Panic. Some governments restricted their populations for weeks, some for months, and some locked down off and on for well over a year. Even as late as July 2021 there were some governments, such those in Australia's states, that were still going at it with relish.

With the benefit of hindsight and the time to reflect on what can and cannot

---

67 https://www.voanews.com/science-health/coronavirus-outbreak/where-did-they-go-millions-left-wuhan-quarantine

be done to control the spread of a virus, it is easy to say what governments should have done, namely very little. The WHO's advice of November 2019 and the blueprints available to health authorities in rich countries favoured social distancing but were equivocal about lockdowns because of their huge social and economic costs. Advice leaned toward doing one's best for particularly vulnerable sub-populations and otherwise simply accepting that diseases will have victims and telling populations to get on with their lives.

Implementing this advice was politically impossible in the circumstances of early 2020. Even countries with many barriers in place to prevent lockdowns, like the UK and the Netherlands, succumbed to the political pressure in March, ignoring scientific objections and legal hurdles. In hindsight, what was needed to prevent the fear from winning were barriers at the national or international level to stop the Panic from getting out of hand and to give politicians a stronger incentive to behave responsibly.

We will return later in the book to what those barriers might look like, but first we need to more fully understand what actually happened and why it was so foolhardy.

Let us begin by surveying the scene after March 2020. What did countries do?

THE COVID CURVE – WAS IT FLATTENED OR FATTENED?

In most countries, authorities acted to reduce human movements by forcibly shutting down businesses deemed 'nonessential', halting most travel, criminalising many forms of social interaction, closing schools, and enacting curfews.

Within countries, there was often significant regional variation and even variation within metropolitan areas in the timing and severity of the restrictions, making for a patchwork quilt of controls that government officials often proudly displayed on colour-coded maps. These maps, which had undoubtedly been laboured over for days by busy bees in the nether regions of health ministries, were sometimes instantly obsolete because localities with the same colour might use their discretionary powers to tweak the rules in different ways. This was apt to cause confusion in the general public, heightening frustration and impatience among Janes and Jasmines alike.

The promise to the population initially was that the tough restrictions — or 'suppression strategies', as some called them — would slow down the spread of the virus such that there would be fewer very sick people at any given time, resulting in a longer, flatter wave. Spreading the wave of illness over a longer period would allow health services to treat more patients as they would not have to turn away sick individuals at the peak of the pandemic. 'Flattening the curve' was the slogan bestowed upon this first reason to control the population.

As weeks became months and months stretched into a second year, the goal posts shifted. The second excuse for all the restraints was 'protecting the population' by preventing the spread of the virus. The third excuse was to provide a 'bridge to the vaccines'. When the vaccines came and threatened to take away the excuse for control, another rabbit was plucked from the hat of excuses: this was to 'protect against new variants'. The worst extremists advocated a 'zero-Covid' strategy that would logically necessitate indefinite total control over the activities of the population.

Every excuse concocted during the Great Panic for suspending normal human activity was dressed up to look as scientific as possible. Governments and their science advisors got almost everything wrong, though not always deliberately. The actions that were sincerely intended to 'flatten the curve' actually made it pointier, increasing the amplitude of the waves of illness because the virus didn't conform to what 'experts' expected.

In March 2020 governments thought it was important to keep people inside to prevent infections occurring outside, which turned out to be counterproductive as nearly all infections happened inside buildings into which people had just been corralled.[68] Worse, it turned out to be important that people get some sunshine and exercise to keep them healthy, so frightening people and hustling them indoors must have needlessly weakened, sickened or killed millions, including some with Covid.

In April 2020 governments started to think masks might help prevent people from inhaling the virus and thus started making masks compulsory. This turned out to be ineffective. Masks failed to turn the tide of mass infections, and the masks themselves became collectors of the virus and other germs, kept in warm, moist pockets and then thrown away, whereupon they became a pollution risk.[69]

The genuine incompetence was ongoing and breathtaking, showing no signs of ending even in the second half of 2021 in the countries still caught in the Great Panic. To ensure people would be queuing up for the vaccines that their governments had provided to save the day, those same governments outlawed the prescription by medics of many cheap early-phase prophylactic medicines like ivermectin.[70] They threatened doctors who flouted these rules with fines or worse.[71] Instead, they forced unhealthy senior citizens to queue close together in indoor testing and vaccination centres where they were more likely to catch the virus.

As was predicted early on by more discerning scientists,[72] the vaccines failed to be the wonder weapons against Covid that they were promised to be. There were deadly or disabling side effects of the vaccines among some groups.[73] Also, they failed to offer 100% protection against catching Covid and

68 McGreevy (2021).

69 https://www.bbc.com/news/uk-wales-56972074

70 Kirsch (2021),
https://trialsitenews.com/do-the-nih-and-who-covid-treatment-recommendations-need-to-be-fixed

71 Health and Youth Care Inspectorate (2021).

72 Shi Lee et al. (2020).

73 https://www.cdc.gov/coronavirus/2019-ncov/vaccines/safety/adverse-events.html

passing it on to others. Worse, the vaccines have been claimed to accelerate the emergence of new variants and even facilitated the progress of Covid in the body in some cases.[74] One possible reason for this is something called antibody-dependent enhancement,[75] which refers to the stimulating effect of a vaccine on the body's production of many different antibodies.

If a vaccine is close to 100% effective, kicking off the production of the right antibodies in sufficient numbers that all of the Covid virus is killed off, then that is great. If a vaccine is far from 100% effective, however, mass vaccination can backfire. Some of the produced antibodies will kill most of the virus in the body, which is what they are supposed to do, but the virus mutations that are impervious to the antibodies will remain at large, enjoying the extra bonus that, thanks to the vaccine, they are now the only ones left to prey upon healthy cells. Other vaccine-created antibodies can fail to kill the virus but instead attach to it and function like a kind of 'entry key' to healthy cells in the body, thereby worsening an infection. In these ways vaccines can be counterproductive and can hasten the emergence of new mutations.

While these are very rare events and hard to prove definitively, it doesn't take many such 'enhancement' events to deliver new variants that make the current vaccines useless in the population. Indeed, using an imperfect vaccine on a grand scale precisely when there are many infected people in a population means that millions of individuals with Covid variants in their systems will be given a vaccine that creates favourable conditions specifically for those variants impervious to the vaccine. The preferable approach is to vaccinate only the vulnerable, reducing the number of bodies in which new variants immune to the vaccine are encouraged to flourish.

With complete eradication of Covid impossible anyway, Covid vaccination

---

74 Doctors for Covid Ethics (2021), https://doctors4covidethics.medium.com/urgent-open-letter-from-doctors-and-scientists-to-the-european-medicines-agency-regarding-covid-19-f6e17c311595

75 This potential problem was recognised early on (e.g., Graham 2020).

programs contained the seeds of their own ineffectiveness, while being costly, disruptive and riddled with side effects. They were in effect a mass medical experiment with unknown long-term costs and benefits.

THE UNFOLDING OF A PANIC

Three distinct periods can be identified in the global reaction to Covid.

The first phase, introduced at the start of the book, was the Great Fear of January-March 2020. In this phase the world became aware of the new virus and obsessed over the perceived threat, as social and mainstream media kept up a deafening drumbeat of negative news. Citizens called loudly on their governments to do something dramatic to protect them.

The Illusion of Control phase came next. In this second phase, governments pretended to be in control of the spread of the virus, while brandishing a stunning variety of regulations and technologies. They spoke of being 'tough', 'decisive', 'firm', and 'taking action'.

Leaders of smaller states seemed to engage in a competitive foot race to demonstrate that they had been tougher than their peers. Martyn Roper, the Governor of the Cayman Islands, typified this tougher-than-thou spirit: 'In Cayman, as we watched the number of COVID-19 cases around the globe steadily rise, the Premier and his Government took decisive, early action, far faster than almost anywhere else.'[76]

Meanwhile, from his perch atop the family of nations, UN Secretary General António Guterres urged his global subjects on to greater sacrifices: 'We must take decisive action to suppress the virus and alleviate suffering.'[77] (Guterres later redeemed himself somewhat by starting to alert the world to the famines and poverty caused by Covid policies.)

---

76 Roper (2020).

77 Guterres (2020).

Leaders everywhere fell over themselves to market Covid as a war that required exceptional collective sacrifice to win. As Sacrificers-in-Chief, they began to appear at their media conferences looking studiedly bedraggled, puffy-eyed, unshaven and shabbily attired. Justin Trudeau grew his beard, evoked the sacrifices Canadians made in the two World Wars, and in a comical attempt to mimic Churchill's famous 'We will fight them on the beaches' speech, he told the Canadian House of Commons: 'The front line is everywhere. In our hospitals and care centres, in our grocery stores and pharmacies, at our truck stops and gas stations. And the people who work in these places are our modern-day heroes.'[78]

When draconian measures were challenged, the official response was, frequently, to jiggle the banner of saving lives. When the Ombudsman for the Australian state of Victoria ruled that the state's imprisonment of 3,000 residents in nine public housing towers was a breach of their human rights, the response of the Housing Minister, Richard Wynne, was to lavish glory on himself and his colleagues, saying 'We make no apology for saving people's lives.'[79]

Depending on the country, the policies enacted in the name of protection from Covid brought quarantines, track-and-trace apps, tiered restrictions, school closures, full lockdowns, partial lockdowns, and many other 'measures'. This period in most countries lasted through all of 2020, though in some places it was off and on.

The third and final phase was the End Games. In this phase, which began in most places in 2021, virus-fatigued populations had to be given some hope that the restrictions to their lives would end with some notion of victory. In many countries this hope morphed into a salvation story of vaccines that would protect populations and allow a return to the situation of pre-2020.

78 https://twitter.com/cpac_tv/status/1249018271493509123?lang=en

79 https://www.abc.net.au/news/2020-12-17/lockdown-public-housing-towers-breached-human-rights-ombudsman/12991162

In this phase, sub-groups and even whole populations started to organise seriously against the restrictions and the abuses of power that had occurred during the Illusion of Control.

These three broad phases of the story board can be seen in almost every country, though the story differs in exact timing and particulars from place to place. Some countries saw none of the slide toward more dictatorial and corrupt government that others painfully suffered. Some populations ignored the hype over the virus and went about their business, while others eagerly complied and still others took a measured approach.

COUNTRIES' REACTIONS: THE MINIMALISTS, THE PRAGMATISTS AND THE COVID CULTS

Based on how each place reacted, we group countries and regions into the following categories: the Minimalists, the Pragmatists, and the Covid Cults.

1. *The Minimalists.* The minimalists enacted few compulsory measures to reduce social interaction.[80] By and large they allowed citizens and businesses to make their own decisions about what risks they were prepared to run, with governments doing their best to deal with the emerging problems such as economic recession due to the loss of trade with other countries, or overflowing hospitals.

Some minimalists, like Belarus and South Dakota in the USA, saw similar numbers of Covid cases to their neighbours while life went on almost as normally as is possible in a major recession. In other places taking a minimalist approach, such as Turkmenistan and Tanzania, governments failed to report meaningful data and the true situation isn't known.

---

80 We define minimalists as having an average 'stringency' for the whole of 2020 of less than 40 points on the scale used by the Oxford Blavatnik Stringency Index: https://www.bsg.ox.ac.uk/research/research-projects/covid-government-response-tracker

While the minimalist landscape featured voluntary reductions in movement and some social distancing mandates, these tended not to be followed consistently by citizens or enforced with particular zeal by their governments. Such places retained their pre-Covid social and political systems.

There were also some isolated cases of Covid cult regions belatedly going minimalist, such as the American state of Florida where in September 2020 the Republican governor Ron DeSantis set about reversing municipal Covid countermeasures and championing normalisation.[81] This included permitting restaurants, businesses and other facilities to reopen at 100% of capacity. The governor even advanced a college students' 'bill of rights' to defend students' entitlement to a student lifestyle, which controversially included having parties. These steps drew the ire of such luminaries as Anthony Fauci, the chief medical advisor to the Federal government, who said the decision to permit people to gather in large-ish groups was asking for trouble.[82]

2. *The Pragmatists.* The pragmatist countries included Sweden, Korea, Japan, Taiwan, Iceland and Estonia. Governments in these countries took actions such as widespread testing and targeted restrictions, but stopped short of extended wholesale lockdowns.[83] Social life was allowed to go on almost normally, though some pragmatists did make it harder for foreigners to enter. They closed few businesses and schools, and made minimal changes to political life.

The loss of life with Covid in the pragmatist countries was about half that in

---

81 It can reasonably be argued that Florida joined the pragmatists group rather than the minimalists. More important, in the authors' view, is that the state escaped from the Covid cults club and remained committed to its position through the ensuing winter as cases rose again, a rare feat. This distinguishes Florida from many regions around the world that relaxed restrictions only temporarily, between intermittent acts of suppression.

82 Nonetheless and in spite of its comparatively geriatric population, reopened Florida did not experience disproportionate health or economic devastation: Finley (2021), https://www.wsj.com/articles/vindication-for-ron-desantis-11614986751

83 In our empirical analysis, these countries are defined as being neither minimalists nor Covid cults during 2020: i.e., having an average 'stringency' above 40 but no more than 60 days of a 'stringency' above 70, which is the cut-off above which we deem restrictions to be equivalent to a lockdown.

the Covid cult regions, but without as much disruption to normal life. For example, in 2020 Sweden experienced Covid deaths on a scale similar to what was seen in the rest of the European continent. By the end of July 2021, Sweden's Covid population mortality rate had slipped to less than that of the European Union.

In East Asia, the pragmatist countries had remarkably few Covid deaths, though they failed to avoid other unwanted outcomes like falling birth rates. Japan, South Korea and Taiwan all had Covid population mortality rates of close to zero.

3. *The Covid Cults.* The governments and populations in Covid cult regions were obsessed with the risks of Covid.[84] The Covid cult club included around 90% of the world population. It comprised most of Europe and the Americas, Southeast Asia, India, China, Australia, New Zealand and much of Africa. Covid cult governments were usually quick to follow China's take-no-prisoners model, with little to no input from experts offering alternative data or holding alternative views. The public discourse that typically precedes major policy decisions in democracies was cast aside in Covid cult regions, under the pretence that leaders needed to act quickly and decisively.

Over time, Covid cult governments quietly upgraded their job description from 'flattening the curve' to eliminating the virus, a transformation that necessitated stronger suppression of dissent and the tightening or extending of restrictions.

These countries suffered enormous collateral damage, widespread abuse of power, and mass invasion of privacy. Their governments periodically acknowl-edged the existence of the damage being done to their own countries, but still dove compulsively into a fresh cycle of obsession with every new wave of Covid. They stuck stubbornly to the narrative that the future depended on sacrificing the present.

Some of the Covid cult regions joined this club late but made up for their

---

84 We empirically define as Covid cults those places with an average 'stringency' above 70 (i.e., lockdowns) for at least 60 days in 2020.

tardiness with compensatory zeal, such as Germany in 2021. Among the Covid cults we see massive drops in numbers of pregnancies and births, little to no interest in sexual activities and the total suspension of all celebrations and festivals. When confronted by Jasmines, the Janes in Covid cult regions often displayed bewilderment at what was said, like a drunk who, when told his kids are dying, has difficulty remembering that he even has kids.

The Covid cults' experiences are of particular human interest because of the huge costs of their actions to themselves and others.

COUNTRIES' COVID EXPERIENCES

Figure 1 below shows, for each of the three groups of countries, how Covid deaths per day evolved over time. In Table 3, more details are shown about selected countries in each group, including the date of the first lockdown and the percentage of Covid deaths that occurred after the imposition of lockdowns.

FIGURE 1

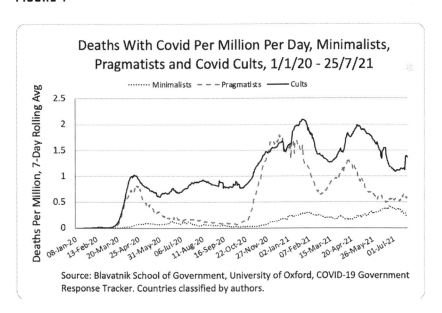

Source: Blavatnik School of Government, University of Oxford, COVID-19 Government Response Tracker. Countries classified by authors.

The most obvious message of Figure 1 is that the minimalists had far fewer claimed Covid deaths than either the pragmatists or the cults. This means that all claims made during the time of the Great Fear, like 'if we don't lock down then something disastrous will surely happen' were simply untrue. It was perfectly possible to have minimal restrictions and also minimal numbers of Covid deaths, although the reasons for those low death numbers might well have been entirely unrelated to policy choices, such as having a population with high prior immunity or very few vulnerable old people.

The second thing to note about Figure 1 is that the pragmatists suffered only a little over half the death rate of the cults. By the end of July 2021, the cults had accumulated around 600 deaths per million attributed to Covid, while the pragmatists were at around 330 deaths per million. The waves arrived in pragmatist countries a bit later, which might explain why they remained calmer at the outset, but the end result was very similar. It's just that the pragmatists did not suffer many of the negative direct effects of lockdowns, such as deteriorating mental health, cancelled health treatments, loss of freedoms, forced closure of businesses, school disruptions and all the rest.

The main message, again, is that there was no extraordinary wave of deaths among the countries that did not lock down for long periods of time. The daily sermons by cult government officials that apocalypse was sure to follow any relaxation of restrictions was obviously wrong. Moreover, the lie was clear early on: no huge waves of Covid deaths came crashing onto the shores of pragmatist countries in mid-2020. Anyone in a cult country thinking rationally would have picked this up as an indication that government policies in her neck of the woods had run off the rails.

The third observation to take from Figure 1 is that the vast bulk of Covid deaths in all three groups of countries occurred between late 2020 and mid-2021, so fully 9 months after most of the lockdowns began in March-April 2020. This immediately makes a total mockery of the idea that lockdowns were preventing anything bad, and instead raises the question of how they may have actually increased the number of Covid deaths. Thinking along these lines, the Jasmines of the world were pointing out very early on that lockdowns make people unhealthy and more vulnerable, and that cheap preventative treatments existed that many cults and even pragmatist countries were ignoring.

TABLE 3

Deaths With Covid Per Million of Population in Selected Minimalist, Pragmatist, and Covid Cult Countries

Selected Countries	Covid Deaths/Million 1/1/20- 25/07/21	Covid Deaths/Million 2020	Date of First Lockdown	% of Covid Deaths Since Beginning of First Lockdown	Maximum Stringency Level 1/1/20 - 25/7/21
Minimalists					
Japan	119.34	26.07	-	-	50.93
Tajikistan	12.44	9.66	-	-	69.44
Taiwan	34.03	0.30	19/05/21	98.22	74.07
Belarus	359.42	151.20	-	-	42.59
Senegal	77.87	25.16	25/03/20	100.00	77.78
Pragmatists					
South Korea	40.09	17.73	22/03/20	94.65	82.41
Sweden	1425.35	849.02	-	-	69.44
Ghana	26.92	11.01	30/03/20	99.39	86.11
Uruguay	1712.15	52.29	4/02/20	99.93	87.04
Switzerland	1270.51	891.52	17/03/20	99.75	73.15
Covid Cults					
Canada	705.02	418.28	20/03/20	99.94	75.46
Argentina	2305.01	962.31	19/03/20	99.99	100.00
Philippines	250.94	85.50	15/03/20	99.96	100.00
Australia	36.19	35.84	24/03/20	99.13	78.24
United Kingdom	1932.03	1099.88	23/03/20	99.72	87.96
United States	1860.94	1072.89	21/03/20	99.92	75.46
Minimalists	74.57	20.78	21/03/20	99.99	97.22
Pragmatists	329.17	143.55	17/03/20	99.85	100.00
Covid Cults	593.87	270.08	2/02/20	99.99	100.00

Countries were selected to give the reader a flavour of the data for the world as a whole. However, the aggregates in the final three rows include all 155 countries in the Tracker with populations greater than 1 million.

The details in Table 3 for particular countries show that policy changes were possible as the Great Panic unfolded. While Senegal was a minimalist country because in 2020 its average 'stringency' was below 40, it did try lockdowns for a short period in March 2020, as shown in its maximum stringency of 77.78 and the fact that it began a lockdown on March 25th 2020. It tried lockdowns but almost immediately abandoned them.

We also see that many pragmatists did experience a lockdown. Unlike the cults, the lockdowns of the pragmatists were less than two months in 2020 in total. Table 3 also shows that well over 95% of Covid deaths in all countries shown came after, not before, the imposition of lockdowns. Lockdowns didn't lead subsequently to any clear prevention of Covid deaths.

For completeness, we note finally that the cults in Europe and the Americas (including Argentina and the US, both shown in Table 3) had much higher numbers of Covid deaths than the average across Covid cult regions. The main reason for this is that India and China are counted among the cults because they officially had very high restrictions for a long time, while experiencing, in relative terms, very few Covid deaths. It's quite possible, even likely, that their low death counts had to do with the structure and prior immunity of their populations, but simply to be consistent we include their numbers anyway in Figure 1. If we were to compare cults to pragmatists in 2021 (so long after initial lockdowns) but limit ourselves geographically to Europe and the Americas, the cult countries would have even higher Covid death numbers compared to the pragmatists.

PHASE II

THE ILLUSION OF CONTROL (APRIL-DECEMBER 2020)

THE EXPERIENCES OF JANE, JAMES, AND JASMINE DURING THE ILLUSION OF CONTROL

JANE'S EXPERIENCE

Jane avidly followed the news on Covid, glad that her government had taken action and keen to make sure that she, her neighbours, and her family would do their bit in the fight against the virus. If she had to give up her job because it was deemed nonessential, she was willing to make the sacrifice. If her children were forbidden to go to school, she was willing to protect them at home. If she couldn't visit her relatives and friends, it was worth it to keep them safe.

She judged the peril of the situation according to whether the number of cases was going up or down. If the number was going up, it was clearly time to tighten things up with greater sacrifices. If the number of cases was decreasing, it was a sign that her sacrifices were paying off.

If masks were said to be useless, she wouldn't wear them. When the authorities said they saved lives, she would wear them and ensure the whole family wore theirs, even inside their own car. If she saw someone outside without a mask she would give them a dirty look or remonstrate with them. If the neighbours had more friends over than the government stipulated, she would report them. If her local pub allowed people to stand where they shouldn't, she would report them too. She downloaded any app the government asked her to download. She hated Covid-deniers and rule-breakers with a passion.

She understood the government's use of words and sometimes enjoyed using them herself, throwing out phrases like 'local lockdown', 'circuit-breaker', 'social bubble', 'office rotation', 'global pandemic', 'greater good', and 'rapid testing'. She supported unquestioningly every other ingenious idea and technology that the government-tech coalition was rolling out.

In the many months following the initial lockdowns, Jane was 100% supportive of 'tough measures'. If it were up to her, the army would enforce social distancing and people not wearing masks would be imprisoned or given draconian fines to punish them for being the anti-social hooligans she took them for. Whenever she heard protests about governments assuming too many powers, she dismissed them as missing the point: of course governments had to take control in these times and they would naturally give up all of their new powers after this emergency. When it was about life or death, there was no time to waste on vague notions of 'liberty'. What use does a corpse have for liberty?

Jane did find the quick changes in rules bewildering and berated the government for not being consistent, tough, and decisive enough. She didn't like the news that jobs were being lost, but would delight in any story about new businesses succeeding and believed fervently that things would eventually return to normal.

In this long period her fears ebbed and flowed, depending on the reported trajectory of cases and how close the virus got to her and her family. Cases at her job, the schools nearby, or in her extended family would increase her worry. Otherwise she tried to get on with her life as best she could, including having safe vacations and planning what to do with the whole family during the year-end holidays.

She did now and then read about some pieces critical of the measures she supported, but was glad to see them refuted immediately in her local media as self-serving conspiracy theories whose authors operated paedophile rings and believed lizard people were running the government. The technical arguments of the sceptics, which of course she didn't read, were debunked in long pieces written by the scientists she saw regularly on the news. Of course, the critics were also denounced by government spokespersons.

She did think that her government was struggling but cut it a lot of slack because of the sheer difficulty of the fight against this evil virus. She blamed the virus for everything that went wrong and was certain that when it was defeated, whatever was lost would return.

BOB PEPPERSTOCK'S STORY (CONTINUED)

The national lockdown in Vietnam started on April Fool's Day, initially for a period of 15 days but later extended to the end of the month for the bigger cities. Schools were closed and nonessential businesses closed too. There were strict physical distancing rules, mandatory face masks in public and travel restrictions. People were asked to not leave their residences except to get medical care or buy food.

The Vietnamese public adhered to the rules and my casual observation suggests they supported them strongly, and would have no problem reporting anyone who didn't obey the authorities.

By the beginning of May, we were 100 days out from the first case in Vietnam and more than 200,000 people had spent time in quarantine camps. By the end of the year it was 730,000.

I was frightened of Covid and realised that extreme measures were necessary. Everywhere I went I had a plastic gun-style thermometer pressed to my forehead and if my temperature was 'above normal' I would be refused admittance and told to go to a hospital for a Covid test. So for example if I went out of the condo compound where I live to go to the 7-11 down the street I had my temperature taken by the security staff at the gate, who then recorded it in a big ledger book. Then I would have my temperature taken again at the 7-11 and have to write my name and phone number in a book there. Same again when I returned to the condo building. I couldn't just avoid it by staying in my room all day because if my name didn't show up in the book for 24 hours the security people would come to my apartment.

Sometimes the authorities would go door-to-door in the building, taking temperatures and administering tests. They have a classification system for people, as follows:

- **F0**: someone who has tested positive. (S)he goes straight to hospital regardless of symptoms and is interrogated by health professionals, civil servants, the military and security personnel to draw up a list of locations (s)he had visited and people (s)he might have been in contact with during the preceding 14 days.
- **F1**: someone who is tracked down from the list supplied by the F0. (S)he is visited, tested, and removed to a quarantine camp.
- **F2**: these had contact with an F1. They only had their temperatures taken and were asked to self-quarantine at home pending the results of the test on F1. If the F1 returned a positive test then the F2 was likely to be quarantined too.

I was always a bit scared of having my temperature taken because if the device was malfunctioning or if my temperature was elevated for some reason (I do have allergies and these cause temperature spikes sometimes), then I was immediately under suspicion. More than once I woke up in the middle of the night thinking I'd heard a knock on the door. And one time I had a nightmare about the KGB. April was not a good month for my blood pressure.

VOICES FROM THE INDIAN SUBCONTINENT (REAL PEOPLE SPEAKING IN THEIR OWN WORDS)

The following is a selection of short letters to the editors of news outlets penned by citizens of India and Pakistan. They are all compliers (i.e., Janes), but some are starting to have critical insights.

SAMEER UMRANI, OF KARACHI, PAKISTAN, IN THE NATION, APRIL 6, 2020

The death toll from the coronavirus outbreak rose to 25 on Monday, with a tally of confirmed cases in Pakistan jumping to 1,762 including 20 deaths.

In Pakistan, Punjab is affected very badly by Coronavirus with 638 confirmed cases and still increasing on a daily basis. The reason behind the firm or fast spread of Coronavirus in Punjab is the unseriousness of the public. They are still taking it lightly and not following a single precautionary measure like regular washing of hands, using sanitiser, wearing surgical masks and avoidance of social meet-ups.

However, Dr Yasmin Rashid the Provincial Minister for Health declared that 'A complete lockdown is the best way to stop the outbreak.' She appealed to the masses to confine themselves to their homes. But still, people can be seen roaming around on the streets, markets and crowds can be spotted everywhere in the province despite a prohibition.

Lastly, I personally salute the doctors and nurses of my nation. They are spending sleepless nights serving the patients and curbing the world pandemic but due to low allocation of budget on health and unavailability of medical equipment, they are disappointed.

I urge the government to take serious measures to eradicate Coronavirus outbreak from Punjab by enforcing lockdown and curfew because the long existence of Coronavirus can damage our economy which is already under the ebb.

G. VASANTHARAJAN, OF THIRUVANANTHAPURAM, INDIA, IN THE HINDU, APRIL 15, 2020

As a person under quarantine after a visit to Kerala, I wish to narrate our experience. Though we did not have any symptoms, we were advised to be in quarantine. We have no problems with the way the health department reached out to us. The issue is about the panic the quarantine sticker has caused in the neighbourhood. We live in a house, which is surrounded by other houses. However the social attitude is distressing. We are an educated family and understand that the virus is contagious and precautionary steps are necessary. Being unable to reduce the panic around us is a challenge. All quarantined persons are not infected. As a close relative says, "we are being isolated by society just for being quarantined". I now understand how tough life is for those who live on the margins of society. Understanding and education are a must.

A. BHUYAN, IN THE TRIBUNE, MAY 30, 2020

It is, unfortunately, observed that the names of Covid-19 patients are being made public by the media as well as the authorities. While we must strongly fight the virus, making public the names of patients is unhealthy and an invasion of privacy. Nobody wants to get infected willingly. The patient and his/her family members get stigmatised for no fault of theirs. Even people undergoing quarantine because they have come from outside the state have started to carry a stigma. Humanity, without doubt, is suffering from the current pandemic. However, our fight should be focused against the pandemic, rather than exposing vulnerable patients and their family members.

AYUSHI BISHT, OF DEHRADUN, INDIA, IN THE TRIBUNE, JULY 22, 2020

Labourers in vehras [an open space inside a house] are accustomed to living in dismal conditions, where they do not even have basic amenities. The small rooms are outnumbered by the people living there, hence the congested areas often have huge gatherings. How can we expect them to practice social distancing under such living conditions? Their health and safety should be a matter of grave concern. The department concerned should hasten work to construct public toilets, or shift workers to a safer place. Moreover, these vehras should be monitored, or else these places will also turn into Covid hotspots.

SANJAY AGGARWAL, SOLAN, INDIA, IN THE TRIBUNE, JULY 13, 2020

The editorial 'For Himachal's sake' (July 11) rightly calls for a review of the decision regarding permission to allow entry into Himachal. Ours is a tourism-dependent economy, but it will not be advisable to let in tourists. As it is, the locals too are taking things lightly and can be seen moving without masks. It will be very late if things go out of hand.

AYUSHI BISHT, DEHRADUN, INDIA, IN THE TRIBUNE, SEPTEMBER 25, 2020

Apropos of 'CM: Violation of Covid protocols worrying' (Sept 23), we need Covid safety protocols and public awareness campaigns because we can see how masks are being treated as helmets by the people. People are not understanding the seriousness of the situation and are wearing a mask when they spot police personnel. Moreover, people have started ignoring social distancing norms and are prioritising their interests over safety. Rather than just wait for the government to take steps, we should do our best to ensure our safety.

DYSTOPIA2'S STORY (IN HIS OWN WORDS)

Dystopia2 is the online name of a Canadian expatriate living in Thailand. He became a regular commentator on Covid-related stories in one of the major national English-language dailies. The following are excerpts from some of his posts between 2 and 10 April, 2020.

Lock down Bangkok, now. Police are useless. Army needs to be on the street to enforce stay-at-home order. Only allow people out for grocery store/

pharmacy purchases. Close all street markets including those selling food. It's difficult to advocate suspension of civil liberties. But, it's evident that there are always going to be selfish, stupid people everywhere (not just Thailand) that are going to ignore the rules. Also, if people upcountry want to continue to ignore this, and gather, even in homes to eat and drink from common sources, then let them get sick and die. Maybe when that happens these fools will wake up.

I'm 68 and if I get this virus, I'll likely die. So, if putting soldiers and tanks on the street keeps people the hell away from me when I absolutely have no choice but to go out, I'm all for it.

[On police breaking up parties in Phuket during lockdown.] Clearly, there's no shortage of irresponsible Thais and foreigners acting in selfish and reckless ways, showing a complete disregard for the well-being of the people of Thailand. Apart from charges they should be put in forced quarantine with ankle monitors as is now happening in the US and Canada for people who violate quarantine.

[On government restrictions so far.] They should be doing what they're implementing in Canada. They announced an even more stringent country-wide lockdown for at least 3 months and will reassess after that. They are fining people $400 CDN (9,000 B) if they are not standing at least 2 meters apart. If people charged for violating social distancing or who are out for no specific reason do not identify themselves, they are fined an additional $700 CDN (16,000 B). As the worry is Toronto will become another NY, they are getting justifiably tough. This should be happening here.

[On international arrivals who avoided quarantine.] Regarding the 152 Thai returnees who rejected the state quarantine, they have shown themselves to be irresponsible, having no regard whatsoever for the safety of their fellow Thais." "Irresponsible" is the key word as it reflects a cultural trait of abiding self-interest at the expense of others, especially among the "Do you know who I am?" class.

[On the number of people infected.] Don't be naive. There are most likely many more infected than officials know about, especially upcountry. There's a stigma attached to having the virus and most people aren't being tested because of the cost. Add to this those that are asymptomatic. There are also likely additional deaths that have been mistakenly attributed to other causes. Since a doctor is not required in most rural areas to sign off on cause of death and the family can just take the body to the Wat for cremation, it's difficult to know exactly the true numbers.

JAMES' EXPERIENCE

James was transformed in the Illusion of Control phase. Whereas in the Great Fear he had sprung into action to defend his people from a terrible new threat, this new phase was a time of great change offering both risks and opportunities.

The first thing he did was deal with foreigners trying to enter the country. By mid-May 2020, only Mexico, the UK and Syria were still open to foreign travellers without any quarantine restrictions. A small handful of countries were open but only with onerous quarantine requirements, while the rest were closed either to specific countries or to everyone.[85]

A few countries even kicked off the process of closing internal borders against their own citizens. In Australia on 22 March, the state of Tasmania began requiring 'nonessential' incoming travellers to quarantine themselves for 14 days upon arrival. The Northern Territory, Queensland, Western Australia and South Australia all followed suit two days later. The premier of Queensland, Annastacia Palaszczuk, was clear in expressing her thoughts about the impurity of Australians from other states: 'Extraordinary times call for extraordinary measures,' she said. 'They [the new measures] are to stop holidaymakers leaving southern states and risking the spread of this virus

---

85 Brumfiel & Wilburn (2020), https://www.npr.org/sections/goatsandsoda/2020/05/15/855669867/countries-slammed-their-borders-shut-to-stop-coronavirus-but-is-it-doing-any-goo

through Queensland.'[86] The quarantine measures were forerunners of later decrees by states to close their borders altogether.

The great change came from new insights on the virus, insights on what actions seemed useful against the spread and severity of the disease, and the acquired experience with the enormous number of new directives. James was heavily involved in the drafting of new rules and recommendations, many of which patched loopholes in earlier rules. For example, when it turned out that parties in one's own home could not be outlawed within the confines of the existing Health Acts, emergency powers were required.

James was also involved in planning the introduction of regional and local rules. The directives brought down by higher entities such as national governments usually allowed for some discretion in terms of implementation at lower administrative levels. In some instances this flexibility was real, while in others it was largely window dressing. This was particularly the case in autocratic states where a phone call from the Big Boss to each of his provincial governors always sufficed to get everyone reading from the same page. In these instances, the result was a uniformity of rules across large land masses, city and suburb, skyscraper and farm, that failed to recognise the real needs of anyone. Often this was ameliorated by local police simply not enforcing the directives, or enforcing them on an occasional basis to preserve appearances.

The entire world around government was changing fast, with many new challenges. As had happened during the Great Fear, opportunities emerged as entrepreneurial Jameses learned how money could be made if they moved quickly. Suppliers of tests, both old and new, could make billions if governments made their test mandatory for schools and travel, which attracted hundreds of applicants and gave James in government an opportunity to sell his support to them.

---

86 Palaszczuk (2020), https://statements.qld.gov.au/statements/89585

Many of the firms vying to sell tests had products that agencies like the FDA in the US couldn't approve because, among other things, 'significant problems' had been found with the tests themselves. The FDA kept a long list of failed applicants who, it said on its website, 'should no longer be offering the tests.'[87]

Likewise, hundreds of new suppliers of face masks, gloves and other PPE equipment knocked on James' door to convince him that the whole of government should use their particular gear, giving him an opportunity to do a private deal with befriended manufacturers and individual entrepreneurs. These entrepreneurs were typically just brokers, often working from their own homes, who acquired merchandise through a long chain of intermediaries. In the spirit of tollkeepers on a complicated road network, each person in the chain took a commission as the merchandise meandered to its final destination. Price gouging was the inevitable result, with comical trades observed like New York State paying 15 times the normal prices for medical equipment such as N95 masks.[88]

Cronyism ran riot. In California, where normal open tender procedures had been suspended, billions were thrown at entities with few or no credentials to supply the equipment they were contracted to deliver. Some of these entities were obscure if not completely fly-by-night, as in the case of Blue Flame Medical mentioned earlier,[89] while others were sufficiently large and opaque to raise red flags. For example, after the Blue Flame deal was snuffed out, California dipped even deeper into its bucket of taxpayer cash to fund

---

87 FDA (2021), https://www.fda.gov/medical-devices/coronavirus-covid-19-and-medical-devices/removal-lists-tests-should-no-longer-be-used-andor-distributed-covid-19-faqs-testing-sars-cov-2

88 McSwane (2020), https://www.propublica.org/article/the-secret-absurd-world-of-coronavirus-mask-traders-and-middlemen-trying-to-get-rich-off-government-money; Salman et al. (2020), https://www.usatoday.com/in-depth/news/investigations/2020/07/23/covid-ppe-face-mask-shortage-draws-new-companies-us-contracts/5459884002/

89 Hamburger & Eilperin (2020), https://www.washingtonpost.com/politics/justice-department-investigates-blue-flame-medical-after-claims-it-failed-to-provide-masks-ventilators-to-maryland-california/2020/05/06/e30b5224-8fa1-11ea-9e23-6914ee410a5f_story.html

a US$1.4 billion contract with a Chinese firm called BYD to supply N95 and surgical masks. BYD, as it happened, was an electric bus manufacturer with a Los Angeles-based subsidiary and a manufacturing plant in Lancaster that employed close to a thousand people. It was also a contributor to Newsom's election campaign.[90]

Meanwhile, in the UK, contracts were also dished out under emergency procedures that skirted normal competitive bidding. As in California and elsewhere, billions in taxpayer funds were dispensed to individuals in private deals. With no official oversight to police what was going on, news outlets launched their own investigations and found that, among others, members of the governing Tory party were massive beneficiaries.[91] To borrow Jim Hacker's immortal words in the British comedy series 'Yes, Minister', officials had 'their snouts in the trough. And most of them have got their two front trotters in as well.'[92]

Companies involved in e-commerce that experienced a boom in business as a result of lockdowns and the general elevated level of fear associated with the virus knocked on James' door to get favourable travel-corridor exemptions for the next round of lockdowns.

Home-office supply companies similarly wanted his business, and of course a large number of companies wanted to be declared essential businesses, while having their competitors named nonessential.

Few industry sectors benefited more than Big Tech. Covid was the perfect alignment of stars for companies like Facebook. Not only because the virus meant that everyone with an internet connection became Mark Zuckerberg's

---

90 Grimes (2020), https://californiaglobe.com/section-2/exclusive-gov-newsoms-byd-mask-deal-profitable-for-insider-dealmakers/; Rosenhall & Morain (2020), https://calmatters.org/health/coronavirus/2020/04/california-coronavirus-face-masks-gavin-newsom-byd/; Associated Press (2020), https://www.marketwatch.com/story/us-regulators-wont-approve-chinese-firms-n95-masks-potentially-scuttling-1-billion-california-deal-2020-05-13

91 https://www.bbc.com/news/uk-56319927; Collins et al. (2020), https://www.thetimes.co.uk/article/tory-backers-net-180m-ppe-deals-xwd5kmnqr

92 See from 3:35 of https://www.youtube.com/watch?v=4kGx2XkWrrs

customer, adding another US$30 billion to his personal wealth.[93] Not only because he had the President of the United States eating out of his hand. Also because all the while he could position himself as the quintessential do-gooder, particularly through the Chan-Zuckerberg Initiative, a philanthropic organisation specifically targeting disease elimination. The charity gave out a lot of money: US$104 million for Covid research, testing and treatment, and also to help communities that were drastically affected by the virus. His causes were good and his optics were great.

Zuckerberg did so much good that it became nearly impossible for his enemies to criticise him for being so wealthy, even as he got a lot wealthier still.

Facebook was also able to use the opportunity to clean up its bad reputation as an information platform. It put together the COVID-19 Information Center and displayed it at the very top of the Facebook app. This carried health information from authoritative sources along with messaging that encouraged people to stay safe at home — where, of course, they would spend more time using Mr Zuckerberg's services. At one point Zuckerberg expressed his concern that shelter-in-place restrictions were going to be lifted too soon, that some of the more vulnerable places would be reopened prematurely and that this would lead to further negative health and economic consequences.[94]

But Zuckerberg's stout-hearted largesse didn't end there. While most companies were laying off workers, Facebook hired more than 10,000 people over the course of the year, many of them in product and engineering positions that would putatively develop better tools for small entrepreneurs trying to build their businesses, on Facebook's various platforms, of course.

The Illusion of Control phase saw a complete restructuring of political

---

93 Tiku & Greene (2021), https://www.washingtonpost.com/technology/2021/03/12/musk-bezos-zuckerberg-gates-pandemic-profits/

94 Bursztynsky (2020), https://www.cnbc.com/2020/04/29/facebook-ceo-zuckerberg-warns-against-reopening-public-spaces-too-soon.html

networks surrounding governments. Many of the old power brokers, such as airlines and hotel companies, were all but irrelevant in the new era as they had no customers and could be punished by the withholding of survival subsidies if they complained too much about the regulations that were killing their businesses. New players were emerging, including large new institutions where tens of thousands of people were enforcing social distancing rules, checking up on business premises or developing the new mobile apps.

There were also opportunities arising purely from the distractedness of the public amidst its Covid obsession. James was able to reduce taxes that he hated, such as steep property and other taxes his rich friends had to pay, while relaxing the environmental regulations that applied to befriended mining companies and others. The fact that the population was looking away also allowed James to grab more executive control for himself and his friends, often bypassing parliament and having nightly news conferences in which it was made abundantly clear who was now firmly in charge.

The Great Fear, in which James had only reluctantly become involved as a defender of the population, now morphed for him into the Great Opportunity for Advancement, though not one that was risk-free. Many others were also vying to capitalise on the new opportunities. James therefore got busy making new alliances, jettisoning old ones that were no longer useful and grabbing as much for himself as possible.

Eager for a seat on the gravy train, some entrepreneurial Jameses overstepped just as they had during the Great Fear phase. One of these was an Australian athleisure clothing chain named Lorna Jane after its founder Lorna Jane Clarkson. The company's marketing claimed that its clothes — sprayed with a substance called 'LJ Shield' — protected the wearer against Covid. It was later fined A$5 million in federal court for misleading the public.[95]

---

95 https://www.abc.net.au/news/2021-07-23/qld-lorna-jane-fined-5m-false-covid-claims/100318840

Meanwhile, the more scientifically-minded Jameses were also busy cementing their new power, but by the rules of the scholarly game. Scientific Jameses churned out large volumes of papers, books, blogs, and op-eds arguing that all the previous decisions were sensible and that it was imperative that the control mechanisms in place stay in place, preferably indefinitely given all the new risks being discovered daily. He derided any critics, made sure sceptical colleagues were fired or at least prevented from publishing and getting new grants, and appeared on the news as often as possible to demonstrate new technology that promised more control over the virus.

Some of the scientific Jameses had successfully grabbed the opportunity for more power offered during the Great Fear. Neil Ferguson was one, but by early May he was forced to resign from the UK government advisory panel for breaking the lockdown restrictions that he himself had advised the government to impose back in March.[96]

Finding himself abruptly on the sidelines, Ferguson needed to find a way back into the public conversation on Covid. His opportunity came on 10 June, when he was invited to testify before the Science and Technology Committee of the British House of Commons.[97] He told them that the number of UK deaths could have been halved if Johnson had introduced the lockdown one week earlier. That got into all the papers, and he was off and running again.

In September he warned the government that without restrictions in place the UK was about to have another wave of Covid that would raise the level of infections to where it was back in mid-March.

Still, there were signs that Ferguson's insensitivity to the plight of the British public was beginning to soften. Indeed, in September he completely contradicted his initial position earlier that year that had pushed Johnson into

---

96 https://www.bbc.com/news/uk-politics-52553229

97 Johns (2020), https://www.imperial.ac.uk/news/198155/neil-ferguson-talks-modelling-lockdown-scientific/

a lockdown. Incredibly, though no one will ever know if he had a straight face when he said it, Ferguson told BBC Radio 4: 'I was always very conscious of what impact it [lockdowns] would have on society and the economy. So I've never been a complete enthusiast for the idea of locking down society. It was a last resort.'[98]

The Imperial College team reinforced that theme in November with its 'Report 35', in which they trotted out more big numbers, claiming that a targeted lockdown by economic sector would raise the UK's GDP by £163-205 billion above the level it could achieve with an undifferentiated national blanket lockdown.[99]

Imperial College's models and the lockdowns they inspired turned the UK into a model Covid cult country that racked up a stinker of a record compared to the rest of Europe and the world in terms of both infections and deaths from Covid. Ferguson will doubtless argue for years to come that if only his advice had been followed more quickly and executed more effectively, things would have turned out a lot better.

Another wonderful illustration of a quasi-scientist whom we introduced during the Great Fear, Brett Sutton in Victoria, Australia, went from strength to strength during the Illusion of Control phase. His boss, state Premier Dan Andrews, never missed an opportunity to remind the media and the general public that the government was following the best public health advice, which was Sutton's. This was partly Andrews' way of setting someone else up for the fall if things went pear-shaped, but it gave Sutton a stupendous public profile.

Sutton's advice virtually imprisoned Victorians for months at a time. In a second lockdown, from June 30 onward, he was behind the enactment of dozens of regulations controlling what people could and couldn't do. He had a curfew going for about eight weeks throughout August and September. He

---

98 Ferguson & Al-Khalili (2020), https://www.bbc.co.uk/programmes/m000mt0h
99 Haw et al. (2020).

dictated how far people could travel from home and for what reason, how many visitors they could have, what kind of exercise they could do, and just about everything else short of what they could eat for breakfast.

All of these directives were given teeth by rigorous enforcement and massive fines for non-compliance. An individual could be fined A$1,652 for not following the rules, for example by being away from the home without sufficient reason. The fine for not wearing a mask was A$200.[100]

Sometimes things got out of hand. In the first week of July, about 3,000 residents in nine public housing towers in Melbourne were prohibited from leaving the towers under any circumstances for five days. The state's ombudsman later ruled that this was a violation of their human rights.[101] The lawyer who took up the case for the tower residents nonetheless had her license to practise law revoked by an organisation of lawyers in Melbourne.[102] Very convenient for Sutton.

Like any clever James, Sutton learned that he never had to be enslaved by the advice he gave yesterday because he could always say the situation was 'rapidly evolving' or 'rapidly changing', or that he had 'new data' or 'new information' that required more stringent restrictions of freedoms. If one of those didn't work as a justification for tightening his grip on people's lives, he simply blamed the people themselves for not doing what they were told.

Sutton understood that the public was looking to follow someone, not hold him to account. He closed schools for three months, just one week after he had claimed that school closures would be an ineffective countermeasure.[103] It was the same story with masks. At first he came out against them. By June

---

100 Beers (2020), https://7news.com.au/lifestyle/health-wellbeing/victoria-stage-four-5000-penalty-for-victorians-who-breach-coronavirus-isolation-c-1214602

101 https://www.ombudsman.vic.gov.au/our-impact/news/public-housing-tower-lockdown/

102 Estcourt (2021),
https://www.theage.com.au/national/victoria/legal-watchdog-cancels-licence-of-lawyer-leading-tower-lockdown-lawsuit-20210415-p57jfo.html

103 Carey & Preiss (2020), https://www.theage.com.au/national/victoria/independent-schools-close-to-ward-off-virus-20200316-p54ai9.html

he was saying that new advice on masks was under consideration.[104] By July he had mandated them.

But Sutton's best footwork and most puffed up rhetoric of all was reserved for the overarching objective of lockdowns themselves. In March he assured people that the restrictions were all about easing pressure on the health system. In July, his macho rhetoric by now commensurate with the power he'd been granted, Sutton declared that his aim was to 'crush the curve.' In August he invoked the language of the US military, saying that he was using 'shock and awe' tactics to obliterate the second wave. Gradually, imperceptibly to many Victorians, he moved the goal to total elimination.[105]

Despite the draconian nature and sheer duration of Victoria's lockdowns, few people publicly questioned Sutton's expertise or his authority. Those who did so were quickly rounded on, even if they were important themselves. Josh Frydenberg, Australia's federal Treasurer, thought Victoria was making a mess of his national economic recovery program and blowing out the national budget.[106] This confrontation with the federal government made Sutton more popular still in his home state.

While the Andrews-Sutton team was justly famous for the missionary zeal with which they locked away Victorians, Sutton himself is only one of hundreds of Jameses in public health ministries worldwide who operated almost without criticism or oversight during the Illusion of Control phase. Every state in Australia had one. The US had Anthony Fauci. California had Mark

---

104 Landis-Hanley (2020), https://www.theguardian.com/australia-news/2020/jun/29/victorians-may-now-be-told-to-wear-face-masks-to-halt-covid-19-whats-changed

105 Burton & Wootton (2020),
https://www.afr.com/politics/federal/victoria-s-covid-19-infection-spreads-interstate-20200702-p558c4;
Ferguson (2020),
https://www.theaustralian.com.au/nation/coronavirus-freedom-the-first-casualty-in-an-anxious-city/news-story/c7dfd4568e9ebdc3d96123cc6dfadb5c

106 https://www.9news.com.au/national/coronavirus-economic-recovery-threatened-by-victoria-surge-in-cases-josh-frydenberg-warns/fa80f8de-22fa-4ddb-8e87-533ef12aa0cf; Davey & Hurst (2020), https://www.theguardian.com/australia-news/2020/oct/19/daniel-andrews-lashes-josh-frydenberg-over-attack-on-victorias-covid-strategy

Ghaly. The UK had Chris Whitty. Canada had Theresa Tam. Every Covid cult country, state and province had its own version. They were ruthless in exploiting opportunities to expand their power at the expense of others. How this was allowed to happen will be explored in depth in the following chapters.

JASMINE'S EXPERIENCE

Jasmine fought an uphill battle in this period. Her writings and other public utterances, whether inflammatory or presented according to the highest of scientific standards, could not reach a mass audience as much of social media was censored by law[107] and by Big Tech companies eager to enforce the views of the authorities.[108] Her papers were rejected by journals she would normally publish in,[109] the words she spoke in public garnered boos, her friends turned their backs on her, and many of her colleagues were now increasing their empires by trying to marginalise and belittle her.

So, over the months, Jasmine organised together with like-minded people around the world. The Jasmines wrote papers, pushed out declarations, analysed data and started reform-oriented movements. They documented the damage and related it to policies. They warned against the abuses of power and the opportunism of businesses profiting from the continued panic. They organised demonstrations and set up new media.

Their main message was that the control measures were doing much more damage than good and should be reversed. They advocated a return to the guidance science had put forward pre-2020 in the event of a pandemic.

In the first few months the Jasmines got nowhere and were totally ignored by most governments. They were derided as 'Covid deniers', 'granny killers',

---

107 For an early example of how governments applied pressure on Facebook to censor, see Field (2020); for what happened in the world, see Human Rights Watch (2021).

108 Niemiec (2020).

109 https://www.standard.co.uk/news/londoners-diary/the-londoner-let-children-be-exposed-to-viruses-says-professor-gupta-a4538386.html

and 'heartless bean counters'. Yet over time, some of those who lost out due to the regulations of the Illusion of Control helped the Jasmines to push their message. The new groups of unemployed, unhealthy, ignored and depressed people increasingly looked to sceptical voices to tell them what was really happening.

In different countries this happened in different ways. In Germany there were high-profile court cases against the government restrictions. In Italy there were violent riots. In the UK, some of the elite Jasmines gave lofty speeches in parliament and organised high-profile declarations. In the US a whole side of politics identified with Jasmine's sceptical message, and was derided for it on the basis of everything normally associated with that side of politics. In France the sceptics had lively debates on television with others. In Sweden and a few other places, the sceptics were actually in charge, and so had to fend off the pressures from those wanting to copy the measures that were in place in many other countries.

However, gradually Jasmines emerged who were regularly given airtime in the media and were increasingly listened to, as the damage of the regulations went on and on while heavily reported Covid waves and variants kept coming, no matter what policies were pursued.

NEIL'S STORY, CONTINUED

Even after being sent back to Australia with much fanfare, I was confident about returning to Boston in September of 2020. I even registered for classes and put down a payment on a university dormitory. However, in June or July the university released a document detailing their policies in the coming semester. These included mandatory frequent testing and universal masking, quarantines in specially-assigned dormitories, restrictions on how many people could occupy the same room, and bans on parties and musical rehearsals and performances. I was shocked and appalled, not merely because I disagreed with the policies, but because it seemed astounding that the university had the authority or desire to exert this much control over its students, given that it was clear even then that university-age students were not a high-risk age group.

The unilateral decision was made on behalf of all students, and you could either accept it or be damned. I chose the latter course. I sent a letter to the Dean of Students in which I firmly, but not aggressively laid out my beliefs. I then posted a petition on the class of 2022 Facebook page with the letter and an appeal to the general student body urging them to consider standing up to the administration if they disagreed with the policies.

It was an utter disaster. Instead of engaging with my arguments, friends and strangers alike preferred to insult me. Someone who for more than a year I considered to be my best friend, posted a comment which is seared into my brain: *I'm so glad we aren't friends anymore after the bullshit I just read. But what would I expect from someone who believes in reverse racism? Unrespectfully, do yourself a favor and shut up.* I suppose I should have been prepared for this – it is social media, after all. But these weren't strangers; they were my close friends and acquaintances. People stopped talking to me, friends lost respect for and were angry at me. And no one was prepared to even consider the possibility that something was terribly wrong. I think that remains the most infuriating thing.

For a short time I believe I experienced what real depression feels like, and I now have greater respect for the difficulties faced by the clinically depressed. Motivation evaporates; humor, music and sex have no appeal; eating brings no pleasure; you are physically and emotionally drained all the time. You want to sleep to stop feeling, but you can't. As I climbed slowly out of this hole, I was contending more and more with a different emotion: anger. More than I've ever felt before. Mostly my anger does not come on suddenly. It builds little by little as my thoughts spiral out of control. Violent, evil thoughts. The desire to hurt others, to take revenge on those who I feel have wronged me, and the joy derived from thinking about their pain. The wishful desire to take my own life, publicly, to make a statement, to take the one bit of control I have left and put it to use in a desperate effort to make people take me seriously. When this train leaves the station, my body temperature quickly and radically rises and I begin to sweat. The urge to break, smash or tear something becomes almost irresistible. Even as I write this I am disgusted with that part of myself. I know that everyone has this darkness in them, but I have not yet been able to forgive myself for thinking in this way as often as I have.

It is the lack of control that is so infuriating. There was no end in sight, I didn't know when I would see my friends again (I didn't even know how many I had left) and I felt like I was wasting my life away at home, bored and listless. Boredom and anger are a dangerous combination. Luckily I have found the drive to engage in projects which have pulled my attention. I also have a wonderful supportive and loving family. I could not have asked for better company through this difficult time.

ARI JOFFE'S STORY [A REAL PERSON SPEAKING IN HIS OWN WORDS]

I am embarrassed to say that I initially favored lockdowns. I thought that my expertise in infectious diseases and critical care medicine gave me (and my similarly trained colleagues) an ability to assess risk. But that training and expertise only gave me blinders — I was only able to see one infectious disease caused by SARS-CoV-2. I saw a pandemic unfolding and thought lockdowns would reduce viral transmission and deaths, as famously (inaccurately and tautologically) modeled at Imperial College.

I soon learned that my expertise was not really expertise at all.

First, I had seen the case fatality rate, and ignored the fact that the infection fatality rate (IFR) was over 10 times lower. In people aged over 70 years the IFR was 0.05%, and for those aged less than 50 years the IFR was lower than for seasonal influenza.

Second, it had somehow escaped me that the IFR had an inflection point at approximately age 70 years. The high-risk groups were individuals aged 60-69 years with severe comorbidities, and individuals aged 70 years or over, particularly in long-term-care homes. Focused voluntary protection of these groups was required, without shutting down all of society.

Third, from my privileged position I had not recognized predictable collateral effects of lockdowns, including loneliness, unemployment, economic recession, interrupted schooling, interrupted healthcare, domestic violence, overdoses and exacerbated inequality. Loneliness, unemployment and adverse childhood experiences I learned are among the top risk factors for shortened lifespan, mental health problems and chronic non-communicable diseases. Though a pediatrician, I failed to recognize that missing school will affect an entire generation with reduced social development, executive function (i.e., decision-making ability), earning potential, and future lifespan. Not trained in economics, I had not considered that government debt and reduced GDP mean less future spending on healthcare, education, roads, sanitation, housing, nutrition, vaccines, safety, social security nets, clean energy, and other services that determine population well-being and life expectancy.

After learning these things, I calculated that lockdowns (if they work to reduce SARS-CoV-2 transmission) cause at least 10 times *more* loss of well-being and life-years than they might prevent. To top it off, more studies continue to be published finding that lockdowns do not work to reduce transmission (and if they do, at best their efficacy has been highly exaggerated).

SANJEEV SABHLOK'S STORY [A REAL PERSON SPEAKING IN HIS OWN WORDS]

I came to Australia in December 2000. I had been a member of India's permanent senior civil service since 1982 but had decided to leave in order to politically change India's socialist model of governance. Since my initial attempt to form a liberal political party in India had not gone anywhere, I migrated to Australia in order to keep learning about good policy and good governance.

In 2005, after three failed attempts to form an Indian liberal party, I took Australian citizenship. Since 2007, I have actively supported the political work of Anil Sharma, an Indian liberal from London, and helped him form India's first liberal party in 2013. I remain a mentor and keen supporter of this party. My writings over the past two decades have thus focused mainly on bringing liberty to India. In these writings, I have often used Australia's institutions as a role model.

It was a shock when I found that Australia's institutions had suddenly and completely collapsed around me like ninepins in March 2020. My belief that Australia was a free nation was shattered. There was not the slightest fight back from any institution. The parliaments, the media, the courts – all went off the Enlightenment standard and hurtled headlong into the black hole of medieval irrationality. Everything I had learnt while working for nearly 20 years in Victorian government departments was breached. Risk-based approaches were tossed out in favour of untested coercive policies imported directly from the CCP [Chinese Communist Party]. The requirement to analyse costs and benefits of pandemic policies was scrapped.

When Premier Daniel Andrews' police started beating up young people for actions that were causing no one any harm, I commented adversely on the Police state on my social media channels. On 9 September 2020 I was asked by my bosses in the Department of Treasury and Finance to remove my social media comments. Within minutes of that meeting, I resigned my job as an economist and turned my attention to retrieving basic liberty in Australia.

When articles and a book (*The Great Hysteria and the Broken State*) that I thereafter wrote did not work, when the International Criminal Court is still twiddling its thumbs on a 68,000-word complaint that I lodged with it in November 2020, when the ASIO (Australia's peak intelligence agency) has not responded to a 40-page Open Letter in which I asked it to investigate CCP's role in the hysteria, I began to look for political, democratic alternatives.

CARMEN'S STORY, CONTINUED

The most 'rebellious' thing I did in 2020 was go on holiday(s). In the summer, most of my Dutch friends decided to go on holiday in the Netherlands, something I had no intention of doing. Instead, a friend and I went on last minute trips to Split, Paris, Prague and Budapest – having researched the countries with the least Covid restrictions, i.e., the countries where bars and clubs were open. Once there, we made friends with many groups who did think like us – that the lockdown was a lot harsher for people who were in the prime of their existence and that many people were being robbed of a future. Some groups

we met live in the Netherlands, and we meet up with them regularly still.

My employer, on the other hand, was quite angry that I decided to go to Croatia, telling me that I didn't take my work seriously as I didn't consider the consequences of going. When I told her that I was still going to go, I was promptly asked to reconsider my employment.

When the second lockdown arrived, one that was actually stricter than the first, it seemed like everyone had adjusted to the 'new normal', and when something became more restrictive this was met with absolutely no resistance. Zoom became the norm, gatherings of 6 people became a party, and no one contested anything. When I made any kind of remark, I was no longer countered with 'well you don't care about people', but 'still? Get over it already, this is just how it is.' The absolute lack of criticism from any of my peers was frustrating, and I felt myself becoming increasingly isolated, except for the few friends who thought about the restrictions in the same way. When it became clear that trying to discuss the regulations had absolutely no impact, I continued to retreat into myself, not seeing the point of engaging.

THE TRAGEDY

The Illusion of Control Phase contained the main tragedies of the Great Panic. The enormous but largely ignored costs of all this control began to surface and James became addicted to power, doing anything to hang onto it. It was James' seduction by power that made the costs far greater than they needed to be, because a person whose power depends on a particular strategic course cannot easily execute a U-turn without exposing himself to the public realisation that he was wrong in the first place. In politics and business, being wrong, and so massively wrong, on an issue that defined you is the worst way possible to secure your place in history.

Let us begin by staring the humanitarian horror directly in the face. We start this chapter by confronting the damage done during the Illusion of Control phase in the currency of human lives. A dedicated website set up in 2020 called collateralglobal.org keeps track of the documented costs of the tragedy, and we recommend it to readers.[110] In this section we give only a brief overview.

---

110 The group that established this website describes itself there as: 'A global collaborative community of academics, health professionals and citizens who document, study and communicate the collateral effects of the measures taken by governments to mitigate the damage of the covid pandemic.' It is funded by a 'range of donors including trusts, foundations, health professionals, scientists and members of the public,' according to the website.

GAUGING THE SCALE OF THE COSTS

Already in mid-March 2020, some observers were predicting that top-down attempts by governments to control the movements of populations would lead to massive loss of life, livelihoods, liberty, reason and happiness. As the months went by and government impositions on their people became worse and worse, evidence of these foreseeable costs rolled in.

The first set of costs to acknowledge, as they are the most gargantuan, are the costs paid by people in poor countries around the world because of the lockdowns and the restrictions on trade and travel that they ushered in. In Table 4, we show a set of effects known in October 2020 gathered by the Canadian medical scientist Ari Joffe.[111]

111 This is Table 2 from Joffe (2021).

TABLE 4

Effects of the COVID-19 Response That Put
Sustainable Development Goals Out of Reach

Sustainable Development Goal	Effect of COVID-19 Response: Some Details
Childhood Vaccination	Programs stalled in 70 countries [Measles, Diphtheria, Cholera, Polio]
Education	• School Closures: 90% of students {1.57 billion} kept out of school • Early primary grades are most vulnerable, with effects into adulthood: effects on outcomes of intelligence, teen pregnancy, illicit drug use, graduation rates, employment rates and earnings, arrest rates, hypertension, diabetes mellites, depression • Not just education affected: school closures have effects on food security, loss of a place of safety, less physical activity, lost social interaction, lost support services for developmental difficulties, economic effects on families
Sexual and reproductive health services	• Lack of access: estimated ~ 2.7 million unsafe abortions • For every 3 months of lockdown, estimated 2 million more lack access to contraception, and over 6 months, 7 million more additional unintended pregnancies
Food security	• Hunger Pandemic: undernourished estimate to increase 83 to 132 million (>225,000/day) from disrupted food chains supplies [labour mobility, food transport, planting seasons] and access to food [from job losses and incomes, price increases]
End Poverty	• Extreme Poverty (Living on <$1.90 per day): Estimated to increase >70 million "Lost ladders of opportunity" and social determinants of health
Reduce Maternal and USM[112]	• Estimated increase of 1.16 million children (USM) and 56,700 maternal deaths, of essential RMNCH[113] services are disrupted (coverage reduction 39-52%) for 6 months in 188 LMIC[114] • Mostly (~60%) due to affected childhood interventions {wasting, antibiotics, ORS[115] for diarrhea}; and childhood intervention [uterotonics, antibiotics, anticonvulsants, clean birth]

112 Under-5 Mortality

113 RMNCH: Reproductive Maternal Newborn and Child Health

114 LMIC: Low- and Middle-Income Countries

115 ORS: Oral Rehydration Solution

| Infectious Disease Mortality | Tuberculosis: in moderate to severe scenario, projected excess deaths (mostly from delayed net campaigns and treatment) 203,000 to 415,000 over 1 year (an increase of 52-107%, with most deaths in children 5yo) |
| | HIV: In moderate projected deaths (mostly due to antiretrovirals) 296,000 (range 229,000-420,000) in Sub-Saharan Africa over 1 year (an increase of 63%). Also, would increase mother-to-child transmission by 1.5 times |

This table only counts physical health effects due to disruptions that took place in the Illusion of Control phase. It considers both short-run and long-run effects. Each of the claimed effects is based on a published study about that effect.

First on the list is the disruption to vaccination programs for measles, diphtheria, cholera, and polio, which were either cancelled or reduced in scope in some 70 countries. That disruption was caused by travel restrictions. Western experts could not travel, and within many poor countries travel and general activity were also halted in the early days of the Illusion of Control phase. This depressive effect on vaccination programs for the poor is expected to lead to large loss of life in the coming years. The poor countries paying this cost are most countries in Africa, the poorer nations in Asia, such as India, Indonesia and Myanmar, and the poorer countries in Latin America.

The second listed effect in the table relates to schooling. An estimated 90% of the world's children have had their schooling disrupted, often for months, which reduces their lifetime opportunities and social development through numerous direct and indirect pathways. The UN children's organisation, UNICEF, has released several reports on just how bad the consequences of this will be in the coming decades.[116]

The third element in Joffe's table refers to reports of economic and social primitivisation in poor countries. Primitivisation, also seen after the collapse of the Soviet Union in the early 1990s, is just what it sounds like: a regression away from specialisation, trade and economic advancement

---

116 UNICEF (2020).

through markets to more isolated and 'primitive' choices, including attempted economic self-sufficiency and higher fertility. Due to diminished labour market prospects, curtailed educational activities and decreased access to repro-ductive health services, populations in the Illusion of Control phase began reverting to having more children precisely in those countries where there is already huge pressure on resources.

The fourth and fifth elements listed in the table reflect the biggest disaster of this period, namely the increase in extreme poverty and expected famines in poor countries. Over the 20 years leading up to 2020, gradual improvements in economic conditions around the world had significantly eased poverty and famines. Now, international organisations are signalling rapid deterioration in both. The Food and Agriculture Organisation (FAO) now expects the world to have approximately an additional 100 million extremely poor people facing starvation as a result of Covid policies. That will translate into civil wars, waves of refugees and huge loss of life.

The last two items in Joffe's table relate to the effect of lower perinatal and infant care and impoverishment. Millions of preventable deaths are now expected due to infections and weakness in new mothers and young infants, and neglect of other health problems like malaria and tuberculosis that affect people in all walks of life. The whole of the poor world has suffered fewer than one million deaths from Covid. The price to be paid in human losses in these countries through hunger and health neglect caused by lockdowns and other restrictions is much, much larger. All in the name of stopping Covid.

Ari Joffe's table highlights many uncomfortable truths. One is that the single-minded attention to the development of vaccines against Covid — over 200 and counting — could have been spent instead on research and direct efforts on the ground directed at preventing or treating much more dangerous diseases, such as tuberculosis, cholera or malaria.

Another uncomfortable truth is that the resources needed to vaccinate the population of poor countries against Covid could save many times more people if spent instead on simple health procedures like cleaner water, vaccinations, basic doctor services and infant care. The logic behind this starts with the fact that vaccination costs approximately US$50 per person. In poorer countries, fewer than 1 in 1,000 people have died with Covid, and those who did so were predominantly old people with underlying conditions that would have limited them to around 3-5 more healthy years to live. This means that the average Covid vaccination effort in a poor country 'buys', at best, 3-5 years of life for one person for every US$50,000 spent vaccinating 1,000 people.

How many years of life could be saved with US$50,000 worth of something else instead — let's call it 'regular health care'? This can be estimated from existing data. For example, a study of the rollout of general practitioner (GP) services in Turkey in 2005 found that the average GP easily saves 30 years of life per year of practice through reductions in infant mortality and improved basic care.[117] Turkey is a middle-income country in which a GP is paid quite a bit less than US$50,000. In the average poor country, US$50,000 would probably buy more like 100 years of additional life if spent optimally on health services. This is twenty times more human life than what can be saved by Covid vaccination programs in poor countries.

In sum, neither lockdowns in the name of Covid nor Covid vaccination policies are sensible in poor countries which simply have much larger health problems to worry about.

Table 5 displays our estimates of costs per month of a UK-style lockdown, per million citizens. The approach of translating damage sustained in disparate areas into units of human well-being, which we initiated, has by now been repeated by independent researchers in several other developed countries.[118]

---

117 Cesur, Güneş, Tekin & Ulker (2017).

118 Ari Joffe in Canada; Andy Ryan in Ireland (Ryan 2021); Martin Lally (Lally 2021) in New Zealand; Foster in Australia; Krekel, Layard, and others in the UK; Frijters in Belgium, Sweden, the Netherlands, the UK, and Australia. All of these have already been published, or are forthcoming in peer-reviewed publications.

Dozens of cost-benefit calculations like this to evaluate Covid policies have been undertaken around the world, sometimes involving our help, in which the damages done to various dimensions of life are translated into a particular single currency, such as WELLBYs, QALYs or dollars, so that like-for-like comparisons can be made across categories.[119]

Similar losses to those in Table 5 are found in many Western countries. We offer these estimates to indicate how much disruption lockdowns bring to the developed West and how many dimensions of our lives they affect.

TABLE 5

Costs per Month of Lockdowns, per One Million Citizens

Disrupted area	Loss in original units	Loss in WELLBYs
IVF services	30 IVF babies lost	14,400
Satisfaction with life	0.5 on a 0-10 scale	41,667
Future health problems	429 extra deaths	12,857
Government debt	US$514 million	51,400
Pollution	no effect	0
Suicide	?	0
Child education	20-30% time lost	5,714
Total		**126,038**

Addendum: by comparison, the total WELLBY loss if 0.3% of the UK population hypothetically dies from Covid (3,000 deaths per million) is estimated at 54,000. It should be emphasised that this is a total cost, whereas the costs of each line item in the table are costs per month of lockdown.

---

119 E.g., Rowthorn & Maciejowski (2020) or the many studies citing that publication, which implicitly claims that the costs of lockdowns outweigh their benefits by about 30 to 1.

The WELLBY ('well-being year') currency we use to quantify damages in Table 5 is formulated based on what individuals themselves answer to the following question: 'Overall, how satisfied are you with your life nowadays?' This question is answered on a scale of 0 to 10, where 0 is 'not at all' and 10 is 'completely'. The question is included on all major surveys conducted by the UK Office of National Statistics and on several other national and international surveys.

One WELLBY is defined as a one-point increment on this answer scale, lasting for one year, for one person. As a rule of thumb, a healthy person living in the UK answers around an '8' to this overall life satisfaction question, while a level of '2' is reported to be as bad as no longer living at all. This means that a healthy year of life in the UK is worth six WELLBYs more than a life not worth living. An intuitive and 'relatable' measure of human well-being, the WELLBY is strongly affected by mental health, social relations, the environment, and pretty much anything that makes life enjoyable and worthwhile. It is now used by the UK government and many others as the basis for judging the quality of life someone is leading.[120]

The first row of Table 5 quantifies a rarely mentioned direct loss due to lockdowns, which is the disruption to births that can only occur with regular medical help. In a country like the UK, around 3% of births each year are the result of in-vitro fertilisation, and IVF services were halted during lockdowns according to the logic that IVF was a nonessential service not worth the 'risk'. That means around 2,000 births per month of lockdown will not happen that otherwise would have, for the whole UK population of around 70 million — translating to about 30 fewer IVF births per million citizens.

Those babies would have been expected to live in good health for around 80 years, and remember one year of good health is worth about six WELLBYs. So, the 30 lost IVF babies could each have expected to enjoy 480 WELLBYs

---

120 A recent Handbook, Frijters and Krekel (2021), lays out this methodology and how it yields the key numbers used above.

in his or her life, meaning the UK lost 14,400 WELLBYs' worth of human well-being per month per million citizens as a direct result of the policy-mandated disruption to IVF services in lockdowns.

To put these costs in perspective, consider the WELLBYs lost per million Britons if 0.3% of the UK population were to die of Covid.[121] That is a higher fraction than recorded in any country of over a million citizens since Covid came onto the radar. 0.3% of a million is 3,000 deaths. Since the average Covid death is of someone above 80 years of age and in poor health, often in a nursing home where those who enter have about one more healthy year of life, the average Covid death takes away about three healthy years of human life, or 18 WELLBYs. The total WELLBY loss of the 0.3% of the UK population hypothetically killed by Covid, per million UK inhabitants, is therefore 54,000 WELLBYs.[122] An equivalent amount of human well-being is sacrificed in 3.5 months of lockdowns via disrupted IVF services alone. Such services were deemed 'nonessential' at the time. But to the IVF child who did not get born as a result of Covid policies, the IVF service was as essential as it gets.

Do Covid deaths alone capture the full physical damages due directly to the virus, against which we are comparing the IVF and other losses in Table 5? As the Great Panic progressed, worry emerged about 'long Covid', the phrase invented for the phenomenon that some people who recovered from an acute bout of Covid infection had lingering health problems for months afterward. If these problems involve significant long-term human costs, then we should include them in our estimate of the potential WELLBY loss due directly to Covid.

121 This number represents 50% more total Covid deaths than have been reported to have occurred in the UK as of August 2021. Only Peru and Hungary have reported a higher fraction of the population to die of Covid than this. See de Best, R. (2021), https://www.statista.com/statistics/1104709/coronavirus-deaths-worldwide-per-million-inhabitants/

122 0.3% of the UK population is about 200,000 people. If they each die, causing the loss of 18 WELLBYs each on average, then that makes about 3.6 million WELLBYs lost in total. To then arrive at a number of WELLBYs lost per million of the UK population from Covid deaths, we divide this 3.6 million by 66 (the UK population, in millions), arriving at about 54,000.

A consortium of Swiss doctors,[123] organised during the pandemic to work quickly through the rapidly evolving scientific knowledge on Covid, noted that recovery from many viral infections can take a long time, so long Covid was not unexpected or unusual. They noted that the percentage of Covid sufferers who still had symptoms after three months varied across studies from between 2% and 10% of patients, and that there was little evidence of permanent damage. Our own reading of the currently available research on this topic concurs with the view of these Swiss doctors.

Our best estimate then is that nearly every Covid victim does totally recover, but it can take several months. During the recovery period life is a bit worse for long Covid sufferers but they are still able to socialise, meaning that their well-being is only marginally impaired. Compared to deaths and other costs in Table 5, this means that the negative well-being effect of long Covid is extremely small — on the order of 1% to 5% of the WELLBY effects of 0.3% of the population dying of Covid.

A bigger worry about the long-run direct costs of Covid is that it is not a single viral strain, but more like an evolving cloud of strains with new mutations emerging all the time, like the influenza virus. How can we approach quantifying the long-run costs of a seasonally returning illness that is always somewhat novel and can to some extent resist previous vaccines?

The notion of a 'fatality rate' applies to an identified strain or a small bandwidth of strains. By contrast, a recurring and perennially evolving group of viruses, like seasonal flu or seasonal Covid, is better thought of instead in terms of its effect on life expectancy: i.e., how many weeks or months does it cost people? That number is unknown at the time of writing because it remains to be seen whether or not new Covid strains will evolve and circulate every year. Yet for purposes of understanding the trade-offs and costs of

---

123 Swiss Policy Research (2020C), https://swprs.org/post-acute-covid-long-covid/

the Great Panic, it actually hardly matters. The costs and benefits of trying to control a mutating virus that comes back every year as a slightly different bug are basically the aggregate of a series of costs and benefits related to each particular mutant strain.[124]

The second type of cost listed in Table 5, under the heading 'Satisfaction with life', refers to the damage done to the well-being of the whole population during the period of lockdowns. We capture here the loss of happiness attributable to the disruptions, and all of the mental health problems caused by increased loneliness, physical abuse from domestic violence, and diminution of purpose. This item also captures the possibility that many people rather like lockdowns and feel quite comfortable locked away with their families: they impact the statistics by moderating the drop in life satisfaction. Yet, on balance we see a high loss of well-being, showing that the costs to the losers far outweigh the gains to the winners. We see evidence of these well-being costs in other statistics such as the percentage of the population with depression and anxiety, which rose from around 16% to 25% in this period in the UK,[125] a scale of impact also seen in other countries.

We also know from many studies that this well-being loss increased as lockdowns dragged on and people became more depressed and lonely. The average effect of lockdowns in the UK up until March 2021 was around 0.5 of a WELLBY,[126] an effect also found for other places like Australia which had well-defined lockdown periods in particular regions.[127] A drop of 0.5 WELLBYs

---

124 In general, restraining a wave in one year makes the population less immune to a related strain, so the costs of restraining in future years only rises with restraints in previous years. Hence if the costs of restraint outweigh the benefits when considering each individual strain, then they certainly do for a whole sequence of strains.

125 Mansfield et al. (2021).

126 See, for example, Figure 2 in Office for National Statistics (2021), https://www.ons.gov.uk/peoplepopulationandcommunity/well-being/methodologies/datacollectionchangesduetothepandemicandtheirimpactonestimatingpersonalwell-being

127 Biddle et al. (2020).

(a yearly measure) translates to a drop of 0.5/12 per month per person, or 41,667 WELLBYs per million UK citizens. So in about three weeks of lockdown, the well-being lost due to loneliness and other mental health effects is equivalent to that lost from all Covid deaths that occurred in the UK through June 2021.

Moving to the third item in Table 5, our estimate of deaths from future health problems caused by disruption to health services comes directly from a UK government report of December 2020.[128] This report claimed that 100,000 Britons would die in the future because of health-service disruption in the six months after March 2020. If we conservatively estimate that each of those deaths — for example, a preventable cancer death attributable to reduced cancer screening — causes the loss of five years of healthy human life, then the total cost of health-service disruptions works out to 12,857 WELLBYs lost per million citizens per month of lockdown.

The largest item in Table 5 is the WELLBY loss resulting from the increase in government debt, which in the UK totalled around US$36 billion per month. This debt paid for the cost of subsidising businesses no longer allowed to operate, a cost incurred directly because of lockdown policies. That debt will eventually have to be paid back and result in a hit to future government investments and services.[129] This materially threatens our future standard of living. If we use the extremely conservative assumption that governments generate one WELLBY for every US$10,000 they spend — the actual cost of delivering one WELLBY is probably half that — then this cost of 'future austerity' works out to 51,400 WELLBYs lost per million citizens per month of lockdown.

During the first two phases of the Great Panic, one often heard the claim that lockdowns were good for the environment because, surely, CO_2 emissions

---

128 Department of Health and Social Care et al. (2020).

129 For the benefit of modern monetary theory enthusiasts, we note that this is the case except in the extreme event that there is no limit to how much money governments can create before the population and businesses lose trust in the currency. As soon as there is a limit, increased debt incurred now reduces the ability of governments in the future to spend that amount.

would be dropping with the reduced economic activity. This turned out not to be true. Many high-energy mass transit systems kept operating, often with hardly any passengers. Meanwhile, private vehicle travel enjoyed a renaissance as individuals avoided low-carbon options like public transport and instead drove everywhere in their 'safe' cars. A similar story yielded other pressures on the environment. For example, the lockdowns led to a waste mountain of masks and additional plastic used by shops to wrap purchases separately 'to be safe'.

The next row of Table 5 relates to something talked about a lot: suicide rates. These were expected by many commentators to rise with unemployment and teenage depression. This did not turn out to be true in all countries. They may have risen in the US, but not in the UK or many other developed countries. The fair loss from lockdowns to report on that line item is zero.

The final element in Table 5 quantifies the disruption to the education of children due to school closures that were mandated as part of lockdowns. The significant direct misery that this caused children is included in the 'satisfaction with life' loss captured already, but an additional loss will be incurred in the future as these less-educated kids enter the workforce and pay lower taxes. Since government expenditures generate a lot of well-being, that matters. A simple calculation by the Institute for Fiscal Studies in the UK suggested that the lockdowns were costing the value of six months' worth of education, meaning around 100 billion pounds less for governments to spend on things in the future.[130]

That report noted the finding of many studies that the disruption in education is worse at the bottom of the education ladder — that is, among children from lower socio-economic backgrounds. Those at the bottom not only failed to advance, but actually saw their skills deteriorate during lockdowns, as they did little homework and became demotivated. Taking

130 Sibieta (2021).

a more conservative estimate that only 20% of that education is truly lost, then this works out at 5,714 WELLBYs lost per month of lockdown per one million citizens.

The end result of these fairly simple calculations is that a single month of UK-style lockdown in the developed West is estimated to cost around 250% of the entire loss represented by 0.3% of the population dying of Covid. This is not even taking account of the importance of lost freedoms or of the catastrophic losses suffered in poor countries. The estimate is based on pessimistic numbers for Covid deaths and highly conservative numbers for the collateral damages. The real collateral damages in the West alone are arguably twice as high. Since lockdowns are now known to have had no clear beneficial effect on the number of Covid cases or deaths, there is no trade-off to be analysed in the area of lockdown policies. There is just loss all around.

Another way to express these numbers is to say that the UK destroyed around 20% of its own total well-being during every month of lockdown. As a permanent policy that would last for generations, locking down the country would therefore be equivalent to killing 20% of the population. Since it also turns out that lockdowns reduce the number of 'normal' pregnancies by 10-20%[131] — something not even counted in Table 5 — it should be clear that lockdowns do immense social harm that will be felt for decades.

COULD WE HAVE KNOWN?

Was all of this anticipated at the time, or at least talked about early on in the Great Panic? Sure it was. Jasmine, as we have seen, was a first-hand observer and commentator. Yet James was already calling the shots, and Jane, from her majority position, was throwing her consequential and decisive weight behind him. Reason was thereby thrown on a bonfire and set alight.

---

131 https://www.brookings.edu/blog/up-front/2021/05/05/the-coming-covid-19-baby-bust-is-here/

Yet already in March 2020 we ourselves were warning of the danger on national radio[132] and writing openly about it in blogs,[133] and there was no shortage of official government reports in the UK and elsewhere making very similar arguments. A UK government report drawn up by actuaries in April 2020, for example, warned of a possible 200,000 avoidable deaths due to lockdowns themselves.[134]

The repercussions for mental health were also clear early. In a survey of its 130 member countries conducted between June and August 2020, the WHO found that 93% of these countries had suffered disruptions to their mental health, neurological and substance use (MNS) services. One in three countries suffered disruption across more than 75% of normal services. The authors of the WHO report noted: 'An important finding is that some life-saving emergency and essential MNS services were reported as being disrupted; 35% of countries reported some disruption of management of emergency MNS manifestations (including status epilepticus, delirium and severe substance withdrawal syndromes) and 30% reported disruption in supply of medications for people with MNS disorders.'[135]

The health damage of forcing populations into inactivity was also in plain sight. By early October 2020, the US Centers for Disease Control and Prevention (CDC) estimated that one-third of the country's 'excess deaths' in the preceding eight months had not been directly from Covid.[136] We can speculate that the one-third was caused by health neglect and unhealthy

---

132 Foster & Reinhart (2020).

133 Frijters (2020A), https://clubtroppo.com.au/2020/03/18/has-the-coronavirus-panic-cost-us-at-least-10-million-lives-already/

134 Knapton (2020).

135 World Health Organization (2020D), https://www.who.int/publications/i/item/978924012455

136 Excess deaths are defined by the CDC as 'the difference between the observed numbers of deaths in specific time periods and expected numbers of deaths in the same time periods.'

lifestyles, both the direct result of government diktats.[137]

So the damage was foreseen, articulated and plainly visible. The trouble was, James had a strong vested interest in turning a blind eye to the damage and, when challenged, to belittle it with propaganda and media attacks. Jane followed along in the slipstream, heaping still more social disdain on those who recognised that we were destroying ourselves.

What was it that people foretelling such future damage knew about humans that policy makers and their health advisors failed to see? To answer this, and thereby isolate the key knowledge that was not at the table where the big decisions were made at the outset of the Great Fear, we must recognise the importance to our species of close social relations.

WHY WAS THE MENTAL HEALTH DAMAGE SO LARGE?

We have evolved as highly social animals, living in constant close physical contact with our loved ones. In the hunter-gatherer period in which humanity evolved and lived for over 99% of its existence, warm social relations and economic relations were one and the same. The people we physically shared our lives with were also the people with whom we produced everything of value. We brought down the mammoth and gathered berries with our family and friends, who were at the same time our army buddies, our co-worshippers and our nurses. We touched each other all the time and kept up a nearly continuous flow of emotions in proximity to those we loved. We have evolved as a species totally used to and dependent upon physical proximity to our loved ones.

In the process of economic development, much of that warm social life was lost, but the human desire for it always remained.

One of the major social revolutions in recent decades has been the 'health and wellness' movement, from which many businesses emerged to improve

---

137 Rossen et al. (2020).

our personal health and small social groups started to openly adopt the idea that they existed for the purpose of improving their members' well-being. Millions of businesses sprang up: massage shops, spa salons, personal trainers, organic food supermarkets, and sports magazines. Peer-to-peer groups became the rage: mindfulness groups, chat groups, family Facebook groups, local heritage groups and yoga groups.

Associated with this revolution was a growing interest in mental well-being and the quality of relationships. We see the effects of this movement most clearly in data on how satisfied people in Europe are with their lives, which has been on a steady increase during the last 30 years.[138]

Key to warm social relationships are regular close proximity, skin touching, eye contact, coordinated movements such as in sports, dance and sex, group singing, hugging, and other forms of closeness. The social system has been evolving to provide more of these to humans for the simple reason that they embody the kind of intimacy that people most crave and thrive on. Previous means of accessing intimacy, such as community parties and extended-family gatherings, are on the decline as societies become more mobile and oriented towards anonymous transactions. But despite our technology we are still just animals, and social ones at that.

There are several elements of warm social relations that cannot yet be mimicked remotely. These elements are crucial to bear in mind when gauging the damage done to mental health from social distancing.

One element is skin contact.[139] Human skin has particular receptors in the form of tiny hairs that only get moved and activated when the skin is stroked with something very similar, such as the skin of someone else. Skin contact between humans stimulates our bodies in ways that are healthy and

---

138 Kaiser & Vendrik (2019).

139 Field (2010).

critical to us. Skin contact calms us down, arouses us sexually, improves our body's immune system and gives us a sense of completeness. It cannot yet be mimicked by any technology and so avoiding skin contact inevitably inflicts a huge loss on people.

Another element is what can be termed 360-degree visual awareness, by which we mean being aware of someone else's presence in a shared physical space such that we notice the tiny movements in their faces, or of their feet and arms. Interacting with someone in close proximity is simply more relaxing, more fulfilling and less taxing if it involves 360-degree visual awareness rather than a disembodied face on a screen.

Perhaps our technology will evolve to allow us the same experience remotely as we are afforded when in actual close proximity, but it is a long way from that yet. Today's people complain of 'Zoom fatigue' and other forms of disappointment with remote contact in part because of the reduction in the many visual cues we receive when actually sharing a space with someone.

A third element of social relations that cannot be replicated by technology is the recognition of the voice and smell of someone we love. Take these cues away and we feel disconnected and strange around the same person. The recognition of these characteristics of a loved one is subconscious and experienced as warm and comforting. Smell cannot yet be mimicked by technology, though the effect of remote voices is not dissimilar to the effect of the same voices in actual proximity: people on the phone sound like they do in real life but don't smell the same.

All of these elements — proximity, and with it skin contact, 360-degree visual awareness, voice and smell — combine to provide mental stimulation and motivation: they keep our minds active and involved in the lives of others. This protects us from mental health problems, feelings of loneliness, dementia and an impaired immune system.[140]

Really, warm social relations give us the will to live. Without them we tend to stop caring about things that used to be important, including ourselves. Even hardened criminals experience total separation from other criminals as a punishment, which is why prisons have isolation cells to deter those who would misbehave.

Even the best-educated and most well-adjusted people change when they are socially isolated, a phenomenon exemplified by scientists in space stations and participants in other isolating events such as expeditions to the poles. Though space-station astronauts select into the job knowing what to expect and possessing a psychological profile that is relatively well-suited to long isolation, petty bickering emerges among them over time, as they are deprived of the warm relationships they need in order to stay socially grounded.[141]

Polar and other early expeditions over land and sea often ended in mayhem among the explorers as their prolonged isolation combined with physical privation literally drove them to mutiny, desertion or insanity. This theme has also been explored in fiction — for example, the ivory trader Kurtz in Joseph Conrad's 1899 novella, *Heart of Darkness*, went crazy partly from the effects of isolation from normal social relations deep in the African jungle.

One of the implications of the crucial role of physical contact with our loved ones for mental well-being is that social distancing has huge costs and is inherently unsustainable, as it will lead to a loss of will to live among many of those who are subjected to it. Depriving people of regular close proximity to loved ones rates among the cruellest things one can do. In normal times, people will take substantial risks with their lives in order to maintain warm social relations. However, as we saw in the previous chapter, under the

---

140 Walker (2017).

141 Flynn (2005).

influence of a large perceived fear they can be led to give up the satisfaction even of this basic need for a while. Yet sacrificing this for a period of time still comes at a cost to mental health and will to live.

The damage done to people forced into isolation is apt to be worse if there are fewer alternatives to accessing their customary social interactions. For example, it is worse in very cold places where going outside just to experience the presence of other people is physically unpleasant and the streets are emptier. It is also worse in institutions where no one can come to visit, and for technologically challenged people who do not have others to help them organise phone or video calls. It is worse too for those already anxious or under stress for other reasons, such as being unemployed or suffering from health problems.

Much of the damage done by lockdowns in Western countries is therefore through its direct creation of enormous loneliness among those without loved ones to live with. It is a heartless cruelty inflicted by those who are comfortable, in large homes and with warm family relations to fall back on. The lack of deep awareness among the early decision makers of how badly humans need social proximity is part of the tragedy.

PERSPECTIVES ON THE DAMAGE

How does the damage seen during the Covid period compare to the impact of other big policy disasters in human history, like World War I or the Great Leap Forward in China, each of which caused roughly 30 million deaths? A precise number for the overall damage of the Great Panic is hard to calculate, partly because we don't yet know when it will end and we don't have a handle on the magnitudes of some particularly important elements of the damage, like future reductions in government spending around the world while public debt is repaid.

Still, if we adopt the rough rule of thumb derived in the analysis above, which is that a UK-style lockdown costs 20% of what makes life worth living in both direct and future costs, then we can make an educated guess about the costs for the world as a whole.

By mid-2021 the world had locked down UK-style for an average of around eight months[142] — longer in much of the Americas, but shorter in Asia and Africa — meaning that we effectively lost 20% of human well-being for those eight months, or equivalently 1.6 months' worth of total human well-being. That may not sound too dramatic, but 1.6 months of life lost by each of 7.8 billion people adds up to 1.04 billion years of life lost, equivalent to 26 million average individuals in the world dying who would otherwise have had 40 good years left. So as human disasters go, the Great Covid Panic has produced a loss to human life and well-being comparable to the losses of World War I or the Great Leap Forward. Those disasters occurred at a time when the world population was much smaller, however, so proportionally the Great Covid Panic is not yet in their league.

On the other hand, it is reasonable to fear that the negative effects are going to turn out much worse for the world on average than for just Western countries, since the social systems in poor countries are much more fragile. Basing a worldwide damage figure on the estimated costs of lockdowns in a Western country may well lead, therefore, to underestimating the worldwide damage.

Part of the long-run damage to both poor and rich countries is the widespread slide towards more authoritarian government during this period. In 2021 *The Economist* magazine summarised the many reports about the large increase in censorship, detainment of political opposition, sidestepping of parliaments and cancellation of elections in poor countries. Their conclusion was that democracy and civil liberties had never been reduced

---

142 The population-weighted average number of days with a stringency index above 70 for all countries above a million inhabitants was just below 240 between January 1st 2020 and August 1st 2021.

in the previous 100 years as fast as they were in 2020.[143] These costs are alarming, not just in their impact on abstractions like 'liberty', but also because in dictatorships neglect of the population is more normal, as the suffering of the poor is hardly noticed. The longer-run danger is an increase in civil wars, famines and mass neglect.

Heavy losses in poor countries might well be occurring at the time of writing. Mid-2021, poor countries are facing famine because the disruption of the world economy impaired food production and distribution. The FAO recorded a 30% rise in prices for essential food[144] by May 2021, which affected the poorest most severely. The United Nations,[145] the World Bank,[146] and the FAO are all in crisis mode to try to lessen the impact of this famine that threatens over 30 million people, while lockdowns and authoritarian governments are hampering relief efforts.

The UN's World Food Program in April 2021 observed the following about the situation in central Africa: 'Measures to curtail COVID-19 spread have contributed to the dramatic increase in food prices across the region.'[147] The fear is that when the dust settles, tens of millions of people will be found to have died of hunger and health neglect. At the time of writing we simply do not know, but with 30% higher food prices, some 10 million unexplained deaths in poor countries[148] and worsening political situations, we fear the worst is happening right now.

---

143 The Economist (2021A),
https://www.economist.com/graphic-detail/2021/02/02/global-democracy-has-a-very-bad-year

144 Food and Agriculture Organization of the United States (2021).

145 United Nations (2021).

146 The World Bank (2021).

147 https://news.un.org/en/story/2021/04/1089982

148 The Economist (2021B).

SCIENCE DURING THE GREAT PANIC: FINEST HOUR OR WORST COCK-UP?

GARBAGE IN, GARBAGE OUT

Some aspects of science functioned brilliantly during the Great Panic, while other aspects became dysfunctional and moved backward.

In the former camp was the science of the virus itself. Chinese scientists worked out Covid's genetic code very quickly. They posted it online and shared it with other groups around the world.[149] The science of how the virus infected different people and how the immune system responded was similarly in full flow, with scientists in disparate research groups sharing new insights almost instantaneously.[150] The vaccine effort also moved spectacularly fast, with Covid vaccines developed, tested, produced at scale, and distributed in record time.[151]

The science of how the virus might spread and cause deaths in the human population also very quickly snowballed into an international effort.

Already in January 2020, just weeks after the discovery of the virus circulating in Wuhan, teams of epidemiologists in the Netherlands, UK and

---

149 Schnirring (2021), https://www.cidrap.umn.edu/news-perspective/2020/01/china-releases-genetic-data-new-coronavirus-now-deadly

150 Dong et al. (2020).

151 Chan Kim et al. (2020).

US had activated models to predict its spread and how many would die in various countries and circumstances. The outputs of these models led to publications in *The Lancet*, a top journal in medicine.[152] The aim of these models was to depict how human interaction would spread the virus through populations and then simulate how various mechanisms could slow down the spread.[153] At this early stage, there was nothing political about these endeavours. The scientists involved were simply trying to do their best to figure out what was going on.

While treating the spread of the virus as a true puzzle, scientists were able to openly speculate about many of the as-yet 'unknowns' — including the relative importance of viral spread through the air and from surfaces, and whether some people might 'shed' the virus in greater abundance and therefore be more infectious than others.

New hypotheses about the unknowns were being generated very quickly on the basis of perplexing data. One puzzle was the quick appearance of the virus in numerous countries despite the few people who traversed airports displaying any of the known symptoms. That suggested to top model builders as early as January 2020[154] that there could be many people carrying the virus and spreading it to others without feeling ill themselves. Since nearly all testing and identification of actual cases was being done among people who had seen medical professionals because they felt ill, the modellers realised that the virus was probably less dangerous to the population than it would appear from fatalities among the hospitalised. They didn't know how many infected people were 'asymptomatic', but they knew that such people were probably numerous.[155]

---

152 Wu et al. (2020).

153 Kucharski et al. (2020).

154 E.g., Wu et al. (2020).

155 See, e.g., Heneghan et al. (2020) or the retrospective discussion later by Tindale et al. (2020).

By around October 2020, a large UK study had found that for every infected person with symptoms there were about six others with mild symptoms at most.[156] Earlier in 2020, that number was thought to be anywhere between one and fifty. If the ratio of asymptomatic to symptomatic cases was 50:1, the virus would be much more spreadable but also much less dangerous than if it was 1:1. That uncertainty lent itself to posturing.

The early studies on Covid's lethality followed the standard approach of comparing the number of people identified as cases with the number who subsequently died while still having symptoms. Again, confirmed cases were predominantly those people sick enough to show up at hospitals and get themselves tested. Within that highly selected group, 3-5% of 'cases' died with the virus, with one study saying it was 15%.[157]

Now, the modellers knew full well that the true lethality of the virus was easily an order of magnitude less than 3-5%. They knew this because of experience with other diseases, where initial lethality estimates were far higher than those reported in later studies based on more representative groups of infected people. They knew that many people with mild symptoms never went to hospitals, so for every patient in a hospital with the virus there were surely many self-caring at home, going untested. Also, they knew that there had to be a rather large group experiencing no symptoms and walking around completely unaware that they had contracted the virus. Yet, while the modelers may have broadly allowed for such possibilities in their technical papers, they had no incentive to emphasise these 'knowns' when addressing the lay audience. The WHO, for example, did not admit these 'knowns' in its reports and statements to the public.

---

156 Laguipo (2020), https://www.news-medical.net/news/20201009/86-percent-of-the-UKs-COVID-19-patients-have-no-symptoms.aspx

157 Rajgor et al. (2020), https://www.thelancet.com/journals/laninf/article/PIIS1473-3099(20)30244-9/fulltext

What happened next is typical of science. In their published studies, scientists calculated estimates of the case fatality rate (CFR) or the infection fatality rate (IFR) based on the number of people identified by tests to be 'confirmed' cases. These studies failed to include estimates of population-wide IFRs or CFRs because that involves guessing how different the broader population was from those who were tested, which would have seemed like speculation: they, and the referees and editors reviewing their work, would have classified this as 'not their job'. However, when organisations like the WHO or the health ministries of individual countries reported that 'studies had shown' the CFR to be, say, 3%, neither they nor the modellers spoke out and said 'but that does not apply to the whole population: the fatality rate for the whole population is probably ten times lower!' The reason, again, was that they did not see this as their job: their studies were getting attention anyway, so why quibble with details that could only serve to cast doubt on the usefulness of their work?

It is thus due to the exaggeration of a very small piece of actual knowledge that untruths get to be the excuse for enormous policy decisions. Lots of insiders see that dynamic happening but have incentives to keep quiet.

This pattern has been seen before. When a piece of scientific knowledge is disseminated widely by an organisation like the WHO, much of its actual information content is lost. What arrives as 'knowledge' to the eyes and ears of a non-specialist can be missing key content that significantly alters the message. In the case of Covid, the message was that 3% of the world's population are to die if the virus is allowed to infect everyone. That is not what the original scientists meant or supported, nor is it even the explicit claim put out by the WHO or national health organisations. But unfortunately the language used would be interpreted that way by Joe Bloggs on the street.

An example of a similar dynamic can be seen in estimates of the rate of extinction of species. Organisations like the World Wildlife Fund advertise that currently the rate of extinction is 1,000 to 10,000 times higher than rates of extinction before the appearance of modern humans.[158] That number has been bandied about in thousands of newspaper articles around the world as evidence of the crimes against nature being committed by humans. It is the kind of number that fits nicely into a 'we are bad' narrative. Where does the number come from? The original number can be found in a 2014 *Science* article that uses a computer model to estimate the number of species and the number of extinctions. That model is fed with a couple of wild guesses about what was normal over the millions of preceding years, coupled with a handful of particular studies about particular types of extinctions, like those of snails.[159]

What could go wrong with a computer simulation like this, one might ask?

Well, for one, the number almost invariably picked up by newspapers, and even by scientists, was the highest such number that the simulations came up with. Other scientists said this was cherry-picking. They claimed that there is no difference between the current rate of extinction and the previous likely rates, and pointed to the fact that the number of confirmed extinctions is only around 900 in the last 500 years.[160] Given the most commonly accepted estimate of around 2 million different species, 900 extinctions is not so many.

A recent *Nature* article explains well how alarmist headline figures about extinctions are in fact based on studies of groups of animals declining in very particular habitats, not on whether whole species that are distributed over many habitats are going extinct.[161] It is like observing the historical extinction of humans on Easter Island and then saying humanity went extinct. These authors' estimates are that around 98.6% of all species show no decline on

---

158 https://wwf.panda.org/discover/our_focus/biodiversity/biodiversity/

159 Aldhous (2014), https://www.newscientist.com/article/dn25645-we-are-killing-species-at-1000-times-the-natural-rate/

160 Pearce (2015), https://e360.yale.edu/features/global_extinction_rates_why_do_estimates_vary_so_wildly

161 Leung et al. (2020).

average, and that the alarmist estimates come from threats to just 1% of all species. They point to the alarmism in the media and environmental organisations typified by terms like 'apocalyptic models', 'biological annihilation' and 'Insect Armageddon'.

It's a well-worn pattern. A particular group of scientists hits upon a particular methodology to come up with a high number on an emotive issue, and that number then becomes the poster child for a whole movement that has its own agenda.

THE FOG OF SCIENTIFIC LANGUAGE

A little bit of knowledge can be a dangerous thing. In careless hands it can be recast as something much greater than what it really is, such as 'scientific evidence' of something extremely important. Once this initial act of exaggeration has been committed, it can have a cascading effect that leaves vast damage in its wake.

This often involves the perversion of language. The language scientists speak is the same as what the general public speaks, but often scientists use words to mean something quite different to what they would signal to the general public.

Even to other scientists only vaguely aware of concepts like 'infectiousness', 'cases' and 'viruses', the headline 'scientists find new virus kills 3% of cases' reads like '3% chance of death for anyone who catches new virus'. That is because the word 'case' is fairly neutral in everyday language. A patient is a case, but so is a person on the street with a slight cold: they have a 'case of the cold'. In common parlance, a 'case' need not be interpreted as something very grave that requires hospitalisation. Immunologists, on the other hand, use the same word for something totally different, namely, 'people ill enough to show up at selected hospitals.' This is totally lost on most other scientists and the general public when they read the words 'Scientists find new virus kills 3% of cases'.

What happens next, as we know from our personal experience in academia, is even worse. Groups of scientists start to treat the advertised number that garnered a lot of publicity and was published in a top journal as having been magically validated, and they plonk it into their models. This is a key reason that the Imperial College London models yielded huge numbers of projected deaths for the UK in their March 16th 2020 calculations: the advertised CFR of 3% was translated into an IFR of 0.9%.[162]

A rival model from an Oxford team around the same time assumed a less ridiculous IFR of 0.14%, but failed to gain support.[163] Others, like the economists who soon started to run their own models, based entire projections on their misinterpretation of the 3% CFR.[164] The headline number had bested its competitors, taken hold, and begun to spawn.

Scientists publishing after the initial 'headline number' is in print do not use more likely numbers because they often will not know that the headline number is inappropriate. Also, they can point to the initial published study as having 'proven' something, even if that is not true at all. In the case of Covid, the headline number gave rise to frightening projections that drew welcome attention to second-round studies.

The reason that using an inappropriate number does not lead to studies being rejected during peer review is that those who judge their calculations are scientists in the same field who start with the same misunderstanding of what the headline number really means. This is the beginning of a process by which a fundamental misunderstanding becomes a new 'scientific fact'.

Worse still, the normal process by which science judges new papers

---

162 Imperial College COVID-19 Response Team (2020A).

163 See the discussion in Panovska-Griffiths (2020), https://theconversation.com/coronavirus-weve-had-imperial-oxford-and-many-more-models-but-none-can-have-all-the-answers-135137

164 E.g., McKibbon (2020), used in Butler (2020), https://www.theguardian.com/world/2020/mar/03/coronavirus-recession-expert-modelling-shows-australian-economy-could-take-huge-hit

in an emerging field involves assigning as peer reviewers those who have already published in the field, because they are seen as the acknowledged 'experts'. These people, of course, have both a professional and an intellectual incentive to reject papers that come to totally different conclusions to their initial work, or that heavily criticise their own papers. In the case of Covid, peer reviewers will have insisted that new papers start from the 'truth' that 3% of people infected with the virus will die.

Science does eventually weed out wrong answers to well-defined questions that can be empirically tested, such as how lethal a virus is in the general population or just how fast extinction rates really are, but that weeding-out process can take years. The initial group publishing the wrong numbers makes it extremely difficult for those who think the truth lies elsewhere to publish their studies, while they will reward those who follow in their own mistaken footsteps.

In this way, a few papers using exaggerated numbers turn very quickly into an enormous flood of studies that use those numbers as inputs into all kinds of follow-on models. In the Covid period, the world was quickly awash with ill-founded pronouncements, from projections of hospital cases to how the general population should reasonably react to the 'shown magnitude' of the threat.

LIES AND TRICKS, DRESSED UP AS SCIENCE

When the panic was well and truly underway, many 'scientists' tried to jump on the bandwagon by 'proving' that politicians should do this or that. In effect, some 'scientists' busied themselves in the role of demanding sacrifices to the new fear, using whatever trickery was available.

A prominent trick some 'scientists' came up with to rationalise lockdowns was a perversion of the precautionary principle. Joseph Norman and his colleagues at the New England Complex Systems Institute exploded off the mark in January 2020 with their precautionary principle argument for lockdowns,[165] pushing their views further in videos and newspaper articles to urge the UK and other countries to shut up shop.[166] They packaged their arguments in mathematics, which made it hard for those not good at maths to see where in the hat they hid the rabbits,[167] but at heart their argument was extremely simple.

They said it was uncertain how many people might die from the Coronavirus and that it might turn out far worse than initially reported in the medical literature. Simply as a precaution, they argued, populations should therefore follow the Chinese into lockdowns just in case the disease would claim far more victims than initially indicated. The metaphor they sold to the world was that when an avalanche is coming one doesn't waste time calculating the costs and benefits of various actions, or even the size of the avalanche. One simply gets out of the way.

Their argument hid two rabbits in their 'model' hat. The first is the implication that lockdowns are actually a means of 'getting out of the way'. This presumes an answer where in fact there is no certain answer to the question of whether and how deaths from a new disease can be avoided. Given the understanding at the time that the disease was endemic and would keep coming back no matter what governments did, their argument that lockdowns were a form of 'getting out of the way' was both implausible and unscientific.

The second rabbit in the hat was to point to risks in only one direction, namely that the disease was more dangerous than it appeared from early medical reports. That too is a sleight of hand, because it ignores the risk in the other direction — that lockdowns would do far more damage than initially realised. Indeed, one could envisage a risk that the economic and

---

165 Norman et al. (2020).

166 E.g., Taleb & Bar-Yam (2020), https://www.theguardian.com/commentisfree/2020/mar/25/uk-coronavirus-policy-scientific-dominic-cummings

167 In mathematics, one would talk of 'right-tailed risk distributions' and 'lockdown-sensitive mortality functions'. In normal English, you'd call such things 'a bunch of misleading assertions'.

social disruption of worldwide lockdowns would lead to a cocktail of war, famine and disease that killed far more than Covid ever could. Norman and his colleagues didn't model that. Nor did they openly discuss the likelihood of various different scenarios. They just assumed that there were risks in one particular direction and that lockdowns would help mitigate those risks.

'Proof by assumption' was thereby badged as 'a result'. Rabbits into the hat, rabbits out of the hat, or to use a less generous phrase: garbage in, garbage out.

HUBRIS AND THE NEED TO 'TALK UP' DISASTERS

What made matters worse is that both scientific journals and the general public are more interested in spectacular claims than in mundane ones. Journals have a strong incentive to publish papers claiming there is a big problem,[168] as long as those papers are based on verifiable data and can therefore be defended. Whether those initial data are representative, or whether the conclusions others are likely to draw from a paper's headline result are reasonable, are simply not questions that journals normally have to worry about. On the contrary, the more controversy the better, as long as a defence is at hand for any spectacular published claim.

The teams of scientists running journals simply don't care that mere mortals, which is to say the rest of humanity, use the words in their papers differently. They dismiss others as ignorant if they do not make the effort to absorb all the subtleties about what particular words mean when used in that particular journal. Yet truly understanding those subtleties would involve years of study, which is not reasonable to demand of others. Their disinterest in assigning to words the same meaning as others assign to them leads to the rest of the population, including other scientists, being misled.

Hubris and a taste of power during the Great Fear led to a further

---

168 Or containing some huge new finding of any sort, for that matter — a cause of what is known as publication bias (Blanco-Perez & Brodeur, 2020).

perversion of truth, inflicted by scientists themselves. The epidemiologists asked to advise governments almost invariably admitted that what they were advocating was only based on their projections of Covid cases and Covid deaths, devoid of any analysis of the effects these actions would have on public health, the economy, education and other important aspects of life. They nonetheless had no problem advocating lockdowns and other draconian measures. Some hedged their bets by saying it was the government's job to generate advice on the broader costs and benefits of these measures to society, while some failed to even mention the likely existence of such other costs and benefits.

The editors of *The Lancet*, the journal that published the earliest studies on Covid, were particularly guilty of jumping the gun. They simply assumed that copying the Chinese lockdowns was useful and worth the costs. In an editorial of March 3rd 2020, the editors boldly wrote 'High-income countries, now facing their own outbreaks, must take reasoned risks and act more decisively. They must abandon their fears of the negative short-term public and economic consequences that may follow from restricting public freedoms as part of more assertive infection control measures.'[169]

They wrote this without having made any calculations of the public and economic consequences of these measures. This shocking deviation from decades of sober writing on public health showed not only an abandonment of responsibility to science and the public, but extreme hubris as well. It raises the question of whether *The Lancet* is fit to continue as a journal.

We now know that governments didn't ask for other kinds of advice and ignored it when it was offered. The epidemiologists close to governments, and their supporters, made things much worse by actively deriding any attempt by others to present a fuller picture of the Covid issue.

---

169 The Lancet (2020).

One form such derision took was to demand 100% certainty about any cost or benefit of actions that an alternative voice was suggesting. This is a manipulative tactic typically employed by the powerful: insist that everyone acknowledge the truth of their uncertain or unreasonable claims, while simultaneously making demands, such as 100% certainty, of any counterclaim. It is akin to a Nazi camp guard dismissing the evidence of millions of deaths in the camps by saying 'prove to me they wouldn't have died of hunger anyway'. This implicitly shifts the onus of proof from those in power to those without it, tightening the stranglehold of the powerful over what is perceived to be true.

GOVERNMENTS IN THE GRIP OF SCIENCE GONE BAD

Once governments started to take action, both the science itself and the organisations directly disseminating it became increasingly corrupted.

The first government to act was China's, which locked down affected cities and actively managed the flow of information about the virus. Officials in the Chinese government wished to be seen to have control over the virus, and to have acted swiftly and appropriately. To assist themselves in this regard they promoted the image, true or otherwise, of having been aware of it much earlier and having acted appropriately by ordering lockdowns. Among the levers China's government could pull to vindicate its strategy was its financial clout inside WHO, where they pushed for recognition that the lockdown approach was appropriate and nothing had been underestimated.[170] China's grip on WHO's leadership was so strong it led Japan's finance minister to refer to WHO as the 'Chinese Health Organization.'[171]

Western governments were no better when it came to the manipulation of

---

170 Mazumdaru (2020),
https://www.dw.com/en/what-influence-does-china-have-over-the-who/a-53161220 Griffiths (2020),
https://edition.cnn.com/2020/02/14/asia/coronavirus-who-china-intl-hnk/index.html

171 Perper (2020), https://www.businessinsider.com/china-who-multimillion-dollar-contribution-political-power-move-2020-4

information. We now know from the book *A State of Fear* by Laura Dodsworth[172] that the British authorities deliberately used fear tactics and disinformation to get their own population to comply. The government changed the definition of a 'case', an 'infection' and a 'Covid death' several times in order to justify the actions they took and to scare people. Only some scientists actively involved in that deception and fear-mongering have so far apologised.[173]

The importance of personal financial incentives in medical science and policy advice should also not be underestimated. A recent article by the investigative journalist Paul Thacker[174] revealed that many of the 'scientists' who sat on the UK and US committees advising governments on the use of vaccines had undisclosed financial links to pharmaceutical companies making those vaccines. These scientists were also actively making claims in scientific journals and influencing the dispensation of billions of dollars of tax revenue, of which they would get a cut. Of course, they professed an outstanding talent for keeping their various interests separate. What else would they say?

We also know that in many countries, governments and their advisors presented outlandish worst-case scenarios to their populations as if they were their central forecasts. They used these scenarios as a basis to mandate measures like masking and school closures without any evidence that they worked, and sometimes even with abundant evidence that they didn't, simply in order to be seen to be doing something. After decisions were made, they brought out official advice on the supposed scientific backing for them.

Governments are known for promising things they don't deliver, but during Covid they went a step further and actually promised things that they *couldn't* deliver. A heinous example is 'total elimination' of the virus, which almost no scientist before had even whispered as being possible for this type of disease.

---

172 Dodsworth (2021).

173 Raynor (2021).

174 Thacker (2021).

Governments, it must be said, did an extraordinary job of pretending to have scientific reasons for the things they decided.

GROUPTHINK INSIDE SCIENCE

In January and February 2020, only the odd scientist was coming up with outlandish arguments pushing governments into forcing their people to give up living. In March 2020, these early birds were joined by a whole chorus of eager, chirping songbirds wanting in on the action. The unthinkable suddenly became the possible: European governments really might follow China and that possibility meant reputations could be made very quickly. Scientists were jumping on the bandwagon, demanding this and 'proving' that.

The conversion of their governments created rewards for those scientists who came up with arguments, data and models that showed the random pronouncements of their national leaders to be sensible. Modelling 'results' and whole papers appeared that rationalised lockdowns after they happened, even though the scientific consensus for the decades prior to February 2020 was that they could at best only delay the inevitable, and at huge costs.

It is almost impossible to understate the popularity of unscientific claims and advice about Covid among scientists during this time. This applied particularly to the advice in March 2020 that Western governments should lock down their economies and social systems. Many groups of scientists signed petitions and wrote articles demanding that their governments 'follow the science' by locking down. For example, in the UK — even before the infamous Imperial College doomsday predictions — some 600 'behavioural' scientists effectively urged the government to follow the lockdown policies of China and Italy, with no apparent interest at all in the victims of such a policy or in evidence of its beneficial effects.[175] Similar advice was tendered,

---

175 https://sites.google.com/view/covidopenletter/home

and followed, elsewhere.[176]

The degree of unanimity in some fields was stunning, particularly in disciplines where one might expect inherent scepticism and a call to quantify the costs and benefits of government actions.

The economics profession, as a leading example, almost fell over itself to abdicate its responsibility to provide useful inputs to policy analysis. Surveys of economists on both sides of the Atlantic conducted in late March 2020 indicated that there was little or no dissent — at least publicly — to lockdowns. Not a single respondent to the IGM Economic Experts Panel survey of top US macroeconomists disagreed with the proposition that abandoning 'severe lockdowns' would inflict greater economic damage than maintaining them. In Europe, only 4% of respondents disagreed with a similar proposition.[177]

Not a single one of these supposed expert American economists said that maybe it wasn't a great idea to inflict such costly, unproven experiments on their people. Apart from a few who were on the fence or had no opinion, these economists claimed that locking down whole societies was the safe and scientific thing to do. Many of them later wrote articles articulating the damage or in some other way dismissing or distracting attention from their personal culpability for the damage that these policies caused.

This all happened even before the Imperial College London modellers hit upon a novel excuse for lockdowns, which was that if one 'flattens the curve' then the hospital system would have longer to deal with the flood of cases.[178] The crucial element still missing from that new excuse is an appreciation of the damage done while 'flattening the curve', something that the hordes of

176 Ward (2020), https://www.theguardian.com/commentisfree/2020/apr/15/uk-government-coronavirus-science-who-advice; Muller (2021).

177 Sandbu (2020), https://www.ft.com/content/e593e7d4-b82a-4bf9-8497-426eee43bcbc ; https://ww.igmchicago.org/surveys/policy-for-the-covid-crisis/; Vaitilingam (2020), https://voxeu.org/article/european-economic-policy-covid-19-crisis-igm-forum-survey

178 Imperial College London (2020A).

scientists loudly supporting lockdowns failed publicly to estimate or, with few exceptions, even to take seriously.

THE MADNESS IN MACRO

Some of the 'mainstream' arguments that various disciplines put forward to rationalise Covid countermeasures are damning. Let it suffice to convey the dysfunction of one discipline near the hearts of the authors: academic macroeconomics. We are not talking here about the applied macroeconomists in central banks, nor the forecasting units of international agencies like the IMF and World Bank, nor even the economists at large commercial banks, many of whom were modelling lockdowns with direct and large economic costs.[179] We mean mainly the academic macroeconomists in universities, members of the larger groups of academic economists who, as surveys found right from the get-go, quickly supported lockdowns no matter what.

These economists were confronted with two significant challenges in building their desired argument that lockdowns caused no more economic damage than would have happened without them. The first was that the virus was known to pose little risk to anyone young enough to work. So, any damage done by a greater number of virus cases in a 'no restriction' scenario would be inflicted mainly on those no longer in the labour force, leaving minimal damage to economic measures like labour productivity and GDP.

The second problem was that the undeniably huge economic damage they saw in their countries was due directly to forced government closure of businesses, which made it impossible to pretend the carnage wasn't policy-inflicted. Other damage too resulted directly from lockdown mandates, such as via closing schools. They had to concoct some argument for why a country without any restrictions would experience the same damage anyway.

---

179 PWC (2020), https://www.pwc.com.au/important-problems/australia-rebooted.pdf

What they came up with, and then copied in dozens more papers, was simply to lie.[180] First off, of course, they started out with very high IFRs of around 1%. Then they simply assumed that the virus posed equal risk to everyone in the population, thereby lying about the actual risks to people of working age. They also claimed that if people kept on going to work it would kill non-workers. For gravy, they claimed the virus was so fearsome that rational workers would take the extreme action of voluntarily staying home from their jobs anyway, just to avoid being exposed to it.

So they first lied about the risks to workers, then asserted that workers would stay away from their jobs anyway just as often as government mandates required. All they had to do now was assume that lockdowns were going to eliminate the virus or lead to some other highly improbable overall benefit, such as a better prepared hospital service, to arrive at the conclusion that lockdowns made perfect sense.

By piling on variations to this cascade of lies and baseless assumptions, the diligent crew of macroeconomists building these models also rationalised track-and-trace systems, border closings, school closings and other extreme measures.[181]

Acemoglu et al. (2020) is a classic in this genre. The authors stuff their paper full of absurd assumptions and exaggerations that all point in the same direction, and then claim that there is no doubt they are right despite the uncertainties: 'We stress that there is much uncertainty about many of the key parameters for COVID-19 ….Nonetheless, while the specific numbers on economic and public health costs are sensitive to parameter values, our general conclusion that targeted policies bring sizable benefits appears very robust …' (p. 5).

---

180 In this paragraph we step through the assumptions specifically of Acemoglu et al. (2020), but many other papers conformed to this model of making absurd assumptions as a means of baking in the desired result.

181 E.g., Grafton et al. (2020).

Papers like this one sprinted along behind the unanimous support for lockdowns shown among American economists in the March 2020 survey. It was a classic case of making up arguments using fancy-schmancy methods to support a conviction already held by the group. It was a repeat of what happened during the American Prohibition period, when as late as 1927, eight years in, support for the alcohol ban was near-unanimous among economists.[182] At key moments in history, it seems economists have a worrying habit of justifying the 'truths' of the crowd.

As with the lies of the epidemiologists, those of the economists and 'risk scientists' very quickly became 'scientific fact'. Papers in this area would be sent for review to the early modellers who had set the lies in motion. These, of course, ensured that follow-up papers toed the line, perpetuating the initial fibs. Worse, junior economists started to harass others about why they were not aware of the 'new findings' unearthed by 'new analyses' using these models. By mid-2021, the policy cupboard was stocked with over a hundred separate papers in macroeconomics looking at the 'optimal lockdown' policies.[183]

Just as with the epidemiologists, many direct negative effects of what the economists proposed were simply taken to be nonexistent unless someone else proved their existence with 100% certainty. There was no mention of the mental health costs of business closures, no actual surveys asking workers if they would go to their workplaces if they were allowed to, and no actual examination of the behaviour of workers in countries without lockdowns. The Great Panic provided a stunning example of how economists can, in circumstances that suit their career objectives, pervert science.

---

182 Tucker (2020), https://www.aier.org/article/the-expert-consensus-also-favored-alcohol-prohibition/

183 A Google Scholar search on June 10th, 2021 returned 100 separate papers containing the phrase 'optimal lockdown' and the word 'macro'. Manual inspection revealed that the vast majority of these were indeed macroeconomic papers in which an argument was made in favour of lockdowns of non-zero length.

SELECTIVE BLINDNESS PLUS COMMERCIAL INCENTIVES EQUALS BAD OUTCOMES

An underlying issue throughout 2020-21 was that very little was known for certain about the virus or the effects of either medical treatments or non-pharmaceutical interventions. This reflects the normal reality of medicine, economics, sociology and other sciences involving human behaviour, in which both scientists and governments need to look at an awful lot of data from different sources to get some reasonable idea of what works and what does not. There is almost never true certainty about anything. That uncertainty creates a space: a range wherein the benefit of the doubt can be claimed or denied.

The huge shift in government policy in this period erased that space. It created an urgency to appear certain about the effects of treatments and policies, which in turn made it purely a matter of politics to ensure that doubts about those effects were suppressed. True science soon became an enemy of the state. Politicians and scientists faced the imperative of finding reasons to agree with what was decided, while belittling arguments to the contrary.

Certainty was claimed for things that were not certain at all. This included the effects of lockdowns, social distancing, school closures, face masks, the use of ventilators in treatments and travel bans. None of these interventions was based on solid science or even on a 'beyond reasonable doubt' analysis of what had been tried and seen to work in the past.

A telling example is masks. Mask-wearing was a commercially lucrative proposition, as governments had to decide where to purchase them and which masks to consider acceptable. There was a lot of money involved in masks, but what was the actual basis for using them? A group of British medical scientists, organised in the 'HART' foundation, gave the following answer to this question:[184]

---

184 Sidley (2021), https://www.hartgroup.org/masks/

Contrary to the Government message that it 'follows the science', the sudden change in advice by the WHO was not based on any new, high-quality scientific studies. By summer 2020, there was substantial evidence that non-medical masks for the general public did not reduce the transmission of respiratory viruses. A review of 14 controlled studies had concluded that masks did not significantly lessen the spread of seasonal 'flu in the community.[] A Norwegian Institute for Public Health review found that non-medical masks achieve no benefit for healthy individuals, particularly when viral prevalence is low.[] From a common sense angle, scientists had argued that cloth masks contain perforations that are far too big to act as a viral barrier and therefore 'offer zero protection against COVID-19'.[]

Inevitably, the public often wear masks incorrectly, or improperly handle them when putting them on, or removing them, constituting an additional infection hazard. There has been recognition of this contamination risk in the scientific literature[] and other researchers have cautioned against the use of cloth face coverings.[] Potential harms to the wearer include exhaustion, headaches, fatigue and dehydration.[] Some doctors have suggested an increased risk of pneumonia.[] Furthermore, the widely varying physical characteristics of the face coverings used by people in the community, that are not standardised for material, fit, length of wearing, changes after washing and drying, and disposal, means that laboratory research on mask efficacy cannot be generalised to real-world situations.

With particular reference to COVID-19, the only large randomised controlled trial exploring the benefits of adopting face coverings in the community found that masks (even the surgical variety) did not result in a significant reduction in infection risk for the wearer.[] A detailed analysis[] of all research investigations, including those purported to suggest that masks might achieve some benefits, led to the view that there is 'little to no evidence' that cloth masks in the general population are effective.

Masks cause psychological harm

Masks impair verbal communication, render lip-reading impossible for the deaf, and stymie emotional expression, the latter effect potentially constituting a gross impediment to children's social development. Acting as a crude, highly visible reminder that danger is all around, face coverings are fuelling widespread, irrational fear.

Wearing a mask will heighten the distress of many people with existing mental health problems and may trigger 'flashbacks' for those historically traumatised by physical and/or sexual abuse. Sadly, going without a mask (even as a means of avoiding psychological distress) can often attract harassment and further victimisation. In response to this, 'exemption lanyards' have been developed, which further stigmatise those who cannot wear face coverings due to health conditions or previous trauma.

Many other groups of critical scientists have produced similar analyses.[185] They detail how masks fit the model of a sacrifice and promote the illusion of control, while in fact being harmful for health, bad for the environment and a source of corruption when governments buy huge numbers of them from favoured suppliers.

That didn't deter medical authorities from advocating the use of masks and deriding those who were sceptical even though the sceptics had 30 years of science on their side. They simply proclaimed certainty, mandated their use

---

185 See, for example, Swiss Policy Research (2021B), https://swprs.org/face-masks-evidence/

and accused naysayers of recklessly endangering all of the fine upstanding citizens who were 'doing the right thing'. Meanwhile, their favoured suppliers laughed all the way to the bank.

The certainty that was projected for the policies and medical treatments adopted early on meant that alternative policies and treatments faced an uphill battle just to get a hearing, much less acceptance. Proponents of any alternative had to make their case while being derided, stigmatised and sometimes even criminalised by their opponents. They received little funding to research their ideas. The 'cancel culture' approach to possible alternatives made it easy for commercial interests to push against cheap treatments and direct attention towards more expensive ones.

THE STORY OF ZINC AND IVERMECTIN

Notwithstanding this dynamic, many groups of doctors and scientists openly defended such alternative Covid treatments as hydroxychloroquine (preferably with zinc), ivermectin (with or without zinc), and fluvoxamine.[186]

As a prime example of the dynamics involved, consider the use of zinc and ivermectin as a treatment for Covid early in the development of the disease. Ivermectin was dirt cheap as there was no patent applying to it, so any and every manufacturer could make it and sell it.

The science on whether these treatments 'work' is not completely settled, even at the time of writing. However, many studies show promising results; for example that in particular patient groups ivermectin reduces the frequency with which asymptomatic patients become symptomatic or severely ill. To be fair, the encouraging studies[187] do not include a large trial in Western countries featuring a substantial group of positive PCR-test volunteers who receive

---

186 This is discussed at length in Kirsch (2021).

187 E.g., Hazan et al. (2021).

either ivermectin or nothing, and then are followed up over time to see which group did better. Such a 'randomised controlled trial', as it is known in the literature, would cost millions of dollars. Medical authorities, governments and pharmaceutical companies refused to organise and fund such studies, preferring instead to claim that ivermectin (or zinc) was dangerous and even illegal. This is despite the fact that these substances had been used for decades for other illnesses, including the common cold.

The studies in favour of the ivermectin alternative were typical of social science studies: not decisive, but not without some merit. In June 2021, the Swiss website swprs.org listed the following summary evidence on the promise of ivermectin and zinc:

- Numerous controlled and observational studies on ivermectin found strong anti-viral and anti-inflammatory effects and a reduction in Covid mortality of 50% to 80%.
- A preliminary WHO meta-analysis found a reduction in Covid mortality of 75%.
- A US-Canadian study published in Nature Communications Biology showed that ivermectin strongly (>90%) inhibits the main Coronavirus replication enzyme (3CLpro).
- A Spanish study found that low plasma zinc levels (below 50mcg/dl) increased the risk of in-hospital death of Covid patients by 130%.
- US studies found an 84% decrease in hospitalizations and a 45% decrease in mortality based on risk-stratified early treatment with zinc and HCQ.
- A US case study reported a rapid resolution of Covid symptoms, such as shortness of breath, based on early outpatient treatment with high-dose zinc.

More exhaustive discussions can be found elsewhere[188] but the reports above suggest that a lack of zinc in the body in Covid patients is associated with problems, and that giving various groups zinc and/or ivermectin may have beneficial effects. One might think that in the face of a global Covid-related panic, these reports would meet the threshold for a serious conversation at least.

Yet the company that originally produced ivermectin itself did not advertise it and even went so far as to recommend against it,[189] trying instead to promote a different medicine that was far more expensive. For over a year, many Western governments went with far more expensive drugs that had no more evidence behind them, funnelling the hopes of the population towards vaccines. The WHO as late as March 2021 advised against ivermectin. Still, ivermectin was used at first only in poorer countries such as in India, and then gradually came to be used in over 20 other countries.[190] There are now finally some large medical trials underway to settle the question.[191]

The story of zinc and ivermectin can be repeated for dozens of treatments and policies: there was a strong case in favour of considering something, but a combination of commercial interests and inertial thinking led to resistance to open debate on its merits or funding more research. This pattern reveals the kind of 'scientific' world we live in, where commercial interests, insti-tutionalised 'science' and politics combine against the interests of whole populations. Western countries and the world as a whole have a mountain to climb in order to return to practicing open-minded science.

To fully appreciate the size of the problem we have to understand how today's corporations, government advisors, and politicians interrelate. This is the focus of a later chapter. For now, we keep to the story of science, and

---

188 Kory et al. (2021).

189 https://www.merck.com/news/merck-statement-on-ivermectin-use-during-the-covid-19-pandemic
190 Kirsch (2021).

191 See Swiss Policy Research (2021B), https://swprs.org/the-ivermectin-debate/

turn to what the more honest scientists tried to do during the Great Panic.

THE COVISTANCE (COVID RESISTANCE) INSIDE SCIENCE

Even before the Great Panic, particular groups of scientists and commentators were warning against overreactions to the new virus.

Jeffrey Tucker was one of the quicker ones, with his January 27th 2020 post called 'Must government save us from the Coronavirus?'[192] He was prescient in that post and many subsequent ones, even writing a book about the human costs of the overreaction.[193] The organisation he headed, a libertarian think tank called the American Institute for Economic Research, spearheaded the sceptical movement in the US. It organised conferences and declarations and published reports and Op-eds throughout the Covid period.

From March 2020 onwards, four different groups of scientists emerged who opposed lockdowns and other Great Panic policies.

---

192 Tucker (2020A), https://www.aier.org/article/must-government-save-us-from-the-coronavirus/
193 Tucker (2020).

First were the top medics who initially found it very difficult to get a hearing because their articles were shunned by the good medical journals.[194] They individually wrote articles and gave media presentations through which they found each other, and many eventually banded together in the Great Barrington Declaration of October 4th, 2020.[195] This statement reestablished the orthodoxy that had reigned before March 2020, calling for public health

194 An instructive example is discussed in Birrel (2021), https://unherd.com/2021/06/beijings-useful-idiots/
195 https://gbdeclaration.org/

policies to be based on an assessment of costs and benefits. It was signed by tens of thousands of public health-related academics and hundreds of thousands of others, including ourselves. Jeffrey Tucker's organisation had facilitated the meetings that led to this Declaration.

The Declaration claimed that the public health and social costs of lockdowns and other measures had been immense, and that a more sensible policy would be for authorities to focus their attention and resources on the most vulnerable while not inhibiting the movements of the vast majority of the population. It called on the young and healthy to work normally. It even advocated that 'People who are more at risk may participate [in activities with high-risks of infection] if they wish, while society as a whole enjoys the protection conferred upon the vulnerable by those who have built up herd immunity.'

These medics were well represented in further initiatives to influence public debates,[196] though as one might expect they were heavily censored and attacked for all kinds of reasons. Their efforts served as a rallying cry, helping those opposed to the lockdowns and social distancing to find and coordinate with each other.

A second group of scientists consisted of lone economists calculating the costs and benefits of the policies enacted in their countries. Many nations had such economists but they were scarce on the ground and not united internationally, largely because their calculations were oriented toward their own countries while the medical scientists could speak in general about appropriate public health strategies. We ourselves were in this group, producing cost-benefit analyses and helping economists in other countries with theirs, as described in Chapter 5.

The third group of scientists had roles in development and political science from which they watched in horror as the lockdowns and economic collapse

---

196 For example, through sites like thepriceofpanic.org.

instigated famine, civil conflict and dictatorships all over the world. This group included people working at the UN, the IMF and charities like Oxfam, and led to reports like those discussed in Chapter 5.

The fourth group of scientists were those in specific fields where the damage of lockdowns became abundantly clear, forcing them to speak out. Critical pieces were offered by scholars of unemployment, child mental health, gendered violence, refugees and loneliness.[197]

SCIENCE AND TECHNOLOGY AS THE 'MAGIC FIX'

The Great Panic gave rise to many claims about how new technology and new means of using it would allow governments to control the socioeconomic system.

Regional testing regimes in hospitals and doctors' offices plus random spot checks supposedly gave governments real-time maps of the spread of the disease, allowing them to 'halt' infections by this or that measure. Tests supposedly also helped businesses to certify their immune workers and isolate the infected from the rest.

Bluetooth-based track-and-trace apps were released, supposedly to alert anyone who had been in contact with a Covid-infected person that they might be infected themselves. Whole workforces became part of track-and-trace efforts to contact infected individuals, figure out where they might have acquired an infection and finger others whom they may have infected in turn.

Mobile labs and remote temperature sensors supposedly helped screen potentially infected people at airports. Mobile-phone-based health-tracking apps allowed millions of users to keep a record of their health that could be misused by authorities. Simple existing technology like face masks supposedly

197 Unemployment: Dreger & Gros (2021); mental health for children: Vizard et al. (2020); mental health and school closures: Lee (2020); lockdowns, gendered violence, job losses for refugees: UN General Assembly (2020); loneliness: Douglas (2020), https://www.psychiatryadvisor.com/home/topics/general-psychiatry/costs-of-social-isolation-loneliness-covid19/ and Kotwal et al. (2021).

would help prevent the spread of infections. Lanes drawn in shops and rules posted on seating would supposedly enforce proscribed social distancing rules, preventing the spread of infection.

All up, hundreds of billions of dollars were spent on a large set of techno-logical 'fixes' during the Great Panic, making many consulting and technology firms far richer than they were pre-Covid.

The general lesson is that most of these technologies were expensive failures. Track-and-trace apps were discarded by the very governments that introduced them soon after they discovered that there was resistance to them within their populations, partly because of privacy concerns and partly because Jasmines were not going to allow their whole lives to be disrupted by positive tests.

With people avoiding the apps, low-tech tracing systems like sign-in books at shops and restaurants were offered in their place. These too were routinely ignored or used to enter false details.[198] Face masks, as we saw earlier, arguably posed a net health risk: they restricted air flow and many people reused the same mask over and over, which meant they were quickly full of germs and a danger both to the wearers and the people they got close to. Remote temperature sensors, instant testing, and countrywide alert systems all produced results too inaccurate to be useful, other than to reassure the public that something was being done.

To illustrate the generic problems, consider just one simple example: the testing of school pupils for infections, whose results led schools to send home whole classes for a period of time if a pupil in some class returned a positive test.

The main problem is that like all tests, the Covid test has a false positive rate, meaning there is some chance a test will indicate an infection that isn't there. The more sensitive the test, the more false positives occur. A relatively

---

198 Anecdotally, many individuals known to the authors gave incorrect information when signing in, including bogus phone numbers. In many countries where such information was being sought from the public, the 'reward' for being in the wrong place at the wrong time could be removal to a quarantine facility. See, for example, Bob Pepperstock's story.

more sensitive test is better at picking up infection in the initial stages, at the moment when information about infection would be most useful. Yet, using a very sensitive test carries the risk that even pure water shows up as 'infected' because of slight impurities in the machine, small mistakes in the 'cycles' that the testing protocol uses, or small levels of contamination from surfaces.

Compounding this, the principal Covid tests do not merely look for the presence of live Covid in the body, but indicate the presence of any residual virus in the testing location. This means that an infection already overcome by the body, leaving behind only broken bits of virus, would still return a positive test even weeks after the infection was over.

A very good test would falsely indicate that someone is infected one time in a thousand, with most studies finding a higher rate of false positives.[199] One in a thousand sounds very little, doesn't it? For a single person tested once, a 1 in 1,000 risk of being erroneously told one is infected seems reasonable. Yet for a school, a mistake once every 1,000 uses makes test results highly problematic as a basis for significant action.

Consider a class of 50 pupils, each tested at the start of the day. With a 1 in a 1,000 chance per test of a false positive, there is about a 1 in 20 chance per day of someone testing positive even if no one is infected. On average, we would expect that once every 4 regular school weeks (20 school days), someone in that class tests positive even if no one is infected. So if the school sends all children home when a positive test result is received, then we would expect that every four weeks the whole class is sent home, perhaps for as long as two weeks.

The reality is that most Covid tests in 2020-2021 were not good enough to yield a false positive of only one in a thousand. One in 500 to one in 200

199 Albendín-Iglesias et al. (2020).

was more common.[200] With that kind of error rate, and assuming that a single positive test sent all children home for a week, classes of 50 would be expected to miss more than half their education even if no one was ever infected. If school policies were more stringent, and a whole school of a few hundred pupils were sent home when someone tested positive, there would be almost no schooling left.

In sum, the available tests were blunt tools for schools wanting to enforce a policy of cancelling classes to prevent possibly-infected students from spreading the infection at school. After a few weeks or months of disrupted education, school staff wanting their pupils to continue to learn will have had no option but to sabotage the test regimes in some way. We are confident that this sort of sabotage has happened all around the world at the hands of caring schoolteachers and principals.

The same goes for the regular operation of many other groups. What appeared as small imperfections in available tests turned out to be so disruptive when amplified in larger groups over time that it was impossible to enact a wide-scale test-and-lockdown regime and keep operating. Offices and travel companies could insist that workers have certificates saying they had tested negative and refuse access to those without such documentation, but they could not isolate large work teams or cancel whole trains, buses and planes based on positive test results.

Over time, populations realise how disruptive tests are to their lives and start to sabotage testing regimes themselves in order to keep living more normally. Someone whose upcoming travel would be disrupted by a positive test simply takes another one, in the hope of getting at least one negative result that can be produced for the airline. Testing agencies with many clients who really wanted negative-test certificates would just use less sensitive

200 Swiss Policy Research (2021B), https://swprs.org/the-trouble-with-pcr-tests/

tests with much lower false positive (and false negative) rates.

The impossible promise of perfect control continued throughout the Great Panic. It seduced governments and populations alike, and traces of it will probably survive its end.

CROWDS

The individual tragedies of the Great Panic — James succumbing to the lure of power, Jane desperate for her government to protect her, Jasmine's voice being drowned out, whole populations suffering for the most part unseen — are only part of the story.

Looking at just the data, the arguments, or the pronouncements in any individual country cannot point the way towards avoiding a repeat, or even tell us what to expect in the coming years in the absence of another pandemic.

Science has mostly been unhelpful during Covid because scientists too often just followed the power. Yet the behaviour of the individual scientist or of the individual Janes during this period can only be fully grasped with an understanding of the groupthink in which they took part. The deeper mechanisms that lead to groupthink and obsessions will not disappear, and we will have to prevent or overcome them the next time around if we want a different result.

The emotional wave that swept through the herd of humanity during the Great Fear turned into a mad dash for lockdowns. The Illusion of Control phase was also a herd-level phenomenon. Particular individuals played prominent roles but no evil genius was behind it all, though of course there was no shortage of people claiming that they or someone else had planned it. It was a whole-group production, out of the control of any single person or sub-group.

While the Great Fear swept across the globe, leaving few stones unturned, the Illusion of Control phase in rich countries crucially involved the reemergence of national crowds. Crowd dynamics can explain the strangest elements of the Great Panic, such as the longevity of the popularity of self-destructive measures and the emergence of totalitarian national governments.

To tell this story, we must first explain what we mean by crowds as distinct from 'normal' groups. We must explain how they relate to emotions, empathy and ideology. To do so we draw on the work of famous sociologists studying crowds 50 or more years ago, including Norbert Elias, Theodor Adorno, Elias Canetti and Gustav le Bon.

These scholars wrote about crowds in a way modern sociologists hardly do anymore: as groups that become insane by the previous standards of the same group. Bystanders to a crowd feel they are witnessing something that looks like people becoming possessed by spirits or demons. While the authors do not believe in demonic possession, this was the normal way to think about crowds for centuries. Le Bon and Canetti thought about them this way too.

Let us then explore the demons of the Great Panic.

WELCOME TO THE CROWD

Crowds are large social groups operating in an emotionally intense mode whose members share an obsession. The obsession can change over time and membership too can evolve, but the presence of an intense shared obsession is the key hallmark of a crowd. Tens of thousands of people watching a game in a sports stadium constitute a crowd, as all are emotionally activated and focused on the same thing — the game — at the same time. They mirror each other's obsession and are aware that they are in a group in which everyone is watching the same thing. Seeing their own obsession mirrored in the reactions of others sweeps them along in a pleasant intense joint experience.

The crowd in a sports stadium is a short-lived crowd and not a particularly dangerous one, as it disbands when the game is over: the joint obsession does not last long enough to support the formation of a strongly bonded group.

Regularly functioning 'normal' social groups, by contrast, have multiple goals that vary at high frequency over time in their importance to members. We have written extensively in the past on what 'normal group' behaviour is and what types of groups there are, with our view close to the 'social identity' school in psychology.[201] In brief, long-lived groups with strong emotional ties among members, like families or nations, pursue the collective interest of their members in a number of ways.

A country as a whole can be a social group without being a crowd, as is the case when its members are worried about a hundred and one things at a given moment with no common, intense focus. A country becomes a crowd when a single obsession absorbs its members' focus, forming the topic that everyone thinks about, talks about and even obsesses about privately.

Often, countries only have a single obsession for a very short period of time, such as on an election day or during a national festival, but sometimes they can be obsessed about one thing for years. For example, France was obsessed with winning the First World War during the whole of the 1914-1918 period. Villages, churches, and political movements too can transform into crowds for periods of time.

Their singular obsession, emotional intensity and size lead to crowds sometimes attaining great power and dictating directions that can change the course of history for a whole country, or even for the world. The inherent danger is that their obsession blinds them to everything else that matters in normal times.

The supreme example of the genesis of a powerful and dangerous crowd is the mass political rallies organised by the Nazis in Germany in the 1930s. In these rallies, hundreds of thousands of Germans stood close to each other in a field, touching each other, all oriented towards the same focal point

---

201 Haslam & Haslam (2012).

— their leader — from whom all truth and morality was seen to emanate. Those in the crowd lost their individuality and their ability to think critically and independently. They became part of a single social entity in which everyone reacted in the same way, cheering this and booing that, and promising undying loyalty to the leader and vengeance to the identified enemy.

Monumental decisions over which people acting individually would have agonised for decades, such as whether their Jewish neighbours who fought with them in the First World War were actually their enemies, were decided in seconds by crowds. The leader of the crowd said they were enemies and hundreds of thousands of voices instantly affirmed it. Lifelong friends became mortal enemies in seconds during these crowd events, and total strangers became blood brothers willing to fight shoulder to shoulder to the death in the trenches.

The Nazis achieved this incredible feat with careful management. Individuals would be 'warmed up' with loud music, military parades and feverish early speakers talking up the importance of the supreme leader. Group symbols like giant flags and shiny uniforms were on display everywhere. Smells and lighting were used to create a homely yet heavenly feel.

The Nazis did not invent crowds, nor how to create and manipulate them. They understood the power of crowds from their reading of history, which is full of examples hardly studied nowadays. The 1910s gave rise to crowds of socialists.[202] The 1880s saw crowds of nationalists.[203] The 17th century saw crowds of American puritans.[204] The 19th century saw religious crowds in Europe, Africa, and Asia. Crowds of farmers were a staple of scientific writing for decades in the era of the Enlightenment, when scientists and merchants saw it as their duty to 'civilise' their populations by helping them

---

202 Smaldone (2020).

203 Darwin (2013).

204 History.com Editors (2019), https://www.history.com/topics/colonial-america/puritanism

turn away from crowd behaviour and think for themselves.

In 1841, the poet Charles Mackay authored the book *Extraordinary Popular Delusions and the Madness of Crowds* in which he describes what he learned from watching cities, villages and countries in times of war, illness, religious and ideological fanaticism. His key message to the future is embodied in this quote: '*Men*, it has been well said, think in *herds*; it will be seen that they go mad in *herds*, while they only recover their senses slowly, *one by one*.' Earlier and later writers said similar things. We take Mackay's pronouncement to be an empirical claim that once a crowd has lasted for a while, it will not dissolve in a bang, but slowly.

THE THREE DEFINING FEATURES OF A CROWD

Three elements distinguish the crowds we are interested in from normal groups.

The clearest distinguishing feature of a crowd is its joint focus on something. The 'something' can be almost anything and need not even be real. Crowds can form around an obsession about a fear of vampires, a religious ideal, a desire for vengeance, a charismatic leader, a coming apocalyptic event, the second coming of a god or the production of a particular flower. The 'something' need not be anything the individuals would in tranquil times care about or even believe in, like vengeance or vampires. Yet, individuals in a crowd will attend to and talk about the 'something' constantly, make plans and promises to each other about it, and berate anyone who wavers in their determination to stamp it out, get it, avoid it, unite with it, or whatever the logic of the obsession demands.

A second distinguishing feature is that in a crowd both truth and morality cease to be fixed things held by individuals. They instead become outcomes of the obsession of the crowd that are almost instantly adopted by all crowd members. Whether or not Jews are the enemy ceases to be an individual moral choice and instead a truth emerges that they are, as an outcome of the group obsession. Whether or not surface cleaning helps to avoid infections stops being the outcome of scientific inquiry, and instead the truth that it does help is elevated to this status as a result of the group obsession. This truth is then instantly adopted by all in the crowd. Whether death is something glorious to be desired or something horrible to flee from can likewise be immediately decided as an outcome of the obsession of a crowd, rather than the result of individual morality.

Everything that individuals normally relate to as if it is fixed becomes fluid in a crowd. It is this fluidity that outsiders find most fascinating, seeing it as a form of insanity. The crowd members see those who do not go along with the new truths and the new morality as either in denial, evil, or outright insane themselves.

Yet how can things as vast as 'truth' and 'morality' become crowd-level constructs if the deliberations and obsessions of the crowd are so limited? To understand this, we envision 'truth' as seen by an individual as a giant canvas on which many elements are painted. Every individual has his own personal giant canvas, normally containing only some elements that also appear on others' canvases.

When individuals merge into a crowd, the crowd's obsession resolves into a new truth, which almost instantly replaces whatever individuals previously had in that part of their canvas. Whatever individuals previously thought about face masks gets instantly overwritten when the crowd leaders pronounce a new view on face masks. Members of the crowd, including scientists, then rationalise that new view and simply assert it to be the truth. If they need to forget that they recently said something different, they will, and they will belittle their former truth with barely a whimper.

Those wanting to argue against any new crowd-resolved truth are given the impossible task of disproving the new truth beyond all doubt to the satisfaction of the crowd. With no mental agony at all, crowd members will pretend to themselves that the new view is totally validated and that all people who say otherwise are lesser beings. The same goes for morality: individual variation is bulldozed by the new crowd-resolved morality, even when it comes to things as fundamental as life and death, and even if crowd members believed the exact opposite only moments before the new morality was resolved. The period of hesitation and ambivalence during which individual perspectives get steamrolled is often no longer than minutes — weeks at the most.

A third element of crowds is that the group as a whole sanctifies behaviour deemed unconscionable at the individual level. The crowd openly does what individuals in it would still see as unethical and criminal to do on a personal basis. Repressed desires often come out at the crowd level as sanctified group behaviour. A crowd will become boastful, domineering, vengeful and violent precisely in societies made up of people who are conditioned to be shy, humble, forgiving, and peaceful. To the outsider it is an extraordinary and chilling phenomenon to see the crowd become an agent of group crimes, while those within the crowd fail to see this transformation.

Group crimes have been richly evident in Covid times. The lonely have inflicted loneliness on others via the edicts of the crowd. Those being bossed around in their normal lives have inflicted humiliation on others through the decisions of the crowd leaders to humiliate those resisting the crowd. Lacking warm social lives themselves, crowd members have been living vicariously through their crowd leaders, while inflicting misery on everyone else. Operating as a crowd, people can do and celebrate things that are otherwise impossible, which is why crowds can be so dangerous. In the wrong circumstances, a lust for destruction can emerge and can then be indulged on an industrial scale.

The three distinguishing features of a crowd – a single obsession, the fluidity of morals and truth, and group criminality – have been studied for centuries. These characteristics describe many cults, mass movements, religious sects and groups of fanatics. We see miniature versions of crowd behaviour in all group events, such as parties, weddings and funerals, where those present join in with crowd-like behaviour for a short while. But weddings, parties and funerals have a clear goal and a clear end point. Real crowds do not have a clear end point, though they do all invariably come to an end, sometimes after days and sometimes after decades.

CROWDS AS BEASTS AND MASTERS

Crowds can be grouped into types based mainly on the nature of the joint obsession that defines them. Crowds unified by a charismatic leader, like cults, are usually kept busy with joint projects such as building something or fighting something. Crowds can also be unified by an initial fear or an initial opportunity. The Great Panic has led to crowds that initially formed from a joint fear, while conquering armies are examples of crowds formed on the back of joint opportunities. Crowds can also be formed by joint grief, a shared god, or some kind of quest.

In all cases, however, crowds have a certain joint intelligence to them. Not only is there a very deliberate intellectual attitude towards the joint obsession, whether that is to exterminate all Jews or to suppress the Covid virus, but a certain rationality protects the maintenance of the crowd itself. As if the crowd was a single smart organism, it senses dangers to its existence and its cohesion that it will counter. This is why all crowds engage in censorship within the crowd, why they resent examples of groups that look like the same crowd making very different choices, and why they see alternative crowds as competitors to be destroyed or avoided. Crowds find enemies and seek to neutralise them.

Crowds also adjust their focus of obsession strategically over time. When one goal is achieved, a crowd will try to switch to another goal in order to keep going as a crowd. We saw this in play during the Covid period when the goal to suppress Covid in order to buy time morphed seamlessly into the goal to eliminate the virus. That second goal allows a longer-lived and more intense crowd than mere temporary suppression. In turn, elimination of the virus easily transforms into an obsession with potential future variants, allowing the crowd to survive even when vaccination or herd immunity was initially seen to have achieved the 'elimination' goal.

Some crowds are looked back upon in total horror, like the Nazis, while others are regarded with fondness, like the early American revolutionaries. Still others are looked back on negatively but more with weary incredulity than high moral disdain, like the American Prohibitionists. The Covid crowds have elements of each of these three well-known historical crowds, but are not exactly like any of them. Finding no perfect match from history, we opt to take a closer look at some of the psychology relevant to crowds and how it has played out in historical examples, aiming to extract lessons for our own times.

What makes crowds appealing to individuals, and what determines whether someone escapes a crowd or fails to become a member in the first place?

Being in a crowd brings several wonderful feelings to its members. Crowd members feel themselves to be part of a great movement, which often brings feelings of deep connection to many others, all experiencing the joys of community. This was definitely a big bonus to membership in the crowds constructed by the Nazis. The Covid crowds have this to a lesser degree because their joint obsession forbids them from physical closeness to many others. This is partly why the Covid crowds are so strongly opposed to social events in which many people meet: the great pleasure of actual physical proximity might allow an emotional high strong enough to overcome the emotional bonds of the Covid crowd, potentially giving rise to a competitor that the Covid crowd cannot allow.

Another wonderful feeling crowds give their members is release from the mental effort involved in deciding upon, updating and maintaining individual truth and individual morality. Both truth and morality are rather energy-consuming things for individuals to construct and maintain. A crowd offers people the opportunity to stop deliberating and making their own moral judgments. They can instead instantly feel virtuous, without having to expend energy thinking about what virtue really is, simply by complying with the strictures of the crowd.

In a crowd, all considerations other than the joint obsession lose their importance, which allows individuals to outsource their individuality to the group more completely than at other times. This frees people from having to think about many things, liberating time and energy for other pursuits which could well include expanding the number and/or intensity of activities related to the crowd's obsession. This is partly why some crowds can be fantastically creative and productive: their members have let go of many other activities and are functioning as one on their new big project.

This joy of freedom from individual responsibility is balanced out by the general tendency of crowds to become dictatorships even if they start out lacking any unifying leadership. This tendency arises for two main reasons. The first is the inevitable struggle within the crowd over who gets heard first about what to do in order to satisfy the obsession. In that struggle, those who manage to denounce their opponents as enemies of the crowd tend to win the battle and grab the reins of group leadership, with the losers either killed or diminished within the crowd. This broad narrative is well known from historical revolutions that famously 'ate their own children' as the initial leadership gradually became captured by one small group that killed off internal competitors. The French Revolution quickly put its own initial leaders, such as Robespierre, under the guillotine; the more fanatical Nazis in Germany killed off close competitors in the 'Night of the Long Knives'; and in the early years after the Russian Revolution, Stalin won the struggle for power and murdered all other initial senior leaders.

The second reason for the tendency of crowds to become dictatorships is the inherent violence of crowds when threatened. Anything not controlled by the crowd becomes an enemy to its existence. Thus under threat, a crowd naturally becomes aggressive, intolerant and even murderous towards those members who begin to waver and no longer subscribe to the obsession. Crowd leaders can take advantage of that intolerance and aggression by promising to punish the traitors.

Crowds naturally become aggressive and eventually murderous towards sub-groups within themselves that fall afoul of the group obsession, as exemplified by Jews who did not fit the story of the superior Aryan race. This further cements a single, intolerant set of rules wielded by adherents as they patrol the borders of the crowd.

This motivation to remain a crowd with the capacity for violence toward those resisting it naturally led, in the case of the Great Fear, to the creation of national or regional crowds because groups can only punish deviants within their own territories. The international wave of fear therefore gave birth to a litter of national crowds which each policed itself domestically. We saw this almost universally in the Illusion of Control phase when countries slammed their borders shut to keep out foreigners, and states and provinces regularly closed domestic borders against neighbouring states and provinces. The Covid crowds wanted to remain cohesive, and in pursuit of that goal it was important to treat all others as 'different' and 'threatening'.

A spectacular example of this tendency was seen in Australia, which for more than a hundred years had been a single country with huge flows of travellers between states. This normalcy suddenly fell apart in 2020 as every state and territory closed itself off from the others for some period of time. The behaviour continued in 2021 when periodic outbreaks of Covid cases sprang up like wildfires in various localities across the country. The border closures were of course always defended on the basis of the obsession — to tame the threat of infection.

Border closures also had an ancillary benefit for the crowd, which was to demonstrate that the crowd had the power to 'do something' about the obsession by simply defining the borders of itself. For a while, individual Australian states acted as separate crowds that were sealed off from each other and even held different beliefs about how to act. When the national government asserted its own power through taxation and spending, much of the 'rally around the local government' sentiment changed into 'rally around the national government' sentiment, causing the Australian Covid crowds to merge. Still, state governments at various times tried to create state-based crowds, and they were not without success.

In all countries that imposed lockdowns and compulsory social distancing, steps were taken towards dictatorship. Governments invoked various legal devices to suspend normal legislative channels and rule by decree. The most popular device was simply to declare a 'state of emergency', 'state of disaster' or 'state of alarm'. Government officials communicated to their constituents directly via the media, bypassed parliamentary oversight on budgets and sidelined elected legislators from decision-making in general.

In nearly all countries, courts reinterpreted laws so that the respect for human rights applying in normal times — sometimes enshrined in constitutions — did not have to constrain government action. Only after many months did courts begin to wake up to this mistake and enforce constitutional provisions. This indicates how judges themselves can be crowd members, sharing the crowd obsession and accepting the excuses the crowd puts forward. If that means they have to pretend a minor risk of Covid deaths constitutes the huge danger needed to justify government violations of the rights of free speech, privacy and protest, then so be it.

We do not expect democracies to relinquish all the trappings of democracy within eighteen months. But neither would it be reasonable to expect most democracies to survive the Great Panic if it were to endure a high intensity for, say, another ten years. It would not be unrealistic in that case to see a slide toward the same phenomena experienced in Nazi Germany, Soviet Russia, the French Revolution and the Nationalist wave in Spain in the 1930s: dissent strengthens, the crowd reacts more murderously, enforcement groups coalesce and are used to command and control, and democracy is killed off.

Fortunately for us all, the Great Panic is unlikely to last another ten years at the level of intensity of those crowds from history. The obsessions of the Covid crowds do not have the same force and appeal as the obsessions of the destructive crowds described in history books.

Nonetheless, a danger lurks that the Covid crowds may fasten onto new obsessions with more potential. There are some worrying signs. In 2021 we see the formation of more sinister enforcement groups enabling governments to act with increasing aggression toward anyone not following the Covid guidelines. We also see increased censorship by scientific institutions, social media channels and national television stations. At the same time, there is increased opposition, which we would expect to become the first victim of totalitarianism if the Great Panic continues to strengthen.

Simply put, we are at a crossroads in 2021 between a gradual dissolution of the crowds formed under the Great Panic, and their further strengthening accompanied by increasing violence.

HOW CROWDS END

Sometimes a crowd comes to an end because the charismatic leader who held it together dies, is imprisoned or is otherwise neutralised. Its members then tend to splinter into smaller groups and gradually become reabsorbed into normal society, relearning that there are other things to live for.

Sometimes a crowd comes to an end because of the total victory of its obsession and the inability of the leadership that formed around the obsession to sustain a sense of purpose. The Russian Revolution exemplifies this: a triumphant ideology that exhausted itself and could achieve no more after about 70 years. Its initial leaders died from old age, the firing squad, poisoning, or the ice axe, and its founding population literally died out, leaving a new generation less fanatical because there was less to oppose and jettison.

The Iranian Revolution of 1979 too followed the trajectory of total victory for its ideology and leading group, before being stopped from expansion on the battlefields of Iraq and losing its founding leadership through death or corruption as the decades went by.

Often, crowds end because a more powerful authority takes over, removes the leadership, and distracts the population from its obsession. This happened to the rural communities obsessed with werewolves and vampires in Eastern Europe in the 18th and 19th centuries. Authority figures from the church and the new state bureaucracies swept into the benighted villages and bombarded their inhabitants with alternative messages for long enough to come to a different view, or at least for them to stop spouting nonsense.

Similarly, Nazi Germany was conquered by opposing armies from countries that organised a complete restructuring of its society, suppressing Nazi ideology for long enough for the Germans themselves to disown it. The same occurred to end the Japanese empire in 1945. The French Revolution likewise ended in military defeat. In many countries, the socialists, communists, puritans, abolitionists and other fanatical crowds experienced actual limits to their power and the gradual demise of their membership.

A crowd can also end when a new obsession comes along that offers the leadership of the existing crowd fresh opportunities, but makes the old structures and priorities obsolete and leaves many in the previous crowd stranded. The obsession of the US military with Islamic fundamentalism that started with a bang on 9/11/2001 gradually faded as that threat diminished and an entirely different enemy emerged, in the form of the challenge to American hegemony by the Chinese. To fight this required new alliances and new military structures to replace those that had worked against the old threat.

In the absence of a crushing military defeat, a clear limit to domestic victory over competing crowds, or the emergence of a new focus for some part of the crowd, the lesson of history is that crowds naturally dissolve, but slowly. As the poet MacKay wrote in 1841, people come to their senses one by one. The crowd dissolves at the edges, like the Soviet Union or the Puritans. The less committed members who got less out of the crowd lose their faith, adopt a different crowd, or simply become disinterested as other things grow more important to them, like family or personal wealth.

Gradually these lukewarm crowd members become hypocrites, paying lip service to the crowd's truth and its obsession but no longer behaving in accordance with its dictates in their own lives. Then they become disinterested and dismissive. Following which they start to oppose it, either quietly or loudly.

HISTORICAL CASE STUDIES: WORLD WAR 1 AND PROHIBITION

Two historical examples of crowd dissolution are most relevant to the Covid crowds that formed in 2020.[205] The first is how the nationalistic crowds of the winning countries in the First World War gradually dissolved. The second is how the US Prohibition movement came to an end.

Countries such as the UK and France that were victorious at the end of the First World War had nonetheless suffered devastation. Millions were dead or crippled and whole regions had been laid to waste. The populations were tired of the nationalist project that had consumed them for years and were glad it was over. However, at the same time, political and economic elites that had benefited from the war effort weren't keen to let go. Whole industries were oriented towards war and many laws giving governments extra powers were in place. How did things get renormalised?

---

205 For a discussion of many other historical analogies relevant to understanding the Great Panic, see Frijters (2021A), https://clubtroppo.com.au/2021/01/08/historical-analogies-for-the-covid-mania/

In both the UK and France, the horrors of the war only became clear after it ended. In the cold light of day, civilians saw the streets of the main cities full of traumatised returnees with hideous injuries. Families and villages that had told themselves throughout the war that life would return to normal found many of their young men were either dead, disabled or deranged. Women had to compete for the few sane and healthy men left, while governments had to reorient to new priorities. In a word, considerations other than the war effort become more prominent, including family formation and all the government tasks neglected during the war.

A second key thing that happened was the casting of blame and an increase in political competition, both of which led to a dismantling of the institutions and industries that had benefited from the war. People blamed their politicians and elites for the stupidity of the war, and that blame was pushed particularly hard by political groups that were opposed to the war already or had other goals.

This is illustrated in the film *J'accuse* of 1919, in which the whole wartime elite in France is accused of stupidity leading to the horrors of the Great War. Socialists, communists, anarchists, and others ran organised blame campaigns which helped to wind down the war industries, the armies and the state propaganda machines that had flourished during the years of conflict.

A third catalyst for the transition was that the institutions born in the First World War started to exert their own pressures in ways that led to new social dynamics and further reduced the obsession with all things war. For example, the war had given rise to universal suffrage in several countries. With all adults entitled to vote, new political parties and their associated media outlets sprang up. The war had also weakened previously powerful groups such as the aristocracy which unsuccessfully tried to regain influence, leading to counterreactions.

In short, at both micro and macro levels, more mundane human priorities returned — the desire for wealth, family life, personal space and power. Still, it took years for the militarism of the Great War to fade.

The Covid crowds may experience a similar 'end of the war' moment in the form of vaccines that supposedly win the day on the Covid battle-field. Yet vaccines do not mean the end of Covid deaths, and of course the crowd machinery can start to reorient towards new variants, other infectious diseases or other obsessions and thus roll on with only minor adjustments. The First World War does not quite fit the Great Panic because the clear dramatic end to the war is unlikely to be replicated this time around.

The analogue of Prohibition in the United States may be even more instruc-tive. Prohibition was a period of 13 years (1920-1933) in which the sale, import, transport and production of alcohol was banned throughout the US.[206] It was the dreamed-of policy of generations of the Prohibitionist movement that grew in strength during the 19th century. The movement leveraged the fanaticism generated in the First World War to press its agenda for a more perfect America.

Unlike the UK and France, which had had their fill of grand projects after four years of death and destruction, the Prohibitionists in the US were living in a country that ended the same war with relatively few deaths and a triumphalist moral attitude. Better yet, the war had politically neutered US citizens of German descent who controlled much of the production of beer and were therefore strongly anti-prohibition.

For a while, the Prohibitionists were a victorious crowd. They managed to get their desired proscriptions anchored in the US Constitution, making them very difficult to overturn. They also managed to plant their flag on the moral high ground and have their views seen as sanctified by the church. Their attitude became the dominant view within science, which churned out studies 'proving' how bad alcohol was for children, mental health, the work ethic and religious probity.

---

206 The interpretation in Stroup (2020) is very similar to what follows.

Similarly, science 'proved' that alcohol was corrupting for society as a whole and had caused nothing but damage in the preceding centuries. Almost no attention was given to the fact that prohibiting alcohol was attempting to eliminate a pleasurable activity that defied suppression, and therefore that it could only lead to criminality on a grand scale.

It took about eight years for US science to quit being the mouthpiece of Prohibitionists and look seriously at the actual effects of alcohol on the wider social system. It took that long for serious opposition to emerge, for example as groups started to argue that the underground alcohol economy was doing more damage than legal sales had done beforehand. Only near the end of the 1920s did it become possible to talk openly about how humans needed some release from the pressures of work and moralising that they had to live with most of the day. Only then did people start to see positive aspects of the use of alcohol, such as improved sociability and lower stress levels.

It took another five years for the political forces against Prohibition to gain the strength needed to overturn it by changing the Constitution. By 1933 most of the population had come to a much more reasonable view on the use of alcohol, as well as the role that drugs in general play in people's lives.

This mass change of mind was not accompanied by any serious punishment for the scientists, politicians and industrialists who had spearheaded the introduction of Prohibition. On the contrary, a massive cover-up occurred, muddying the question of who was to blame for the immense damage that Prohibition had caused.

The organisations directly calling for Prohibition did see their membership dwindle to nothing, but there was no culling in academia or anywhere else. There was simply a temporary reduction in the volume of moralising, followed quickly by new moral crusades like the New Deal. The zeal for Prohibition also became dwarfed by the misery of the Great Depression that started in 1929 and offered plenty of clear and present concerns unrelated to alcohol.

There are many analogies between the US Prohibition period and what we have seen in the Great Panic. In both cases, the rise of the main crowd was preceded by decades of minor scares and groups arguing that an Armageddon was in the offing, in the form of a pandemic or population-wide drunkenness, that would destroy humanity.

Like the Prohibitionist crowd, the crowd of the Great Panic immediately moralised upon all actions related to its obsession — Covid infections — and spawned a cottage industry of dubious science 'proving' the appropriateness of the actions taken.

As with the truths of the Prohibitionists, the truths of the Great Panic crowd quickly became enshrined in law and co-opted the major ideologies and religions of the day. And as was true during Prohibition, the elites themselves eventually tried to circumvent the consequences of these changed laws, while the broader public likewise learned to avoid actual compliance while still preaching their subservience.

The Great Panic sits somewhere between these two historical experiences of France and the UK after the First World War, and of Prohibition in the US around the same time. The Great Panic is doing damage on a similar scale to the Great War and has now created nationalist crowds like those seen in the war, but it also contains the same long-running trail of hypocrisy observable in the Prohibition period.

As was true at the end of the Great War, many coalitions stand to benefit from the continuation of The Great Panic, yet counter-movements have developed as in Prohibition. The Great Panic has considerable geographical policy variation like that seen during Prohibition in which some authorities were more zealous about enforcement than others. Yet within countries, the Great Panic appeals to the same nationalism that propelled the crowds of the Great War. Like Prohibition, the Great Panic can only truly end by a dismantling of the control industry set up to enforce its impossible edicts, but like the Great War there is a promised end date of 'victory'.

On balance, we expect the Great Panic to fade and end like Prohibition, with a jolt in that direction if the rollout of vaccines does not produce the immediate return to normal that many have been led to hope for. That disappointment will slowly erode the credibility of the authorities, just as during Prohibition. Yet, a danger exists that the Covid crowds will latch on to a new obsession through which they will persist even after a failed vaccine effort. At the time of writing, crowds are not unwinding everywhere yet and we fear what would happen if a more appealing obsession presented itself to them.

The absence of any threat of foreign invasion can be expected to limit the strength of the Covid crowds and lead to a gradual reawakening. Only if the obsession switches from Covid to something more inherently violent as an obsession, such as the threat from China, do we expect mass physical violence in the West.

CROWDS: SOCIOLOGY'S COMEBACK KID

The big surprise of the Great Panic was that the lockdowns of early 2020 created a social phenomenon not seen for nearly 50 years in much of Europe or the Americas. Crowds were not instantly recognised because social science has rather neglected them as a topic during the last few decades.

The main clue that crowds had returned was that people did not quickly come to their senses during the early lockdowns. They did not start to resent the costs to their own mental health, the disruption to the schooling of their children or the endangerment of their own economic futures. That was truly remarkable because people normally cared a great deal about these things. Somehow, the normal sensitivity to bad outcomes had been switched off. Also, hardly any interest was shown among Western governments or their citizenry in what one could learn from experiments in other countries, or even what the optimal medical treatments for the new disease actually were.

This too was strange to observers outside the crowd, including ourselves.

Both the blindness to personal costs and the open hatred toward outsiders doing different things signalled that we were not witnessing merely a wave of fear. If a population is only afraid then its government should have a keen interest in looking at all options to address the problem, and should be eager to learn from others that have tried different approaches. However, many governments during the Great Panic showed no interest in study tours. Rather, they expressed highly derogatory views, if not outright contempt, of other countries such as Sweden that did not opt for lockdowns. This makes no rational sense if the underlying issue is simple fear and there is no other agenda. Some strange group phenomenon was occurring, and very few recognised it.

The crowd phenomenon was probably very surprising even to the governments implementing the wishes of the crowd. It locked them into policies that were not in their countries' interests and were potentially dangerous to the governments themselves. After all, crowds are obsessive, and if what they want cannot be delivered then they can easily look to blame their leaders. Leaders who were otherwise secure can be suddenly ousted if the crowd turns on them for failing to deliver. History provides many such examples.

Kaiser Wilhelm of Germany had to flee Germany in disgrace after the Great War because he was seen to have led the losing side. He was the last in a line of kings going back centuries and had been revered as god-appointed merely a year before the nationalistic crowds created in the Great War turned on him. If Wilhelm is anything to go by, politicians in 2021 and beyond have something quite real to worry about. Kaiser Wilhelm at least got away alive, something not true of many other leaders who were seen to disappoint a crowd, like Robespierre in the French Revolution.

The fact that the fear of early 2020 led to the reemergence of crowds offers a major social science lesson for the future. Crowds formed because the lockdowns meant a huge change in the lives of much of the population.

This 'activation' of the population via the implementation of different daily habits was the modern-day analogue of wartime mobilisation for the armies which led to the crowds of the Great War.

As the Covid crowd morphed from an international one into dozens of territory-specific crowds, populations suddenly started to think of themselves as a united national or regional front that was there to purge a virus through sacrifice and control.[207] Once formed, the national crowds then gradually shifted their focus, finding excuses to keep going.

Understanding crowd behaviour requires a way of looking at humans and society that goes beyond understanding a virus, the economy, or individuals. Trying to understand crowds as a complex phenomenon 'emergent' from individual behaviour is akin to trying to understand a beehive by watching how each individual bee behaves and fits in with the others. It is much easier and more instructive to look instead at what the beehive does as a whole, thinking of it as an organism itself. So too for human crowds, wherein the individuals involved change their minds almost on a dime, making it extremely difficult to understand crowds by tracking individuals within them. A crowd is more helpfully conceptualised as a kind of beast with certain characteristics, as in MacKay, Gustave le Bon and Canetti's depictions. It is a beast that wants to live and grow.

Crowd members display some tell-tale signs that were highly visible among people within the Covid Cult countries of 2020-2021 and will also be evident in the members of future crowds, providing a diagnostic tool. Is someone a crowd member, or not?

A first clue is that a crowd member is averse to adopting any clear, fixed goal as the thing by which to judge the future and the past. To adopt a fixed goal, such as 'flattening the curve' in the time of Covid, makes an individual vulnerable to being at odds with the crowd when it inevitably changes its

---

207 For a similar analysis, see Moloney (2020), https://thehill.com/opinion/international/492253-coronavirus-is-accelerating-the-advance-of-nationalism-over

mind. The need to stick with the crowd means that no individual member can judge the future or the past on the basis of the crowd's current obsession. One can always identify a crowd member by asking him which fixed goal he thinks his group should care about in the past or future. The kind of question that catches him out is of the form, 'If your government in 3 months declares something totally different as the goal to what it declares now, will it then be immoral?' The fluid nature of the morality of crowds means that the crowd member cannot himself afford to adopt a moral position that is fixed over time.

A second clue is that crowd members are not willing to commit to any truth about their obsession (like 'the IFR is 1%') because, again, when the crowd changes its mind the individual may be left hanging out to dry. While they want to belittle those who do not believe in the current truth of the crowd, crowd members are also reluctant to commit themselves to any of its future truths either. Jasmines can identify crowd members with bets like 'I will give you 100 dollars if in a year's time the government models still produce an IFR of 1%, and you will give me 100 dollars if they produce a different IFR'. Bets that point to what the crowd will believe in the future will identify crowd members because their crowd truth does not exist in the future. It only exists for sure right now.

Yet another clue is that crowd members will adopt crowd-referential reasoning that cannot be refuted. This includes reasoning like 'How can all of us be wrong?' and 'The courts and the media say so, so it must be true'. With such circular reasoning, they are in effect appealing to the power of the crowd as their source of truth and morality. One can always challenge that by asking them to apply the same logic to the past or the far future with questions like 'Were the courts and governments always right? Will the population never make mistakes in the future?'

In the individual stories of Jane and the adventures of James in this book, this type of circular reasoning can be observed. Individuals believe something is true and good *because* they think the crowd they feel part of believes it.

This core aspect of crowd psychology reveals the deep need that drives so many to remain blinded: they want, desperately, to belong.

THE DYNAMICS OF POWER BEFORE, DURING, AND AFTER THE GREAT PANIC

I n this chapter we sketch the political and economic realities underpinning the events of the Great Panic, particularly in Western countries. This narrative includes the gradual formation of a coalition of politicians and businesses that benefited from the Panic and had a keen interest in keeping the Covid ball rolling.

We also link the virus story with the personal interests of leaders of corporations and large institutions, which provides insights into how future stories might play out. We assess the durability of trends that were already in train but received a Covid 'boost', such as increasing inequality[208] and escalating tension between national ideologies and the ideology of international elites.[209]

By exploring the dynamics of the past 40 years that accelerated during 2020-21, we aim to show what our societies are really up against as we emerge from the Panic. This look at history will also show who is 'on our side' — i.e., which forces of history are pushing towards human thriving.

We start by sketching the main developments of the economic system through history as it evolved together with politics and culture, focussing

---

208 Alvaredo et al. (2013) and Alvaredo et al. (2018).

209 See Moloney (2020), https://thehill.com/opinion/international/492253-coronavirus-is-accelerating-the-advance-of-nationalism-over and Hammond (2018), https://www.politicalanimalmagazine.com/2018/12/14/nationalism-and-anti-nationalism-a-matter-of-perception/ for good topical discussions and introductions to the relevant literature.

mainly on the West. We pay special attention to the feudal period of the Middle Ages in Europe around 1300 CE, because of sobering similarities between that period and the current era.

ECONOMICS: THE BIG PICTURE[210]

From a long-run perspective, the reason why we are so much richer and healthier now than we were as hunter-gatherers ten thousand years ago is because we trade and specialise. A hunter-gatherer had to do everything himself. He had to make his own clothes, gather his own food, collect his own medicine, keep up his own religion, educate his children, and entertain himself and others. There is some sharing within the small group and some-times with other groups, but hunter-gatherers do not specialise heavily. Each is a Jack-of-all-trades, and the level of knowledge of the whole group is not much more than the level of knowledge of the individual.

Through the gradual deepening of trade ties, humanity has transformed its economic system completely. Nearly everything we consume today requires the work of millions to produce, without us being aware of who those millions are.

Take the modern supermarket. The food there, much of which derives from plants grown from seeds altered in labs, comes from all over the planet. The beef in the TV dinner comes from carefully cross-bred cattle that over generations became fast-growing, immune to the most prevalent bovine diseases, and docile so as not to get into fights with other cattle. Hundreds of steps were taken along the way between cow in the meadow and beef in the TV dinner, involving, for example, the trucks that brought the cow to the abattoir and the freezer technology that allowed the beef to stay unspoiled as it was moved from slaughterhouse to processing factory, where it was sliced and blended with herbs, preservatives and other ingredients. Likewise, the shampoo on

210 This section largely follows Frijters and Foster (2013).

the shelves is the product of thousands of laboratory tests and chemical processes refined over centuries by millions of engineers and other workers.

Buying a basket of goods at the supermarket is equivalent to trading with hundreds of thousands of people around the world you have never met. By exchanging money for your groceries you have traded the result of some of your time for the result of some of their time. Our trade ties also extend to non-physical goods ('services') like education, entertainment, and health care. Services account for approximately 80% of the economies of Western countries, and thus 80% of the activities from which individuals earn income in exchange for their labour — income that they in turn exchange for goods and services.

The interconnected economy is a wondrous system and has made us easily a hundred times materially richer than our hunter-gatherer ancestors. The specialisation that allowed this staggering increase in wealth is still developing in modern times, if anything more rapidly than before, leading to higher average wealth, better health, and safer living environments. Increased long-run specialisation is a good thing.

Economic development has taught us that gradual specialisation goes together with more international trade and has, on the whole, been great for humanity. People who view each other as potential clients and suppliers are far kinder to each other than those who see each other mainly as competitors for resources. By extension, if whole countries were to withdraw from international trade, the result would not just be greater poverty but more war as well. Other elements help keep a healthy economy humming along, such as currency systems, the education system, and international migration. Yet to understand why things went so badly during the Covid period, specialisation of trading partners and competition between people with plans are the key elements to appreciate.

The world economy — a huge, interdependent web of networked producers, suppliers, and clients — is built on countless specific micro-level ties that cannot be easily or quickly replaced. To see this, imagine that the tyre supplier to a car manufacturer stops producing tyres. That car manufacturer cannot replace the tyre he used to buy with just any alternative. It takes time to find a new supplier that builds to the exact same specifications in terms of the wheel the tyre has to fit, the electronics it has to respond to, the load it must carry, the aesthetic it must match, and so on.

The same goes for network ties in the service economy. One cannot replace a Canadian company tax advisor with one whose specialty is household taxes, or with someone whose expertise is in the Russian tax code. One cannot replace a personal running trainer with a personal dance trainer, or a private maths tutor with a private French tutor.

Economic history teaches us what happens if you break a lot of existing ties, such as during an economic recession or because of exogenous shocks like floods and wars.

Break all the ties completely and we'd be back in the hunter-gatherer world, in which case more than 99% of us would starve because hunter-gatherers are not capable of taking the millions of steps involved in modern agriculture and industrial food production.

Breaking a large number of the ties (say 50%) will not immediately result in starvation, but it will still take quite a while for ties to form again. Like trust, trade ties are much more easily disrupted than built up. During major downturns in an economy, like the Global Financial Crisis after 2008 or the Great Depression after 1929, the period in which the economy actually shrinks is shorter than two years. The period of recovery, by contrast, lasts a decade or more. This is because of the time it takes to find new trading partners — consumers, employers, employees, raw material suppliers and so on — to replace those that were lost in the early stages of a recession.

Judging from history, we should expect it to take several years for the economic system to recover from the disruption of the Great Panic, particularly in the poorest parts of the world that were only just starting to benefit, pre-Covid, from being included in international economic networks.

THE BEAUTY OF THE MARKET SYSTEM

Another key lesson from economics is that attempts at central State organisation of the economy can work well for a few years but invariably end with stagnation and mass corruption. This is mainly because the big rewards in a planned economy flow to expertise in politics, rather than to innovation or efficiency.

In a region under centralised control, ambitious individuals find it more advantageous to lobby politicians and ministries for favours than to try to discover new ways of doing things. Innovation and efficiency are the casualties. In contrast, in a properly functioning market economy system, many ambitious people know they can only enrich themselves by making better products more cheaply than their competitors.

However, even in a market economy, corporate executives will game the political system as a means of advancement if they can. The more this happens, the more unhealthy the economy. In dysfunctional market economies, corporate CEOs spend their time lobbying for subsidies, tax breaks or favourable regulation instead of looking for efficiency gains or developing new products. Big firms always tend to have more influence over government decisions and so make life harder for small firms. A market economy must inevitably contend with the problem of keeping the biggest companies from becoming too politically and economically powerful.

This dynamic has led to breaking points in the past, such as at the end of the 19th century in the US, a period during which governments broke up the biggest companies or took them over. A leading example was Standard Oil, co-owned by the Rockefellers, which was such a large and powerful company that it was forcibly dissolved in 1911.

Yet when it works well, a market economy is full of myriad corporations led by ambitious people convinced they have brilliant plans to become super-rich, leading them to invest in a variety of different technologies and trade ties. Most of these plans fail, but the ones that work out not only make their creators rich but get copied by millions of others, leading the system as a whole to advance rapidly.

At its best then, the market economy is fuelled by countless trade connections between firms, workers, suppliers and customers. It exploits individual hubris to generate collective knowledge about what works. Many smart, ambitious people follow their own ideas about new products and new ways of doing things. Those people are put in competition with each other, with visible success informing others of what worked well and what did not. Ultimately, these discoveries bring advancement to everyone's lives. Trusting that this happens is largely what is meant by 'trusting the market'.

The centralisation of economic activity seen in the West during the Great Panic moved the whole system in the opposite direction. History and economic logic tell us that it cannot be sustained, and that it is damaging the underlying health of the economy and depressing human life.

POLITICAL ECONOMY

At its core, politics is about who gets to spend the fruits of taxation levied on the activities of the population. Here, 'taxation' basically means demand on the productive system from individuals outside it.

A local duke demanding to sleep with all the virgin daughters of the peasants in his territory is, in essence, taxing the peasants by demanding a slice of the desirable services they have to offer. The warlord's grab of half of the grain produced by his vassals is equally a form of taxation, by he who has the authority over those who produce the goods.

Nowadays of course, taxation is an intricate system of state, but the principle is the same: the business of politics revolves crucially around the questions of who taxes whom and what the tax revenues are spent on. A king is no king if he cannot choose how to spend his own tax collections.

The history of political economy traces the coevolution of the economic system and the political system. Sometimes those who tax are simply committing a form of theft from the economic system, destroying it along the way. Sometimes they are supporting a vibrant economic system by using tax revenues to fund wise investments.

The more altruistic the politics, the larger the share of taxation invested in productive institutions. Think, for example, of the tax revenues spent by states on basic education and health. These investments are extremely beneficial to the economy and the population, and generate more long-run tax revenue than they cost. By contrast, the less altruistic the politics, the more politicians are involved in siphoning off the wealth produced by others and using it for their own private purposes instead of making productive investments.

In the long arc of history, politics has become more altruistic, with fewer dukes demanding sexual access and more competing politicians spending on useful investments. The high point of altruistic politics was probably around the year 2000 CE in the West. This was not a time without wars or problems, but fewer of them were in evidence then than at almost any previous moment in human history. The year 2019 was not bad either, but already by then society was dropping hints about many unaddressed, festering long-term problems.

OUR INSTITUTIONS

The institutions that function before our eyes today — universities, courts, parliaments, police forces and so on — have embedded in them a deep knowledge accumulated from their experience over the course of generations. This knowledge has been codified into institutional practices and appearances because this makes the institutions work better. Through this lens our institutions can be thought of as a showcase of our cumulative historical intelligence.[211]

Past generations have helped current generations largely through the institutions they have passed on to us.

Consider as an example of a long-running institution, the primary school system, which in much of the Western world is run cheaply and efficiently by the state. This system's key purpose is to provide a multi-year program for children that gives them basic skills and social habits required to function effectively in their society. At the commencement of secondary school, the primary school hands over this child-moulding process to another institution.

To function properly, the primary school system first needs to know how many young people there are and where they live, since this information will determine where schools should be set up, expanded, downsized or eliminated.

The system needs to include techniques and protocols for dealing with disruptive children, children from different ethnic backgrounds and children with different learning styles. It needs to be cognizant of the changing nature of the labour market for which pupils are being prepared. It also needs to ensure there is an adequate supply of teachers, so it must arrange for some fraction of adults to be educated into the profession. Then, teachers must be provided with teaching materials, methods and curricula.

The primary school system also needs to fit in with the religious and social ideals of the communities of which it is a part, thus helping to prepare kids to become well-adjusted and valued adult members of their communities.

It really is incredibly complex — a marvel of an institution developed over more than a century in the West and incorporating encyclopaedic knowledge of how humans learn and are moulded into social groups. That knowledge continues to accumulate daily, although most of it is implemented without

---

211 It is this fact that underpins the convictions of many thoughtful people who self-identify as politically 'conservative'.

much thought by the particular individuals applying it. Only very little of the complexity of the primary school system is realised by any single individual, including those who work inside it. As a system, on the other hand, it evinces formidable intelligence and efficiency.

To illustrate that 'deep knowledge' embedded in the primary school system, consider how children can be taught to remember particular knowledge well for the rest of their lives. Roughly speaking, imprinting a piece of knowledge into long-term memory requires that it be repeated a couple of times, applied in memorable settings, and actively remembered several times. Not every child learns the same way, nor are all types of knowledge remembered in the same way. Yet, the practise of primary school teaching almost perfectly fits the requirements of long-term learning for most children.

Material on, say, language structure is introduced in a simple way one week, then repeated and added to the following week, then tested as a package a week later, then tested again a month or so after that. Teachers in well-functioning schools explain the structure in different ways to different pupils based on their individual psychology and learning style, while both the tests and the lessons exploit the latest technology. The same material is not repeated five times on the same day or five years later, because that would not work as well: the timing itself reflects — indeed has been customised over centuries to embed — our collective knowledge of how memory works.

Very few scientists are masters of all the elements of basic psychology, learning styles, media technology and social interaction that feed into the present-day method of teaching students to remember language structure. Instead, experts specialise in different pieces of the whole learning trajectory. Some focus on language structure and how it is remembered by individuals with different learning styles. Some know about the optimal timing of tests. Some are experts in 'experiential learning' and how to optimise the way material is explained and visualised. Some know how tests are best set and organised — on paper, open- or closed-book, time of day, and so on. Some are experts on the interactions between teacher and pupils, or the interactions between pupils, or the interactions of the school with parents and the rest of society. No single person has perfect oversight of the whole learning trajectory, but as a system it works fantastically well and quite cheaply.

Getting a diverse group of children to set material in deep memory is only a tiny component of the whole primary school institutional package. In addition to knowledge about lessons and tests, the system also includes knowledge of the importance of play, holidays, arts, pastoral care, building codes, school buses, lunch organisation, after-school care, and many other elements.

The many institutions and associated habits in a country embody a kind of 'deep capital' available to it at any time. Human capital, social capital, institutional capital and physical capital, discussed in different economics literatures, all reflect some portion of this deep capital. The collective institutional space and the deep capital it reflects sets the rules of the game and the opportunities in a country at any point in time.

In order to help future generations, the lessons we draw from the Great Panic must be embedded into the 'deep capital' of the West through changes to existing institutions.

The essential role of politicians in the development of economic and political systems is to create, copy, change and destroy institutions. Political leaders inherit and then adjust institutions like the school system, the legal system, physical and virtual infrastructure, the habits of interaction between people, social groupings and relations between them, the public and private health system, the police and army, the tax system, and so on. Because politicians are the main gatekeepers of institutional change, it will be politics that determines whether or not institutional changes are taken up as societies emerge from the Great Panic — including those changes we suggest will help avoid a future Panic, as discussed in Chapter 10.

The economic system, whose development has led to increasingly intricate networks around the world, has coevolved with the political system. Many institutions under the influence of politicians have helped improve economic specialisation. Government-issued money can be used to trade. Government-organised education prepares people for specialist roles in the economy. Infrastructure organised by governments helps lower the cost of trade and thereby increases specialisation. The legal invention of limited liability was crucial in the emergence of large companies. In sum, the story of how we arrived at the complex societies of today is one of political and economic coevolution, involving wars, inventions, coercion, cooperation, and many other joys and sorrows.

Centrally planned economies fail not only due to poor incentives, as discussed earlier, but because they are based implicitly on the incorrect assumption that the planners at the centre of it all can grasp the whole system. The 'span of control' of the centre is limited in its usefulness because of this limited understanding.

A key role in the learning of the market system is played by market-determined prices for both goods and types of workers, which reveal to all those looking to get rich what is highly lucrative and what is not. Without the guidance of market prices, a centralised system learns only weakly from observing the outcomes of the grand experiments carried out inside the whole body of society. Moreover, far fewer people have an incentive to pay attention to those outcomes anyway. This does not mean there is no role for planning, but rather that any particular plan is simply another experiment.

A well-functioning market system has not just one, but countless experiments running all the time with incentives for millions of people to pay close attention to the small number that work. A market system over time learns much more, collectively, from the experiments continuously conducted by companies, individuals, and other countries.

LEARNING FROM HISTORY

To understand the political economy of the Great Panic, we examine sequen-
tially the economic and political realities of two stylised periods in history,
chosen for the similarities they bear to the modern day: early agriculture,
and the Middle Ages in Western Europe (around 1300 CE). What we sketch
below is highly simplified. Readers interested in the huge complexities of those
times are recommended to turn to Bar-Yosef (2001) and Anderson (2013).

Early agricultural villages

Early agricultural societies, such as those in the Middle East or China 10,000
years ago, had evolved from the hunter-gatherer days when groups of 20 to
100 humans were largely self-sufficient and traded infrequently with other
groups. The early village settlements of a few hundred to a few thousand
peasants that followed the hunter-gatherer era were able to stay put by
growing crops and raising livestock. This required a technological package
of winter food storage and water for the livestock, building construction,
weapons assembly, cooking technology and some metallurgy. Threats to
the village from bandits and productive needs like harvesting or primitive
irrigation would have been dealt with at a village level.

Not everyone was peacefully cultivating. 'Big men' with their bands of
armed retainers regularly either raided villages or taxed them. In a sense,
each 'big man' political group was akin to its own village, but specialising
in warfare and sustained by parasitism on the villages. The more secure a
warlord was over 'his territory', the more stable the environment would be,
with more predictable taxation, less coercion, and more security against raids
by rivals. Such conditions made for more productive farmers.

Since more productive territories yielded correspondingly more tax
revenue, secure warlords might make some virtuous investments, like
organising better irrigation, making trade routes safer, or spreading knowledge

about successful agricultural techniques within their territories. This, in turn, paid for larger armies with which to conquer more territories. In this way, the competition among rival warlords to be the most successful parasite provided an incentive for individual warlords to invest some of their exactions in productive institutions.

This coevolution of the economic and political systems of early agricultural proto states shows the inevitability of some degree of 'warlordism' wherever parasitism is a viable means of subsistence.

Politicians are always somewhat parasitic. They perennially face the temptation of power and will rarely fail to succumb to it. If only to protect their turf against rival politicians, those in charge will always use a sizable portion of what their territory produces for their own personal advancement. Humans are just not good at resisting the allure of power, as the Great Panic has once again reminded us. One can point the finger at particular politicians for their weakness, but this is as futile as being angry at the rain.

Still, just because politics always has an element of warlordism doesn't mean that it serves only to hinder economic development. 'Warlords' with the right incentives have a history of setting up beneficial institutions that help future generations. The long-run challenge for humanity is to nurture institutions that make warlordism as a lifestyle difficult, while simultaneously making the population as a whole wealthier, healthier, and happier. It is the job of intellectuals to suggest institutions like this that might be taken up by politicians.

The Middle Ages

Consider now the much more intricate political economy of the Middle Ages, around 1300 CE, in the European regions that are now occupied by nation states such as Italy, Spain, Germany, France, the Netherlands and the UK. Roughly 90% of the population in those regions lived in agricultural villages in 1300 CE, but a handful of cities were involved in manufacturing and trade, with some degree of specialisation. Europe was sufficiently crowded at that time to be vulnerable to new diseases like the plague. The politics of the time featured two rival systems, each with its own internal rivalries.

The most important political system was that of kings and nobility, who in different regions were called dukes, lords, barons, earls or other flashy labels. They owned nearly all of the land and controlled the majority of the population. These 'big men' specialised in warfare and surrounded themselves with professional soldiers, called knights. Kings were the head honchos of the warlords. They taxed the lower-level warlords, who in turn resisted in various ways. The Magna Carta is an artefact arising from the efforts of a coalition of warlords — barons in that case — in their struggles against the exactions of the king.

Picture then, across Western Europe at this time, hierarchies of warlords all vying with each other for power.

Taxation was apt to occur at sword point but could also be less dramatic, because to obtain protection peasants and villages often acquiesced to coughing up regular rent and levies to their local warlords. Such levies were not limited to grain and other foodstuffs; peasants could owe the warlords prizes like the virginity of their young women as well.

The warlords also taxed trade routes that ran through their territories and formed alliances to raid territories belonging to others. The Crusades were a particularly spectacular example of this genre, in which the more ambitious and rebellious warlords of overpopulated regions organised armies to raid other regions in the name of religion. Cities were somewhat independent, but usually had to pay levies to kings and could not really avoid taxes on trade.

The scrap over tax revenues between the lesser warlords and their kings in the Middle Ages is reminiscent of the friction today between large corporations and national governments. Today's corporate chieftains are politically similar to the barons of 1300 CE. They are sometimes so powerful that they pay little or no tax, while simultaneously coopting governments to help force their products onto consumers. This is a modern-day analogue to feudalism, when powerful barons avoided being taxed by their kings, while simultaneously having the latter write laws to make it illegal for peasants to run away from the barons' territory, or to marry without their permission.[212] A population not allowed to travel more than 5 kilometres from home, forced to conduct all its social and business activities online and bullied by its government to get an expensive vaccine that boosts corporate profits is politically similar to a population of peasants forced by kings to stay in one place and donate some of their production to the local baron.

The second political system of the Middle Ages reposed within the Roman Catholic Church, an independent international organisation that dominated the markets for education, spirituality, religiosity and pastoral care. The Catholic Church was organised in a similar way to the larger secular kingdoms. It had cardinals who were somewhat akin to 'princes', military bands like the Teutonic Knights, monasteries and local churches analogous to fortresses, and so on.

The Church also took a lively interest in taxing the peasants. It had its own territories to tax but also demanded taxes from peasants living in the territories of the barons and kings. In this respect the Church was in competition with the kings and nobility, a competition which it eventually lost hundreds of years later.

Many medieval tensions resonate strongly today. Consider, for example, the ideological alliance between the Church and the nobility against the peasants. The clergy openly told the peasants they were inferior beings and that they owed fealty to their local barons despite the latter's brutality, since the barons were appointed or approved of by God. For the barons, this conveniently made screwing the peasants much easier. It made the Church a useful tool for them, even though in the sphere of taxation they were rivals.

The ideology of the feudal period, enforced by alleged divine rights and

---

212 Bishop (2001).

engendering large-scale submission to authority, is comparable to today's mainstream ideology of blind adherence to the Covid edicts of governments, underpinned by the claim that governments inherently know what is best.

As a second example of a common theme between the Middle Ages and today, consider the ideology that pitted individual against individual and thereby reduced resistance to authority. In Covid times, the essential storyline is that each individual is a potential threat to others and should therefore not be trusted by those around them. The feudal period featured two versions of this type of ideology. A key plank of the Catholic Church's ideology was that everyone is born a sinner, that the devil always lurked in other people to tempt them and that they would go to hell unless they found salvation which only the Church itself could deliver.

In this way, the Church positioned itself as the Stairway to Heaven, the necessary and only route between man and god: the Church, and nothing else, could offer salvation from original sin. Any contrary claim about different means of achieving the same outcome was denounced as heresy, and the Church encouraged the barons to destroy the heretics. Thousands of heretics were burned at the stake, allegedly for the good of their own eternal souls, conveniently leaving their property to be divided among the barons themselves.

Another medieval story that catalysed submission by stoking distrust was that the 'end of times' was near, at which point life on earth would cease and everyone would be judged by heavenly powers. This 'our doom is nigh' story was useful in keeping the peasants anxious enough to want to be in the Church's good books. Barons too could be kept in line because their immortal soul could be barred from heaven by excommunication from the church.

So, both the 'you are born sinners who will go to hell' story and the 'our doom is nigh' story were highly effective ideological weapons of the Catholic Church, keeping both peasants and nobility in line. Fear was wielded systematically by an international organisation — the Church — for centuries, both to help the nobility and to threaten them. The modern-day analogue is visible in the government scientists, academic public health experts, the WHO, and other loose networks of ideologues who propound similar stories of sin, mistrust and fear, working both with and against governments as it best suits their ambitions for power. It is not exactly the same, but eerily close.

Another deep similarity between the feudal period and today is in the functioning of royal courts. Royal medieval courts were the centres of medieval power, as the chief organisers of taxation, armies and elite relationships. They concentrated functions that today's governing apparatus is set up to distribute across multiple institutions: making laws, passing judgments and taking executive decisions. They were the institutional seed from which modern state bureaucracies would eventually grow, and had already developed several habits that were highly efficient and have been retained. For example, the current institution of a cabinet of ministers with joint responsibility for a country's policies has its origin in the kings' councils of those days.

Royal courts were also awash with what we would now call bullshit. Machiavelli, who wrote about the courts around 1500 CE, called the majority of people in royal courts 'flatterers and pretenders'.[213] Machiavelli was simply describing what he saw courtiers do. He observed how they would constantly flatter a king, agree with all his utterances, and ridicule those who openly expressed doubts. They pretended to have useful expertise but their actual effect was to create a huge fog between a king and the truth. Simply by coming up with convoluted rationalisations for why his every utterance was true and meaningful, they made it almost impossible for a king to maintain a realistic view of the world. Machiavelli believed this was a deep problem and one for which his only solution was to have a king smart enough to see through the bullshit.

The bullshit of his royal court was not entirely without its uses to a king.

213 Machiavelli (1513).

The mere fact that so many in his court would openly agree with everything he said made him look powerful to any visitor. Power must be seen to be obeyed. It also meant that whatever he said would be explained to the rest of the population in the most favourable light possible, without him having to understand or rationalise anything himself. In this way the court protected stupid kings. It also gave the king a sense of control and brilliance. Flattery felt good. One might say that the king 'bought' flattery and the semblance of power by spending much of his tax revenue on a perennial retinue of bullshit artists.

Naturally, the bullshitters were looking for opportunities to expand their sphere of influence and control, and so were always in competition with each other, but also, in a very subtle way, with their employer. They looked for ways in which they themselves, rather than the king, could make decisions on how to spend tax revenues. To this end they used the levers of vanity available to them, for example by pushing for useless rituals that the king supposedly needed to abide by. These clogged up his time with form rather than substance, leaving the courtiers with more power over actual policy.

Similar observations have been made about other courts, like those of the Chinese emperors or the courts of the Ottoman sultans. The Chinese emperor, for example, had his own colour (yellow) and his own dragon (with five claws) that were both forbidden to others.[214] The 'Mandarins', eunuchs and multiple wives at the Chinese Imperial courts were famous for their plots against each other,[215] and for trying to usurp the actual power of the emperor as much as possible.

An Ottoman sultan had a formal title about a page long, starting off with 'Sovereign of The Sublime House of Osman, Sultan us-Selatin (Sultan of Sultans), Hakan (Khan of Khans), Commander of the faithful and Successor of the Prophet of the lord of the Universe, Custodian of the Holy Cities of

---

214 Zhou (2012).
215 Jay (2019).

Mecca, Medina and Kouds (Jerusalem), Kayser-i Rum (Caesar of Rome)'.[216] Simply hearing his own title would have kept the sultan occupied, leaving the actual governing to others. The flattery extended in further directions too. Some historians with a sense of humour noted that paintings of a particular sultan would exaggerate how pretty and noble he really was, glossing over the actual shape of his nose.[217] There was no plastic surgery in those days, but their own version of photo-shopping was well-developed.

The lesson we draw is that highly concentrated power, which in the feudal period was in the hands of the royal court, invites large groups of bullshit artists who make the leader blind to the real world with their sycophancy and, plainly speaking, keep him stupid. In Covid times, an increased concentration of power had the same effect on the collective intelligence of governments. A retinue of medical advisors and other opportunists served as the flatterers and pretenders, expanding their own power and elevating their public profiles. This led to huge distortions of policy as the advisor-pretenders obscured governments' view of what policies would truly be useful.

In feudal times, what held for royal courts also held for the largest international organisation, the Catholic Church. Today, in parallel, not only governments but large international organisations too are swarming with bullshit artists who board up the windows while saying exactly what the decision makers want to hear. Today's international organisations are often hubs of concentrated money and influence, inevitably inviting bullshitters eager to say things that the leadership and audience of those organisations find useful or enjoyable, even if they are patently false. Some international organisations do also have productive roles that constrain their ability to stray too far from reality, but the mere fact of having large budgets inevitably

---

216 https://en.wikipedia.org/wiki/List_of_Ottoman_titles_and_appellations
217 Rodini (2017).

makes them hubs of flattery and pretence.

Autocratic power attracts sycophants, without exception. Whatever the flavour of the week — from 'zero carbon' to 'total inclusivity' — the sycophants will sing its praises and pretend their organisation will deliver it.[218] This is also a major problem for the modern corporation, but competition in the private sector tends to keep companies sharper than non-government organisations (NGOs) like today's powerful international institutions.

Many others have noted how in recent times in the West, a whole class of sycophantic insiders have become important in governments, bureaucracies, companies and even charities. Christopher Lasch talks about them in his book *The Revolt of the Elites*. He believes these insiders have betrayed their public mission. In Michael Lind's book *The New Class War*, he calls them the 'managerial class'. We agree with these authors. Bullshitters are a problem for society as a whole, making their organisations less efficient, more opaque, less public-spirited and more self-serving.

The modern courtiers who form a subset of the 'managerial class', who are not the top politicians or owners of companies and charities themselves but rather just lackeys, spend their time trying to usurp as much power as possible while constantly flattering the truly powerful. These courtiers depend for their livelihoods on the real power, meaning that pro-social reform would have to address what happens above them in the hierarchy. The betrayals committed by the bosses are in a different league to the bullshit of their lackeys.

In sum, the feudal period of the Middle Ages featured three political-economy dynamics that are seen in modern form today. The tug-of-war over tax revenue between kings and barons is similar to the tension between large corporations and governments. The role of church ideology in feudal times to belittle and divide the majority is similar to the modern story that every

---

218 Frijters (2020C), https://clubtroppo.com.au/2020/06/29/from-being-to-seeming-why-empirical-scientists-failed-in-times-of-covid/

citizen is a potential 'virus vector' who is a menace to all other citizens. Finally, the incessant bullshit of the royal courts and the church hierarchy in feudal times is repeated in spades within the increasingly autocratic governments and international organisations of today.

POLITICAL AND ECONOMIC SYSTEMS IN THE WEST: WHAT'S SHAKING?

As a result of thousands of years of increased specialisation and steadily improving institutions, the world economy at the start of 2020 was highly interconnected with huge flows of goods and people between countries. Hundreds of millions of people flew around the world as tourists, scientists, businesspeople, athletes and government officials. Hundreds of thousands of boats, trains, trucks and planes brought essential physical products all around the globe — everything from oil to grain to computer chips to sex toys. Tens of millions of people lived as temporary migrants in countries other than those where they held citizenship.[219]

All that trade and information flow had great benefits. Humanity in January 2020 boasted more people than ever before, the highest life expectancy in human history and probably also lower levels of violent crime than ever before. For humanity as a species, life in January 2020 was better than ever. Specialisation and improving institutions had achieved this. Yet challenges and underlying problems remained, and some of these became more visible in the events of the ensuing two years.

Three elements in the political economy of early 2020 would prove pivotal in catalysing the changes during the Great Panic: international media connectivity, monoculturalism in the politics of many countries, and the rise of large corporations.

---

219 Migration Data Portal (2021), https://migrationdataportal.org/themes/migration-data-relevant-covid-19-pandemic

GLOBAL CONNECTEDNESS: WHEN NEWS SPREADS QUICKLY, SO DOES PANIC

Increased trade ties over many centuries led to a high degree of media connectivity by early 2020. Radio, television, and online and print media were also highly concentrated. Illustrating this, a group of scientists at the Australian Centre for Policy Development issued a table on media concentration in various rich countries in 2011 that we reproduce as Table 6 below.[220]

The table shows that in some countries, well over 80% of the newspaper market is cornered by just three papers. Concentration levels are similarly high in television and online news, though we do expect that to be challenged by a lot of new media in the near future. Still, at present in the United States, for example, it has been claimed that merely six companies own over 90% of all media.[221] That is the sort of pattern reflected in the table below by the label 'highly concentrated', applying to most countries' TV networks in 2011.

TABLE 6

Media Concentration in Selected OECD Countries

Country	Population in 2019 (Millions)	Approximate Circulation Share of Top 3 Newspapers	TV Networks Herfindahl-Hirschman Index Concentration (lower is better)	Radio Networks Herfindahl-Hirschman Index Concentration (lower is better)
Australia	25	98%	1600 (moderately concentrated)	1200 (moderately concentrated)
United States	328	26%	2164 (highly concentrated)	1750 (moderately concentrated)

220 Harding-Smith (2011), https://cpd.org.au/wp-content/uploads/2011/11/Centre_for_Policy_ Development_Issue_Brief.pdf

221 E.g., https://www.webfx.com/blog/internet/the-6-companies-that-own-almost-all-media-infographic/

Spain	47	55%	2207 (highly concentrated)	3366 (moderately concentrated)
Japan	126	39%	2116 (highly concentrated)	1000 (moderately concentrated)
France	67	42%	2025 (highly concentrated)	1311 (moderately concentrated)
United Kingdom	67	62%	2550 (highly concentrated)	2616 (moderately concentrated)
Sweden	10	85%	2834 (highly concentrated)	1516 (moderately concentrated)
Netherlands	17	88%	2549 (highly concentrated)	2500 (moderately concentrated)

Apart from this high concentration of ownership in media production, connectivity around the world has also been boosted by the high concentration of internet-based services in the hands of a few major platforms. Most of the world's news-sharing takes place on Facebook, Twitter, Telegram, Whatsapp, Weibo, WeChat, Instagram and a few others. These are the platforms on which people look for news and through which they alert their friends and families to what they have found. The platforms are international, facilitating the rapid global spread of stories that resonate.

By 2020, knowledge of major events in any country would quickly spread across the planet, thanks to a combination of mainstream media and social media networks. Something picked up initially in local media, in a local language and owned by a local company, could soon spread via thousands of channels into the mainstream and across the world — and this was more likely when the event involved or evoked emotion.

The importance of the global connectedness of information feeds was shown in the spread of the Covid panic from China to East Asia and then to the rest of the world in early 2020. It was virtually unstoppable by any government in the absence of a massive, quickly organised media effort against the contagion. The world proved its emotional connectedness in early 2020 as panic spread from country to country slightly in advance of the virus itself.

Just as we do not think on balance that any evil genius planned the spread of the panic in early 2020, we don't think any individual country had much hope of stopping it. The WHO and China both played parts one can critique — for example, there are credible reports that both deliberately tried to influence Western countries to instigate lockdowns, against previous WHO advice[222] — but the WHO and China, like other institutions and nations, were just 'going with the flow' and following their own immediate self-interest. Propaganda was a normal business model way before 2020.[223]

Media connectivity is a recent phenomenon, and the Great Panic was the inevitable moment in which the world learned about the disadvantages of that connectivity. Just as stock markets can fall into panic traps whose damage we might try to stem by halting trade for a while, so too can a connected information system lead to panics whose damage we might try to stem through temporary 'cooling-off' periods. This would require an early-warning system, and governments prepared to counter a panic. We explore these ideas more towards the end of the book.

EMERGENT MONOCULTURALISM

There was a second key element of the prevailing political economy of early 2020 that drove us into the Great Panic. It was that the internal politics in

---

222 Mazumdaru (2020), ,https://www.dw.com/en/what-influence-does-china-have-over-the-who/a-53161220; Griffiths (2020), https://edition.cnn.com/2020/02/14/asia/coronavirus-who-china-intl-hnk/index.html

223 Cook (2020), https://freedomhouse.org/report/special-report/2020/beijings-global-megaphone

many countries, including those in the West, had become monocultural.[224] By 2020, in almost all Western countries with the important exception of the United States, a political class had arisen consisting of very similar people with very similar views of the world. They belonged to parties that supposedly disagreed, but despite a lot of bluster about their differentness they really only disagreed a tiny bit. Western politicians were no longer radically different from each other. Neither were they necessarily even true representatives of their constituents.

In the West, this political mono-class is a novel development in the democratic era. Not since the days of dominant royal houses populated by a 'clique' with similar manners and world views have we seen such homogeneity of political vision. Democratic leaders since the beginning of the twentieth century had been famously diverse. Different political parties had different religions, spoke with different accents, went to different schools, followed different media and had totally different beliefs about how to run a country.

This was still true for most countries even in 1970. Media outlets were still divided along religious, ethnic and class lines. Political parties were still made up of politicians with prior careers and worldviews different from those of the members of other parties. Populations were still very diverse in their beliefs and their information feeds, with little knowledge of far-off regions or ideologies. Western political parties in the 1970s could be depicted as representing distinct large groups in their society, like 'socialists' or 'liberals', with political leaders beholden to the interests of the groups their party represented.

By 2020 however, that view was completely outdated. As political scientists Richard Katz and Peter Mair discuss at length, parties now operate more like cartels with minimal influence from voters, meaning that elections have become mainly 'spectacles'. Like many other political scientists they contend that political parties are now primarily vehicles for career advancement, with voters

---

224 Throughout this section we mainly follow Katz & Mair (2018), though we use slightly different language.

only one of many sources of influence on policies and institutional change.[225] We agree with these observations and place them here in a wider context.

Many Western politicians in January 2020 had entered politics in their mid-20s or even younger, rather than coming into politics from earlier professions or other lines of work. This meant that their collective knowledge of how the 'other half' lived and experienced the world was almost nonexistent. In becoming its own separate profession, politics reverted to knowing as much collectively about everyone else as any single profession knows collectively about other professions. Politics had thereby been dumbed down, with traditional expertise simply absent from governments.

This situation had not arisen by evil intent but because of the unfortunate reality that less-specialised politicians lost out to the professionals who were better versed in the skills of politics, like messaging and spinning, which is to say bullshitting.

Politics had become its own specialisation. The parties to which politicians belonged had become vehicles for their careers, run by central party 'machines' that selected candidates. Parties ran their own little training programs for young politicians, in which ambitious young people who had joined up and were deemed to have talent would be strategically placed in particular think tanks or on the staff of top politicians.

Different political parties set out slightly different trajectories, but the diet they fed their fledgelings was similar and led to the development of similar skills. This diet would include reports from governments and international organisations on political topics, the opinions of focus groups on many possible party programs, extensive media training, a couple of old books on the supposed ideology of the party, and not a whole lot more.

The ready-for-prime-time politicians emerging from such programs,

225 Katz & Mair (2018).

whether supposedly populist right-wingers or vegan green warriors, were in reality largely the same as each other, speaking the same language and watching the same media as those in other parties. The monoculture produced by this system absorbed very little of the true diversity that still existed, and was even still developing, in social groups outside politics.

The monoculture extended even beyond national borders, helping to create a somewhat unified international Western political class. This spread was assisted by national politicians appointing people to international organisations like the UN or the WHO, suggesting people for opportunities like the European parliament, and appointing foreign ambassadors. National politicians used their powers of appointment to reward former politicians in their own parties, and equally to get rid of those in their parties they didn't like. The monoculture spread to envelop not only international organisations but much of local politics too, for example through the influence of national politicians on candidate lists for city mayors. With both local and international careers now related to national politics, lobbying and influence occur across levels and in all directions.

This monoculture has its advantages. It gives national politicians a strong incentive to remain friendly with peers who are involved in appointments for the same lucrative international posts. In this way, it is a kind of pacifying force. It also limits misunderstandings, as people who speak the same language do not go to war by mistake. It stabilises national politics, providing a predictability that helps both companies and populations to plan. If essentially the same crew is in power all the time then there is little need to worry that the next leaders will steal the business that the previous ones didn't.

Yet the monoculture lacks the collective intelligence of a group that contains true diversity. The collective intelligence of the West's political system has eroded not because today's politicians are individually stupid, but because they all have the same sort of intelligence. This turned out to matter when Covid arrived on the scene. Covid exposed the inability of the political class to understand a complex phenomenon and to absorb new information. They were sitting ducks for any wrong-headed notions proclaimed by supposed 'experts'.

A further problem related to political monoculturalism in early 2020 was that the professionalisation of politics had made the system more corrupt. This happened through the gradual silencing of many critics and the formation of alliances with the principal new sources of money.

How did this gradual corruption of politics happen? Developments happened at somewhat different times in different countries, with places like Italy and the US seeing changes very early on. For example, Italy's Silvio Berlusconi in the 1980s was one of the first rich celebrity politicians. Still, the basic trends are similar across the West.

First, politics and media grew closer together. Professional politicians became celebrities and political parties, with their rich backers, actively started to control the media.[226] Selected stories were drip-fed to befriended journalists, who thereby became roped into the preferred narrative of politicians. Political events ranging from weekly media updates to presentations of government budgets were increasingly stage-managed. Politicians even participated directly in the media, such as US President Trump who provided a daily Twitter deluge, or Canadian President Trudeau who ran to stardom on Instagram.

Because the politicians ultimately held the power they were able to grab control of the key information streams and narratives. With that control, the political class as a whole had less to fear from the media: the media as a group struggled to gain traction in attempts to expose corrupt activities because politicians could use channels they controlled to create deliberate noise as a pushback. What's more, much of the media, including the newspapers in

---

226 See, e.g., Wheeler (2013) on the rise of celebrity politics.

many Western countries, were unprofitable and only had market value as propaganda outlets for rich people and politicians. Independent journalism was simply overrun by the increased influence of money on the content of news stories. You don't bite the hand that feeds you.

The second corrupting element is that money became more important for politicians in their public roles. In order to produce 'deliberate noise' through media channels, politicians needed rich backers or friends in the media. Without such networks, a politician would be easy to frame and marginalise. Someone accuses her of something horrible, different media sources repeat the accusation, and lacking any platform from which to defend herself she is a dead duck. So while top politicians allied with some part of the media became more resistant to being uncovered as corrupt, those politicians without serious backing would struggle to get attention and find themselves easily sidelined by powerful interests.

We saw these pressures abundantly during the Great Panic. When the system of deliberate framing of opponents was let loose on critical scientists, such as the authors of the Great Barrington Declaration of October 2020, they became subject to an enormous campaign of disinformation and accusation. The perpetrators of the GBD disinformation campaign included opponents who added fake signatures and then pointed to the signatures they had added as evidence that the whole thing was a fraud.[227] Similar campaigns were waged throughout the period, something Robert Wright in May 2021 despairingly labelled 'Dismisinfoganda'.[228]

The deeper point is that money really matters in modern politics and this practically forces politicians to be corrupt. Any politician who makes no deals with deep pockets that allow him to become a big media player simply

---

227 E.g., Magness (2020), https://www.aier.org/article/the-fake-signature-canard/
228 Wright (2021), https://www.aier.org/article/dismisinfoganda/

gets benched. The same is true of whole political parties. To survive in their chosen profession, today's politicians simply cannot afford to ignore all the implicit offers they get to buy their political support for this or that. Becoming a senior politician in many countries now means becoming seriously corrupt. Those who refuse are smeared and marginalised out of contention long before making it into something as lofty as a parliament.

The numerous links and deals made during the Great Panic have been noticed. Transparency International now releases weekly stories on how bad corruption has become, even in Western countries.[229] The rise of corruption has gone hand-in-hand with reduced press freedom, now regularly documented by 'Reporters without Borders' who publish a World Press Freedom Index in which scores plummeted in 2020.[230]

Perhaps comfortingly, these developments are not unique to our times. The Great Panic did not reveal for the very first time that many governments manipulate media and that many media self-censor so as to remain onside with power. Both phenomena have occurred many times before in the West.

A famous example comes down to us from the Napoleonic era. Newspaper headlines in Paris in 1815 reported on Napoleon's escape from exile on the island of Elba and his subsequent journey through the south of France to Paris, where he was greeted by cheering crowds. The royalist government that had been restored by foreign powers nine months earlier sent soldiers to stop him, but they joined him instead. Parisian newspapers told this story as follows, in their headlines over the course of less than two weeks:

9th March: The Anthropophagus [a monster] has quitted his den
10th March: The Corsican Ogre has landed at Cape Juan

---

229 https://www.transparency.org/en/news
230 Reporters Without Borders (2020).

11th March: The Tiger has arrived at Gap

12th March: The Monster slept at Grenoble

13th March: The Tyrant has passed through Lyons

14th March: The Usurper is directing his steps towards Dijon, but the brave and loyal Burgundians have risen en masse and surrounded him on all sides

18th March: Bonaparte is only sixty leagues from the capital; he has been fortunate enough to escape the hands of his pursuers

19th March: Bonaparte is advancing with rapid steps, but he will never enter Paris

20th March: Napoleon will, tomorrow, be under our ramparts

21st March: The Emperor is at Fontainebleau

22nd March: His Imperial and Royal Majesty, yesterday evening, arrived at the Tuileries [in Paris], amidst the joyful acclamations of his devoted and faithful subjects.

The same individual described as an ogre, a monster, a tyrant, and a usurper as late as the 14th of March 1815 was once more referred to as Emperor and Imperial Royal Majesty on the 22nd.[231] Reading the writings of power on the wall, the media will readily belittle today the opposition that they will cheer tomorrow.

THE BARONS OF MODERN CAPITALISM

The third and most important facet of early-2020 political economy is that by this time, the rise of large corporations in the West had already spanned about 50 years. Many world markets had come to be dominated by a shrinking number of companies. Just two — Boeing and Airbus — dominated the

231 https://en.wikisource.org/wiki/Napoleon%27s_March

airline production market and fewer than 10 companies had the lion's share of pharmaceuticals, led by Johnson and Johnson, Sinopharm and Roche. A small number of firms — including Facebook, Twitter, WeChat and LinkedIn — dominated the social media market. A single company, Luxottica, gobbled up most of the eyewear market and really only three players dominated e-commerce — Amazon, Jingdong and Alibaba. The same held for dozens more industry segments producing goods from laptops to mobile phones, from furniture to home appliances, from e-taxis to e-books, and from flowers to genetically modified crops.

Two statistics illustrate this change most clearly. The first is that the share of labour in national income has dropped substantially,[232] meaning that 'profits' have become more important relative to 'wages'. The graphs below show that for many Western countries, a declining share of observed national income has gone to 'the workers' since the 1980s. The definitions vary a little across countries, so cross-country comparisons of the absolute levels can be misleading.[233] Yet the changes over time within most countries show a clear drop of 10 percentage points in labour's share of income: from around 70% in 1975 to 60% or below in 2010.

---

232 The labour share figures that follow are taken from Autor et al. (2020); see also Aum & Shin (2020), https://research.stlouisfed.org/publications/review/2020/10/22/why-is-the-labor-share-declining

233 The UK for example is far more unequal than Japan despite these graphs showing the opposite, basically because UK statistics on income are very unreliable, as detailed in a very recent piece by Stephen Jenkins for a large national review on the topic (Jenkins, S. 'Getting the measure of inequality', Commentary prepared for the IFS Review of Inequality (chair: Professor Sir Angus Deaton), Revised version, May 2021, mimeo.)

FIGURE 2

International Comparison: Labour Share by Country

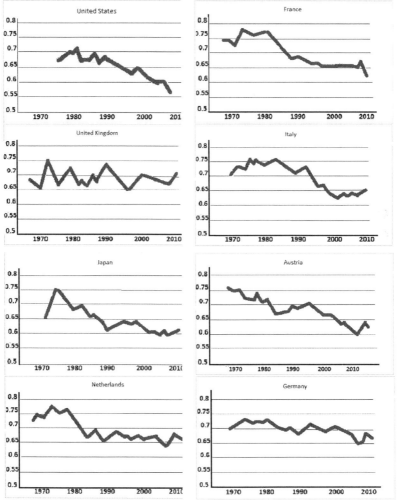

The share of national income attributable to 'capital' rose commensurately, according to the data shown in Figure 2, from 30% to 40% or more. The data do not yet include the large changes since 2010 that would have continued the trend toward a lower labour share. The graphs also likely heavily overstate the share of labour in national incomes even in 2010, because the super-rich are better than the average worker at hiding their financial flows and many of their gains will be disguised as labour income.

While the large decrease in labour share started earlier in the US than elsewhere, the average secular trend since the 1980s is evident. Ordinary employees are increasingly losing out to managers and owners, and particularly to those of 'superstar' firms, which is to say large international corporations. On top of this, even in well-paid jobs, workers are increasingly powerless, with less and less say over how they do their job. Even highly educated workers are increasingly following very rigid rules on what to do and how to do it.[234]

The clearest information on just how unequal today's world is emanates from the über-rich themselves, when they show off how wealthy they are. Official data on income and wealth usually exclude what the super-rich own and earn because of all the tricks that can be used to obfuscate it. Many of these individuals hold wealth in the form of creative instruments, such as patents they have nominally put on barren rocks in the Pacific Ocean in order to avoid taxes.[235] The annual Forbes rich list,[236] where the rich brag to each other, reveals the truth.

Oxfam generated the following graph in 2019 based on data it sourced from Credit Suisse, a Swiss bank, which in turn took it from the Forbes rich list.

234 Lopes et al. (2014).

235 See, e.g., Tørsløv et al. (2020), https://missingprofits.world/

236 Dolan et al. (2021), https://www.forbes.com/billionaires/

FIGURE 3

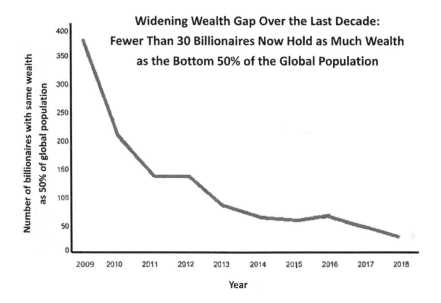

This graph shows that from 2009 to 2018 the gap between the richest and least well off widened shockingly, though one would never suspect this based on official statistics for income and wealth in individual countries. In 2009, the 380 richest billionaires on the planet held as much wealth as the bottom 50% of all humanity. But by 2018, the combined wealth of only the richest 26 billionaires equalled that held by the bottom 50% of us. Each of those 26 billionaires individually owned as much of the visible asset stock of the world — land, buildings and so on — as about 120 million people. That is not just your average baron. That is a very big and powerful baron, far wealthier than the European kings of old.

On the basis of the most recent updates to that Forbes list, the *Financial Times* was able to gauge what happened in 2020 to the world's level of inequality by showing how the share of GDP owned by billionaires changed in that year.[237] We approximate the *Financial Times* graph below.

FIGURE 4

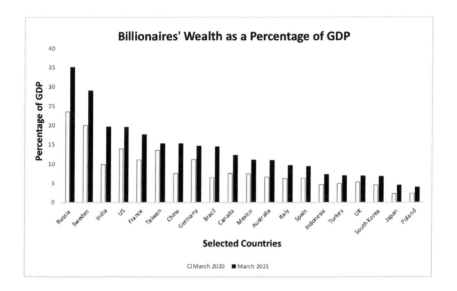

This graph tells us that in 2020, a year in which the International Monetary Fund (IMF) estimates the world economy shrank by 3%, the world's über-rich gained some 30-50% more wealth. Historically speaking, that is a stunning increase in inequality and one of the significant outcomes of the Great Panic.[238]

Billionaire CEOs and their large companies are barons in the modern struggle for power. All up, there are not that many barons in today's world. Thinking of a baron as the richest and most powerful individual in every 100,000 or even fewer, all the billionaires belong to the modern baron club, plus plenty who have wealth in the US$50 million to US$1 billion range. The

237 Sharma (2021), https://www.ft.com/content/747a76dd-f018-4d0d-a9f3-4069bf2f5a93

238 Gabriel Zucman, a follower of inequality trends, also documented a ten-fold increase in the wealth of the top 400 wealthiest Americans, with a large jump from January 2020 to July 2021: https://twitter.com/gabriel_zucman/status/1411697337693396993

rise in wealth and influence of these people, and their families and associates, has led to political dynamics very similar to those seen when barons rose to power in the feudal era. The reason for their ascent was also similar.

Large companies arose partly because of their efficiency advantage over smaller ones: large firms can quickly apply the latest technology throughout their global operations. In economic parlance they enjoy 'economies of scale' in production and organisation. This competitive advantage means that larger companies can produce more cheaply than many smaller ones operating in similar industry sectors.[239] The same was true for the most powerful barons in the feudal era — they could more efficiently tax and organise activities and resources than many of the second- and third-tier nobles.

The growth of large corporations has led to a corruption of politics and was also facilitated by that corruption. Large firms lobbied governments for favourable tax treatment and regulations that made things harder for their competitors, just as the barons of the feudal era lobbied their kings. Large firms that lobbied successfully expanded even further, buying up small ones.

Tax favours granted by governments (or kings) are obviously advantageous, but the role of regulation is also pivotal. Complex tax codes make it easier for the super-rich to hide their money, since even well-meaning regulations invariably contain ambiguities that can be interpreted 'creatively' and used to squirrel away money.

Eventually, a court may decide the chosen accounting trick is acceptable. Adverse court decisions, however, can be a long time coming, and in any case alternative 'interpretations' of the rules may be exploited for hiding the cash. In practise, the supposed distinction between 'tax avoidance', which is legal, and 'tax evasion', which is not, blurs for the super-rich: what is 'legal' becomes a matter of interpretation, retainers for expensive lawyers, and

---

239 See Autor et al. (2020).

regulations that can be influenced even after the fact.

Ironically then, the more complex the tax code the more likely it is that people with deep pockets will find ways to avoid taxes. Legal scholar Katarina Pistor has used the term 'code of capital'[240] to describe the process by which money buys favourable regulation, which in turn enables tax evasion and other unethical behaviour. A recent letter by concerned legal academics expresses their belief that large corporations use international trade agreements to buy legislation from politicians that allows them to dodge their responsibilities.[241] Only when whistleblowers send sufficiently damning information to the general public do these corrupt deals become public.

Annette Alstadsaeter and her colleagues[242] nicely illustrated both the scarcity of the new barons and the fact that they have completely beaten the official systems supposed to keep them in check. The graph below, adapted from their 2019 paper, represents what they learned from trawling through the Panama papers, an infamous stash of secret documents held by a company in Panama that helped rich people avoid taxes. The authors also used information from tax amnesty programs in which people were allowed to declare, years later, the offshore resources they had 'forgotten' to claim in previous years. They compare what they uncovered from those sources with what was uncovered during official random audits, to reveal how much tax the rich were effectively evading via offshoring.

---

240 Pistor (2019).

241 https://www.citizen.org/wp-content/uploads/migration/case_documents/isds-law-economics-professors-letter-oct-2017_2.pdf

242 Alstadsæter et al. (2019).

FIGURE 5

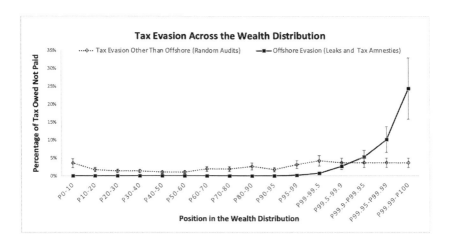

This graph organises the population on a continuum from poor to rich. So 'P0-10' for example denotes the (supposedly) poorest 10% of the whole population, according to what is claimed in their tax returns. 'P60-70' denotes those people who hold less wealth than 70% of the population, but more than the bottom 60%. The mostly flat dotted line shows that if individuals are audited randomly, the level of tax evasion discovered is below 5%, even for those in the P99.99-P100 group who are the richest in every 10,000 individuals.[243] This implies that according to the random audits government officials use, nearly all Americans, including the super-rich, are upstanding tax payers.

The solid line shows by contrast what the Panama papers and tax amnesties revealed. Up until P99.9, meaning for the least-rich 99.9% of Americans, hardly any tax they are supposed to pay is evaded. It is only the very richest .01% of people who are found to cheat, and they hide a large part of their wealth.

Billionaires typically have no need for somewhat sleazy and illegal

---

243 There are too few audited people in the top 0.01% to generate a data point for that group, so the authors use a prediction.

tax-evasion services provided by companies like the one in Panama. This is because they employ accountants and regulation-influencers to help them avoid tax in a manner that is entirely legal.[244] Without that assistance they would be paying more tax in line with the social norms of their countries.

In sum, the inequality one finds in Forbes numbers, which is fed by the tax-evasion dances of billionaires, differs significantly from what you would conclude from official statistics on wealth and income. Increased complexity in national tax codes and even international governmental efforts to curtail tax evasion have an unfortunate habit of enabling new ways of hiding wealth from the tax man.[245]

The new barons are more like the richest in 100,000 people, rather than merely the richest in 10,000, and that money comes with significant pull. Legal courts do not serve as the places where these new barons are held to account, but rather as the places where their lawyers pursue their opponents and fend off government officials on the trail of their wealth and activities. This is exactly how it was in the Middle Ages.

Regulations in spheres other than tax often help barons in their struggles with competitors. This should not come as a surprise because the barons use their political connections within governments to help design regulation. The modern analogue to 'raids by barons' takes the form of labour regulation, ethics regulation, environmental regulation, industry standards, safety procedures and so on. Having to comply with thousands of pages of complicated regulations is easy for a very large company, but a major problem for small ones. Compliance costs can cause small companies to go bankrupt, while the companies of the barons grow. Only after his competitors have been run out of business will a baron possibly complain about the extra hassle

---

244 For the latest revelations about the tax behaviour of some of the biggest billionaires, see https://www.theguardian.com/business/2021/jun/08/richest-25-americans-jeff-bezos-elon-musk-tax

245 E.g., Johannesen & Zucman (2014).

of regulations, which have done their job for him and are no longer needed.

Through this lens, Covid regulations during the Great Panic have served as a weapon of big companies in a 'raid' on small businesses for market share. This is the modern equivalent of what occurred in the Middle Ages when communities of peasants were prevented from moving away or in other ways challenging the power of the local lords. Control was applied with laws upheld by the King and the local sheriffs, after the king had been lobbied by the barons.

The gradual corruption of politics pre-2020 by large vested interests is something we and others have written about previously. *Game of Mates: How favours bleed the nation*, a best-selling book from 2017 by Cameron Murray and Paul Frijters, exposed the increased corruption in Australia. It documented how in each sector, big businesses form alliances with politicians from the major parties in order to defraud the public through changes in tax rules, government contracts and regulation. Similar exposés have been written by others for the US, Germany, the UK, France, Italy, Spain, India, Russia and many other countries.[246] This work has detailed how the rise of big businesses has occurred in tandem with their increased influence on politics.

In the last 40 to 50 years, a new class of barons has arisen virtually everywhere in the world. This trend has been resisted successfully in very few countries. The ability of barons to buy up the best lawyers, regulators, media outlets and international connections has allowed them to amass enormous political power. These new barons have caused a huge increase in inequality, higher taxes on the middle classes, lower taxes on the rich, and a hundred and one other changes detrimental to the population as a whole.

UK readers may have noticed that taxes on selling housing were lower during Covid and that people travelling in order to buy houses were exempt

---

246 E.g., Ledeneva (2018), Leung et al. (2020).

from travel restrictions. This reveals the power of property-owning groups. In the UK, property ownership is increasingly concentrated among the most wealthy, particularly in the most expensive areas like London where increasingly many homes are owned by few and rented by many. A recent paper looking at these dynamics was titled 'Game of Homes'.[247] When Covid threatened to reduce demand for housing and therefore depress prices, money spoke and politicians listened: they reduced taxes and gave exemptions that allowed the 'Game of Homes' to continue. Many other industries were not so lucky.

The feudal nature of politics is even worse in some ways today than in the Middle Ages. At least in the Middle Ages there was a king who kept the barons somewhat in line because he needed to keep his country productive in order to ward off invasions by other kings. In the modern era kings have been replaced by professional politicians who will only be in power for a short time, after which they will have to find something else to do that is ideally of high status. The long post-politics careers over which they salivate make today's politicians very susceptible to lucrative offers by the new barons.

These offers may be overt or implicit. A normal pattern today is for a politician to do a firm a favour with a juicy regulation, and then after retirement from politics that same politician is hired as a lobbyist by that firm. Favour exchange also occurs more indirectly: the politician is in a network that includes very rich firms and people, who are prepared to use their wealth to help the politician, not only to get elected but also to reward people he wants them to reward. So already during his stay in political power, the politician receives favours from the barons that increase his power. As long as he remains in the network, the retired politician will be looked after, both by the barons and by the next person in a position of political power. These are the common ways in which modern politicians sell out their own constituents.

---

247 Bangham (2019), https://www.resolutionfoundation.org/app/uploads/2019/06/Game-of-Homes.pdf

Unlike medieval kings, politicians have less incentive to compete with the barons for tax revenue. Also unlike those kings, politicians of Western countries do not really need to fear being invaded by other countries, so there is little to make them resist the barons' temptations. It is mainly the sense of unity in a country — the patriotism of the whole population — that imposes some degree of restraint on politicians and barons who step too far out of line. That patriotism is the main enemy of both.

The rise of the new barons has been accompanied by the rise of somewhat toothless international organisations and a substantial increase in the number and activities of think tanks subsidised by the barons. Many international organisations, like the WHO, are directly subsidised by people like Bill Gates, who is of course a prize example of a new baron.[248] The barons want their puppet organisations to say things they like, and often get their way because money talks so loudly.

Would a new baron want to hear that the regulation being supported by his funded think tanks is bad for human progress because it kills off small companies? Or would he prefer to hear the story that the current regulation doesn't cut it because it fails to address the concerns of the population, while the suggested new regulation would only help that population? Does he want it widely known that the new regulation would also, conveniently, help him?

Would a baron want attention directed to the tax left unpaid thanks to international regulations and trade deals that his company had a hand in writing? Or would he prefer to hear that taxes on large companies and very rich people are too high and bad for the population as a whole because they cost jobs and reduce investment? Would he want intellectual property regulations that make his monopolies harder to maintain, or easier to spread to more countries?

---

248 Gates' foundation gave US$455 million to the WHO in 2018-19, making him the WHO's third-largest donor: https://www.who.int/about/funding/contributors

There are no prizes for guessing the answers to these questions. Financial incentives rule, just as they did for the barons of old. This is not evil at work, but human nature revealed in the modern context.

The gradual corruption of politics and international laws has not been all bad. It has empowered the large companies that have been major players in rapidly spreading knowledge of efficient production methods throughout the world. These companies have an interest in maintaining the peace and stability needed to do business, so they are naturally opposed to devastating wars. They want high-quality education and healthy workers, and have rewarded countries that invested in those things by setting up more businesses there, increasing the incentives for other local leaders to invest in health and education. In these ways, large corporations have served as tremendous engines for human progress over the past half-century.

As with viruses, one should not want to eliminate all large companies or all of their political activities. Their power has simply grown so large as to become a real problem, just as state bureaucracies, armies or unions become a real problem if they become overly large. We revisit this issue and what can be done about it later in the book.

MODERN SIN STORIES

A very effective way to dominate people is to convince them they are sinful unless they obey. Sin stories are therefore always political. There is never a shortage of groups shouting out that everyone outside their group is sinful. However, the powerful have used the sin stories at their disposal differently over time.

Big companies benefit from the sin-based ideologies that had already grown legs before the Covid era. Stories that divide people benefit large corporations because they divide both their workforces and the national populations that are their natural enemies in the political space. Like the Catholic Church of the Middle Ages, large international companies use stories about sin and fear as weapons, even if they didn't create them. The Covid-era story that everyone is a potential risk to everyone else is the latest handy tool for breaking the bonds between people.

Among pre-Covid sin stories are the idea that humanity is destroying the planet with its hyper-consumption, the idea that Western nations are evil because they are responsible for empires and slavery, the idea that men need to apologise to women for the patriarchy that has run for thousands of years, the idea that 'white' owes 'black' and other colours an historical debt for generations of oppression, and the idea that that those 'recognised at birth as female' are sinful to exclude anyone else who claims to be female from female-only spaces.

These ideas have been kicking around for a long time and were certainly not invented by large companies. Rather, they have been championed by people genuinely upset at this or that grave injustice that they had personally experienced or seen others experience.

Many of these ideas have some merit. After all, humanity is not a saintly species and communities do both good and bad things. There are always legitimate grievances against any community, particularly in hindsight. Yet to explain their rise to prominence, the place to look is how such stories fit the agenda of the barons.

Consider first how the stories damage local and national groups, which are natural enemies of the economic interests of the barons and of international organisations.[249] A story in which every community and nation is sinful loosens people from their obligations as members of those communities and nations. When a country is portrayed as sexist, transphobic, racist, imperialist and otherwise despicably evil, a conscientious person will feel obliged to criticise and disown it. The natural defenders of the community are thereby

---

249 For a similar argument (though using the word 'patriotism' where we say 'nationalism'), see Ariely (2012).

turned into its enemies. Modern sin stories enable and support an internationally oriented group of workers who are key ingredients in successful large companies and international organisations.

Precisely because the new sin stories divide communities, they are also used within countries by rival groups that think of themselves as being in competition with each other. Rival ethnic groups for example will push the idea that another group is sinful and should pay restitution. The state bureaucracy itself can also be a player in such fights: by 'talking down' the largest ethnic group — say, Caucasian-Americans — the state can elevate itself as the 'unifying group' that is above ethnicity.

Sin stories are therefore a useful political device for powerful groups in competition with each other. Because they are so useful, a continuous flood of new sin stories will emerge that individuals and groups will use to undermine each other. The arrival on the scene of the new barons has simply given the existing sin stories greater impetus and has made it harder for pro-community stories to be heard.

Modern sin stories are also useful within large organisations, including private companies, as they provide a perfect excuse for managers to set up internal police that belittle the whole workforce and keep them docile. As an example of this, consider how the idea of being 'gender sensitive' is useful for the CEO of a major company.

By adopting the stance that everyone in the company has to be gender sensitive and is monitored for compliance, the CEO can achieve two things simultaneously. First, any particularly outspoken internal champion of the employees can simply be accused of lacking gender sensitivity, after which (s)he must self-defend from the doubts of others in his or her camp. Second, the policy also will create 'local enforcer' jobs such as membership on monitoring and compliance committees, which will appeal to those workers already inclined to bully others. The policy will encourage complaints to be lodged by some employees against other employees. In this way, an internal policy based on a modern sin story gives rise to an internal police force that the CEO uses as a stick to bully the workforce.

This pattern is basically a carbon copy of how barons ran their estates in the Middle Ages. They too allowed local priests to belittle the peasants. They too had informants. They appointed a token number of peasants as local enforcers, who in turn were allowed to abuse their positions a little. At the same time the barons ran their own local police and court system supposedly to enforce ethical rules, but with the larger agenda of securing and enforcing taxation of the peasants.

The same logic holds for university managers or the top bureaucrats in government. These people have a strong incentive to divide their knowledge workers, the most potent group of workers in their organisations. They do so by setting up internal police to monitor those knowledge workers for compliance with policies based on sin stories. In universities taken over by professional managers, new forms of internal police arise based on various sin stories whose primary role is to belittle the academics. This dynamic is not well-understood by outsiders, who often mistakenly believe that all academics are in favour of the new sin stories. In reality, while a few serve as their outspoken champions, many are themselves being repressed by these stories.

In a sign of the times, Peter Singer, a Princeton Professor of Philosophy, recently helped set up the *Journal of Controversial Ideas* in which authors are allowed to publish under a pseudonym in order to avoid being hounded by the new priesthood policing thoughts on university campuses.[250] This is intended to help scholars freely debate new ideas around racism, sexism, nationalism, climate change, and other modern sinful topics. The journal was set up in response to death threats and career threats faced by academics

---

250 Singer (2021), https://www.project-syndicate.org/commentary/pseudonyms-to-uphold-open-intellectual-discourse-by-peter-singer-2021-05

willing to speak out against the new sin stories that have become dominant in Anglo-Saxon universities.

There are now many names for these sin stories and their use as weapons against the free speech and free thought of others:[251] political correctness, wokeness, grievance culture, identity politics, and so on. What few realise is that it is the rise of large corporations led by those who think themselves opposed to national identities that has lent these sin stories the muscle to become so dominant.

What is happening on university campuses relates to wider changes. When previous community ties weakened, political opportunists jumped on stories that allowed them to divide and rule, helping to set themselves up at the tops of universities and enjoy their largesse. That further weakened community ties, leading to a spiral of anti-social changes. What is known as 'corporatisation' or increased 'managerial control' of universities is in perfect lockstep with the use of these new sin stories.

Many corporations have undoubtedly succumbed to the new sin stories out of convenience because managers want to play along with the idealism of their 'woke' kids or workers. After all, corporations too want to blend in with influences from outside. A company leader may feel a pull to be seen to go along with the local political power of this or that ideology, hoping that lip-service to a particular sin ideology will distract from his firm's unequal pay structure, tax evasion behaviour, or the poor working conditions in his foreign factories.

Yet these 'marriages of convenience' between corporations and sin stories are not deeply felt and therefore only a small part of the picture. The pull of sin stories because of their usefulness to internal corporate operations — e.g., as an excuse to set up an internal police force, and as a trigger for releasing employees from community loyalty — is deeper and more enduring.

---

251 Duncan (2019), https://joemduncan.medium.com/oppressive-wokeism-needs-to-stop-3e0c1283e4f6

From the perspective of politicians and large companies, Covid made for an almost perfect sin story. It set everyone in the population against each other as potential sources of infection; it kept people away from each other which made it harder to organise a counter-movement; it made it easier to hide standard-issue corruption and control flows of information; it killed off much of the small-time competition in the form of small businesses that couldn't afford the rolling lockdowns and reams of new regulations; and it allowed vast new sums of money to be allocated quickly in secretive arrangements. It was, in a word, a corruption bonanza.

Yet the Covid sin story also supported the emergence of national crowds, which in itself contains the potential for both renewal and destruction.

The political coalition in favour of the new sin stories is by now quite large and stable. It will not go quietly into the night with the demise of Covid-related excuses, but will instead try to latch on to new sin stories in order to keep the people divided. On this basis we expect an outpouring of more vigorous sin storytelling once the Covid mania subsides. Candidates are the threats of global warming, extinctions of species, or other diseases, and the sins of previous generations such as slavery and colonialism.

Neo-feudalism, complete with its enabling sin ideologies, will hang around for a while. Its immediate rivals are the national crowds it gave birth to during the Great Fear, and its longer-term rivals are its own incompetence and the competition between countries.

NEW BULLSHIT STORIES

A final effect of the rise of big companies on the stories of our time is seen in the aggrandisement of the bullshit industry. Bullshit benefits the new barons every bit as much as it benefited the barons and kings of the Middle Ages.

For one, layers of bullshit create a fog around what is true and what is not, and this fog is much easier for a well-organised large company to see through and manipulate than for smaller companies or families.

Second, layers of bullshit inside the national governments that naturally compete with the barons for tax revenues make those governments easier to manipulate and harder to run. While the new barons do not want excessively poorly functioning governments because they partner with governments in many ways, such as on education investments and keeping the population quiet, they take a very keen interest in obscuring governments' view of what their companies are really up to.

Third, just as the ideologies of the Catholic Church in the Middle Ages appealed to the innate wish among the population for religious and spiritual meaning, so too are today's large companies implicitly asked to provide a semblance of religion and meaning to their own workers, customers and other connections. Yet like the barons of the feudal era, they don't want to be hindered in their own actions by an ideology that is too proscriptive. From their perspective, a vague and malleable ideology is preferable, because it can be flexed as needed.

There are dozens of stories to tell about the rise of bullshit, but perhaps the level of its current penetration into our lives is clearest in the open confession of a bullshit artist. In a hilarious essay for the Centre for Public Impact from which we excerpt an extended quotation below, a modern 'company man' tells of his 10 years of lying:[252]

> I spent 10 years of my life writing. I wrote neighbourhood plans, partnership strategies, the Local Area Agreement, stretch targets, the Sustainable Community Strategy, sub regional infrastructure plans, funding bids, monitoring documents, the Council Plan and service plans. These documents describe the performance of local

---

252 https://www.centreforpublicimpact.org/insights/public-sector-porkies-10-years-of-lying-up-the-hierarchy Hat tip to Nicholas Gruen for the referral to this source.

government and its partners.

I have a confession to make. Much of it was made up. It was fudged, spun, copied and pasted, cobbled together and attractively formatted. I told lies in themes, lies in groups, lies in pairs, strategic lies, operational lies, cross cutting lies. I wrote hundreds of pages of nonsense. Some of it was my own, but most of it was collated from my colleagues across the organisation and brought together into a single document. As a policy, partnerships and performance officer in local government, this was my speciality and my profession.

Why did I do it? I did this because it was my job. My manager told me it was "to get the best for the local area" and that "you have to play the game". When I attempted to reveal the absurdity of the situation I was criticised for not being in the real world. I quickly learned that in the real world, data is cleansed, re-presented and re-formatted until it tells an acceptable and neat story.

My can-do attitude was rewarded with promotion in the hierarchy and respect from my colleagues. Stretching the truth was seen as harmless and normal. Our behaviour was rational. We told lies in order to:

Get funding

Keep councillors happy

Keep management team happy

Impress government departments

Get a good inspection rating

Compete with other organisations in our region

The purpose of our behaviour was to maximise the chances of looking good and to minimize the chance of upsetting or embarrassing important people in the hierarchy.

This confession of a professional bullshitter illustrates how the manufacture and gilding of turds happens naturally in a large hierarchical organisation. 'Looking good' has pushed its way to the forefront of what matters. The growth of hierarchies within governments has gone hand-in-hand with increased media and corporate concentration, because government departments need to 'control the message' so they are not exposed by opponents. The increased threat posed by the corporate barons that are now the new power brokers has led to more hierarchical bullshit inside governments, as politicians need money and a steady generation of propaganda to 'win' the media wars.

The rise of big companies over the past half-century explains many of the changes in culture and politics of recent decades in Western countries. The uneasy alliance-cum-rivalry between corporations and governments explains much of the increase in inequality, corruption and bullshit in Western countries. The increased power of the new barons over both media and international organisations also explains the rise of sin-based ideologies, just as the ideologies of the Middle Ages fit the needs of a smaller layer of nobility to keep the vast majority subservient.

CORRUPTION IN THE TIME OF COVID

Corruption blooms when an emergency arises that allows politicians to spend a lot quickly, particularly when the media and general public are looking the other way. The Great Panic was a classic case of this.

Alliances were formed between local politicians and other Jameses to take advantage of new money-making opportunities.[253] Anti-corruption researchers from around the world have documented how the pandemic created opportunities for the new barons to form fresh alliances through which vast

---

253 Rose-Ackerman (2021) documents how corruption increases during crises and surveys some of the emergent evidence on 'rent-seeking' in government contracts and pharmaceutical expenses.

amounts of tax revenue could be obtained.[254] That alliance formation involved misinformation, direct bribery, lobbying and of course regulation to kill off the competition. Some of this corruption is becoming the target of watchdogs and anti-corruption institutions inside Western countries. Some of it was so obvious that academics and journalists simply pointed it out.

In the US, less populous states with more senators per citizen ended up with more federal money spent on them per citizen than was spent in other states because politicians were trying to buy their votes.[255]

Meanwhile, in the UK, the National Audit Office found that business friends of members of Parliament got priority when it came to Covid-related subsidies or contracts.[256] Also in the UK, most of the 1,644 contracts awarded in the period before August 2020 had irregularities,[257] ranging from contracts given by politicians to friends with no transparency or normal verification checks at all, to simply being late with the paperwork.

Again in the UK, activities from which the rich made a lot of money, such as selling houses and playing golf, were exempt from the Covid regulations and even given huge subsidies. The favoured activities of the poor, such as selling cars and playing football, were made extremely difficult by regulations. In many other countries, the corruption was blatant, though journalists reporting on it were met with state violence and suppression, as a Human Rights Watch report detailed.[258]

The weaponizing of regulation to serve the interests of the new barons was on grand display in Covid times. Regulation that banned small shops

---

254 See, e.g., the study for Columbia by Galleco et al. (2020) and the dozens of similar studies around the world that cited it.

255 Clemens & Veuge (2021).

256 Read (2020), https://www.bbc.com/news/business-54978460

257 Comptroller and Auditor General (2020), https://www.nao.org.uk/wp-content/uploads/2020/11/Investigation-into-government-procurement-during-the-COVID-19-pandemic.pdf

258 Human Rights Watch (2021), https://www.hrw.org/news/2021/05/20/bangladesh-arrest-journalist-investigating-corruption; https://www.aljazeera.com/news/2021/5/18/rozina-islam-bangladesh-arrests-journalist-for-covid-reporting

from opening was a direct hindrance to the business of those small stores. If politicians had wanted to 'help small business', they could have insisted that only smaller companies be allowed to deliver supplies to people's homes locally. Compelling consumers to look for small stores capable of supplying them would have helped preserve the smaller stores' market share. It would even have helped create more local economic bubbles, as local stores use local workers.

Instead, almost everywhere in the Western world, corporate James was allowed to raid his competition. Regulations were enacted that made it very difficult for local stores to supply people at their doorsteps, but relatively easy for large companies. Not only did politicians fail to direct customers to local shops but they instigated many Covid-based compliance rules on home deliveries, further beating down small business.

Goods had to be packed and transported in a certain way. Workers and deliverers in the supply chains had to abide by rules on distancing, mask use, and testing regimes. All these extra rules posed little problem for huge chains with enormous warehouses, thousands of delivery vans, and links to suppliers of everything from tape to test kits. They could figure out how to abide by the new rules efficiently enough to preserve some profit margin, and then implement those methods rapidly across their organisations.

Each smaller business, in contrast, had to individually work out its compliance strategy. This was a huge new fixed cost of production that many were incapable of absorbing. Instead, many small shops tried to piggy-back their products on the supply lines of the big companies, which pretty much laughed them out of cyberspace because their own bulk-bought supplies inevitably outcompeted them at the online checkout.

Similar stories held for financial rules, rules on outdoor seating for pubs and restaurants, rules for trying on clothes in stores, rules for cleaning goods to be sold second-hand, rules for visiting sites where companies could showcase their wares, and so on. Such activities were regulated very heavily by zealous civil servants who in turn were increasingly egged on by large companies in a raiding bonanza.[259]

Covid regulations also automatically handed a competitive advantage to larger entities because they were more likely than smaller firms to have preexisting technology platforms. In the retail sector, when governments shut down shopping malls, large mall companies used their digital infrastructure to turn themselves quickly into online marketplaces on which only their own tenants could sell — leaving smaller, unattached shops out in the cold. For example, in April 2020, Frasers Property, which operates 14 shopping malls in Singapore, launched a delivery service for mall tenants to members of its 800,000-strong loyalty program, requiring only some tweaks to infrastructure already in place.

What was the result? Small coffee shops in London disappeared by the boatload in Covid times, while the stock price of the large coffee shop companies such as Starbucks increased even though their costs went up.[260]

An early survey in the US found many small and independent businesses folded in the first two weeks of lockdowns in March and April 2020.[261] A 2021 survey of 2,500 US businesses then found that 'the smallest offline firms experienced sales drops of over 40% compared to less than 10% for the largest online firms.'[262] Losses were particularly large for firms with female or black owners.

What held in the US also held across the globe. Reporting on the results of a survey in the middle of 2020 of 120,000 businesses in 60 countries, researchers at the World Bank reported that '[m]ore than half of micro and small businesses (those with fewer than 20 employees) are in arrears or expect to fall in arrears in the next six months.'[263] Tellingly, that same survey

---

259 Táíwò (2020); https://heated.world/p/the-right-is-using-covid-19-to-wage
260 Edgecliffe-Johnson & Gray (2020).
261 Bartik et al. (2020).
262 Bloom et al. (2021).
263 Cirera et al. (2021).

also found that small firms were only half as likely to get government support as large firms. Complex regulation was harder for small firms to navigate, while they were also more affected by restrictions, than large firms.

So all over the world, small businesses lost out to big ones, with regulations and government-fanned fear to blame.

Covid mania produced a modern-day equivalent of a raid by medieval barons on the remaining independent peasants. When the dust settled, the value of stock markets, which is to say the largest companies, increased, while small companies whose value is not captured in stock markets disappeared.[264] For many years to come, when the subsidies for being idle at home disappear, large groups of workers will find themselves begging to be employed in some way by the big companies that thrived in the Great Panic. For independent businesses, the Great Panic has mostly been a tragedy.

Not all big businesses benefited. Some barons lost out, like those leading the airplane manufacturing companies Boeing and Airbus. They received billions of dollars in subsidies, but still had to fire thousands of workers, saw their share prices drop 30% at least, and can expect a much less rosy future than before. Big Oil saw its share value remain roughly constant rather than reaping huge benefits. Though they did protest, these losing barons could not resist the tide of the Great Panic and were sacrificed by the politicians.

Yet many big companies, to their own surprise, found out mid-2020 that the Great Panic was turning out well for them. After dropping 30% from January to March 2020 when the prevailing wisdom was still that everyone would lose from the economic collapse of the Great Panic, by mid-2020 the big internet companies saw their share values rise above what they were at the start of the year. Such a surprise gain was due to the increased use of the internet in work activities, greater reliance on technology to socialise

---

264 Frijters (2020C), https://clubtroppo.com.au/2020/12/10/what-stock-markets-tell-us-about-the-covid-mania/

with friends and family, and e-commerce.

Subsequently, the big internet players were more than happy to start censoring critical voices and supporting extensions of lockdowns. For instance, Cephas Alain in June 2021 unravelled the story of how Big Tech was involved in a wide attempt to censor the theory that Covid escaped from a lab in China.[265] Since China is a big market, the Big Tech companies were keen not to offend the Chinese authorities. Just like the barons of the Middle Ages, the barons of the internet acted in ways that made them richer and more powerful. They were glad to round up the dissidents in their realm and call for more regulation that was useful to them. Lockdowns were an unexpected gift, for which they became vocal supporters.

However, self-interest ordained that some of the barons would turn against each other. Nowhere was this more evident than the spat between Facebook's Mark Zuckerberg and Tesla's Elon Musk. While Zuckerberg was an ardent lockdown fan, profited hugely from it, and expressed concern that stay-at-home mandates would be yanked too soon, Musk demanded, sometimes in belligerent Twitter storms, that the lockdown be lifted in California where he had his biggest factory.

The good fortune of the internet companies was emulated by the pharmaceutical companies, home-delivery services, mask producers, test producers, track-and-trace system producers, and car manufacturers. Their share prices all dropped in March 2020, only to rise above their previous levels by late 2020 as they found to their own surprise that they were the big winners of the Great Panic. Particularly car manufacturers could not have hoped to gain, even months in, but the growing fear and avoidance of public transport meant more demand for cars and delivery vans.

---

265 Alain (2021). A broader discussion on technology-industry censorship can be found in Mehta (2021).

DID THE BARONS (OR SOMEONE ELSE) PLAN THE GREAT PANIC?

Those critical of lockdowns and authoritarian measures felt a strong need during the Panic to identify a clear culprit who was to blame for all the damage. Having a clear enemy was also important for the 'Covistance' to organise around. This search for a scapegoat is nearly inevitable whenever large groups no longer trust mainstream sources of information and the pronouncements of their governments. Everything starts to be thinkable, especially when it concerns something as vast and complex as societywide reactions to a pandemic.

Expectations were high for conspiracy theorists and they didn't disappoint, coming up with many colourful suggestions ranging from a cabal of paedophiles, to the Chinese leadership, to a global network of freemasons, to the CIA that supposedly planted the virus in China. Each story had a bit of suggestive truth to it, such as that the Chinese leaders indeed lobbied the rest of the world to copy their example, and that some key politicians were involved long ago in juvenile sex scandals. But none had much direct proof and so the spinners of these stories needed to cobble together a lot of circumstantial information, inevitably leading to highly arguable results.

The most prominent of the stories became known as *The Great Reset*, the title of an early 2020 book by Klaus Schwab and Thierry Malleret, whom one of the authors of this book knows personally. Schwab and Malleret headed the World Economic Forum, an annual conference in Switzerland attended by the world's biggest companies and political leaders. The organisers liked to promote this conference as the place where true decisions were made and where the future of humanity was decided. A bit like the UN, but posher and more expensive, and hence suitable for company executives to attend.

In *The Great Reset*, Klaus and Thierry speculate far and wide about all sorts of things, including the idea that humanity will blend with robots, change its own genetics, and achieve a kind of socialist paradise in which everyone is equal. The book proposes a radical future in which inequality disappears, world politics becomes obsessed about the quality of the environment, and private property is abolished. The future they envisage is somewhat reminiscent of *Star Trek*.

The book, which was clearly written for the most part before the Great Panic, was subsequently marketed under the guise that the pandemic offered a 'unique opportunity' to reset global politics. Many world leaders during 2020 and 2021 adopted the slogan and started talking about the need for a 'great reset'. Was this proof of a large conspiracy of the 'barons' who planned the pandemic and foresaw the responses to it?

The script of the grand 'great reset' conspiracy starts falling apart when you consider both the particulars of the organisation of the conspiracy, and the nature of the 'great reset' claims themselves.

The original book and its authors' marketing of it, and the World Economic Forum itself, certainly talk about the pandemic as if they are directing world events. Yet these authors have been writing like that for decades. It is their business model to pretend that the super-rich run the world because that supports the success of the conferences they run.

We have personally attended several of these conferences. What you see there is many rich people pretending that they run the world, drinking vats of champagne and mountains of caviar canapes, after which major world problems like melting ice caps get solved in 5 minutes flat and just in time for dinner.

The conference ends with lengthy pronouncements that tick all the boxes, ranging from the need for recognition of transgender rights in the upper-Volta delta to the crucial importance of not forgetting to fix the extinction of the polar bear in Nova Zembla and the disappearing languages of Papua New Guinea. Everybody goes home flattered to think they have just solved every major problem, but no one is truly obliged to do anything. In the backrooms a few interesting business deals will have been made, usually of a quite mundane variety that were in the clear interest of powerful attendees — around trade disputes, monopoly TV rights, or marginalising some mutual enemy. Lots of exchanged business cards for rolodexes worldwide.

In fact, the World Economic Forum is just one of many enterprises using the same business model. The UN's pronouncements, such as the sustainable development goals or the millennium development goals, are cut from the same cloth. The global warming treaties of the past 30 years were also of this ilk, consisting of beautiful-sounding pronouncements by rich and important people about how, in a future world, their countries would not be rich and important. In those pronouncements, the supposed path to the utopian world involves the leaders becoming even more important, and of course the pronouncements do not actually commit anybody to anything solid. It is bullshit distilled to its purest form but it sells very well. And the champagne is good.

Think of the organisational capacity of the new barons that would be required for them to create and implement a plan for the pandemic. It would take tens of thousands of people in the know, huge coordination, and enforcement. Yet many of the most important and powerful barons pre-2020 lost out during the pandemic, such as the CEOs of hotels and airlines. Whole countries did not play along. The super-rich do have a great degree of influence, but they simply do not have the military organisation required to form a unified bloc with a realistic conspiratorial plan to rule the world.

We think of *The Great Reset* less as an operational manifesto and more as a convenient narrative for some to pretend they agree with for some time. Politicians who want to hold onto their power, for example, would find it appealing to be told they should keep the population under total control in order to 'fight climate change'. They may even actively do things that can be spun as being related to 'zero carbon'.

Consider a key quote from *The Great Reset*: 'First and foremost, the post-pandemic era will usher in a period of massive wealth redistribution, from the rich to the poor and from capital to labour.' Does that sound like the kind of thing the wealthy and powerful truly want and are steering towards? Of course not. It sounds more like the promise of anti-establishment revolutionaries. What is actually going on is that a loose coalition of politicians and barons happen to have the same interests at a point in time and are picking out bits in a convenient existing narrative. They ignore the bits they don't like and change their coalitions as their interests change. In a word, normal politics.

Looking more closely at what the authors of 'The Great Reset' have said in the past reveals that they have been running essentially the same flattery business for decades. They also talked of an historic opportunity for change following the Global Financial Crisis of 2008. They talked of historical opportunities in Africa in 2016. In each case, their message is of the following variety: 'The current problem is a huge opportunity for you to do something that sounds amazing'. They are able to see an historic opportunity in everything, though what they call for has changed with the seasons to suit the bullshit of the day. The continuous production of this flavour of bullshit is a form of flattery of the powerful that works as a business model. Maybe Klaus and Thierry even believe it themselves, or maybe they care only about a part of their message and use the flattery to drive sales.

One can delve in similar fashion into each of the 'grand plan' stories doing the rounds, but they all fall apart for similar reasons. Just think: how many paedophiles can there actually be in order to keep up a world coalition, and how can they avoid the general disgust that nearly everybody has for them? Where have the lizard people who are supposedly running the world been hiding all this time? How did the Chinese leadership get brilliant enough to foresee the policy choices in 150 countries for 15 months ahead, and yet not manage to avoid their own population's plummeting birth rate and reduced economic growth?

Yet, of course, this period was one with conspiracy stories on all sides.

We know from personal experience that even the Jasmines were accused of being funded by libertarian think tanks or of being embedded foreign agents.

All of this wild speculation was additional 'fog of war'. When the personal power of top politicians rides on a particular version of events, there is such a distortion of state media and politician-aligned media that it is extremely hard for critical parts of the population to know which information to trust and which to doubt. A thousand and one well-meaning intellectuals then start searching for what might be true. They gradually sift through the more unlikely stories as an increasingly organised group. That takes time and is hampered by the fact that the sceptics too are naturally attracted to simplistic stories that sound good to them, such as that there is a clear enemy somewhere who planned everything.

There will always be some people who hold on to stories no one else has come to see as likely. Nevertheless, groups that have a strong need to develop a reasonable understanding usually do find one. Humans wanting to truly understand something have an incentive to agree with others who have found good explanations. This insight is the basis of problem-solving solutions that involve juries and diverse work teams, to which we return at the end of the book.

CAN WE EXPECT A RETURN OF SMALL SERVICE INDUSTRIES?

We have now sketched the key political and economic developments that sped up during the Great Panic. Large industries employing millions of workers were simply shut down as governments and the private sector formed new alliances and social distancing policies closed businesses. Millions of these businesses have never reopened and are unlikely to in the future. As a case study, consider the particularly hard-hit sector of personal services. Will this sector flourish again, or be gone forever?

Prior to February-March 2020, a huge and growing industry in personal services featured close physical proximity. Growth and 'nichification' was occurring in beauty salons, hairdressing shops, massage parlours, personal fitness centres, yoga retreats, cinema complexes, sports stadiums, dance studios, bars, hotel wellness services, night clubs, restaurants, coffee shops and a million and one other businesses that customers frequented in order to benefit from closeness with others. Other jobs were being created involving incidental human interaction, particularly with in-home services where technicians and tradespeople visit homes to fix the computer, tend the garden, or install wifi.

The logic behind all these close-contact activities involved three elements: humans absolutely need close physical contact in order to be healthy and sane; people can bond more effectively when in close proximity; and the more densely people are packed in, the more creative the whole group becomes.

We discussed the first of these in a previous chapter. To recap, humans need to be close to other humans, to touch and be touched, and to sense the presence of others. But it is not necessary that we do these things for the whole day or with the people we produce and trade with. The social need for physical proximity is not a pressing reason on its own to say the world economy must have, for example, lots of handshaking in order to preserve health.

The second of these reasons is more central to the modern economy as it goes to the importance of group formation in workplaces. In order for coworkers to form bonds that lead to caring about the output of the team and having each other's backs, close proximity is important for the same reason that it is crucial in families. Without the physical nearness, people are just not as emotionally involved and will not bond as well. This is why companies and organisations have company retreats, Friday night happy hours, staff clubs and all the other forms of joint social activities and supporting infrastructure. Events need to take place at which coworkers become friends.

In industries requiring intense creative effort by groups to develop new products, workplaces have become 'campuses' with facilities and incentives such as upscale cafeterias and gyms that are designed specifically to keep people together for extended periods, to enable them to socialise and to make them feel disinclined to go home. The Googleplex, the headquarters of Alphabet, Inc. in Mountain View, California, and the Microsoft campus in Seattle are good examples.

For the same reason, business trips and academic conferences involve joint dinners and face-to-face meetings. Such events were never only about sharing information. They were also about participants sharing subtle social cues and letting down their guards around each other. Good business is always mixed with pleasure because it makes for stronger bonds, deeper knowledge of trading partners, and more trust.

The third reason for the pre-Covid rise in personal services relates to networks and specialisation. When in close proximity to many others, we spontaneously interact with them, hear new things and compare ourselves to them. The more densely packed people are, the more of these accidental meetings and exchanges of information occur, so the spread of ideas quickens. A lot of preening goes on in these settings because there are so many eyes to impress and people use the opportunity to draw the admiration of others.

This is also one of the reasons that modern office designs deliberately pack so many people into open-plan spaces. It's also the reason that very dense cities like London and Shanghai are so much more productive per person than small cities. It explains why you see many similar businesses in the same geographic area within a town — they all benefit from the flows of people and relevant information generated by the close proximity of many individuals working in similar lines of business.

These reasons have not gone away with Covid. Once restrictions are lifted we expect the return of central business districts, office life, and close-proximity personal services. Close proximity makes for much more productive, creative and fun working lives. The countries that make close proximity harder will lose business. Further, small-scale operations will out-compete larger-scale ones in personal services because personal services are most effectively delivered on a small scale.

THE FANTASY OF THE BUBBLE ECONOMY

A central question in predicting our economic and social future is whether and how a radically separated economy would work in the long run. Can we envisage a 'bubble economy', in which people are highly productive and engage in trade with many others, but where they spend most of their lives physically interacting only within small bubbles? This futuristic question is crucial to consider in deciding whether we should fear a slide toward permanency of populations being locked away from each other.

In such a hypothetical society, most trades, including service trades, would happen without the physical proximity that makes the exchange of diseases inevitable. It would take the global economy many years to adjust to such a change, but once established, small communities of, say, 50 people would operate physically in separated bubbles, producing and trading with the rest of the world.

Because of the limited degree of individual specialisation possible within such a small community, this would mean the demise of high-quality versions of many physically proximate services such as massage, dancing lessons and choral singing, but insofar as those practitioners could not be replaced by robots, people could conceivably just go without. The quality of production of many other products and services would also fall and costs would rise: the returns to scale that large organisations presently exploit and that flow through to lower prices would be unavailable for any industry that could not fully transition to online work, such as car manufacturing, health care or airplane travel.

We know that people can in principle have a full social life while just interacting with 50 others. Indeed, we have been evolutionarily selected for that kind of lifestyle. Yet if each person lived in a social group of 50 while still retaining the modern economic system and producing goods for millions, then unlike in the days of the hunter-gatherers, the social group would no longer be the economic group. This is already true today — recall our anonymous exchanges in supermarkets with unseen growers of our food — but could 50-person-strong communities survive in a hypothetical 'bubble economy' that retained these anonymous trades?

History tells us that our social group is far less dear to us if it is not also our economic group. If we need others less, then we love them less and respect them less. This is one of the reasons why extended families have been whittled down to nuclear families in the West. Extended families used to be economic units, giving people reasons to keep up with distant aunts and nephews as they would be the avenues through which new jobs are found and new trades occur. When that overlap of the social group and the economic group was replaced by more anonymous trading, we gradually lost interest in keeping up with extended families.

Nuclear families remained powerful because so much of value is produced in them: childcare, sex, everyday companionship, and children. Our deep need for such outputs sustains the nuclear family as a core group in Western society. What would sustain a social group of 50 people in a world with global trade?

Quite apart from considerations about the sustainability of such a new system, the path from the modern social structure to strict 50-strong social groups is also fraught. Nowadays, our families and friends are regionally dispersed and belong to disparate groups. By physically interacting with parents, siblings and children, a person also inevitably comes into physical contact with their friends and families, connecting us to the broader social world. This social structure would allow transmission of the same diseases we are exposed to now. Constructing a 50-person-bubble social world in which we can control and eliminate infectious diseases requires a sacrifice of more than just the pleasures of in-person services (barbers, massages, personal trainers), low-cost and high-quality goods and services of all types, and our physical isolation from the millions with whom we trade. We would also have to overhaul the social system such that the 50 people we live with include our family and friends, and all their families and friends.

This means returning to a world in which local communities have very little to do with each other except when exchanging wives and husbands. When exchanged, presumably without any prior in-person interaction with the intended spouses, young people would have to agree to give up the community they came from and, presumably after a long quarantine and cleansing, come and live in the community of their new spouses. Such a setup recalls the royal courts that exchanged princes and princesses in the medieval European game of political alliance formation, but with more medical exorcism.

Clearly this would not work with groups of 50 people. But how about with, say, 50,000?

Communities of 50,000 would be like small towns, with something like a few thousand extended families in each of them. They would have schools and small hospitals, and the citizens would be allowed to physically interact fully, so quite a lot of close-proximity services would be available. They could exchange more complex, lower-cost, and higher-quality services with other communities around the country and the world.

Even with communities of this size, large offices, large cities, and large exchange programs with other regions and countries would need to be abandoned. Specialised services like large-scale performance-based live entertainment and stadium sports would also be gone. Anything needing a large crowd could only proceed virtually.

With communities of 50,000, productivity would also decline materially. Education would be less specialised and excellence degraded because the very brightest of the various communities could not mingle together on campuses and push each other to excel. The high-rise office-work lifestyle, which facilitates the rapid forging of networks and drives creativity, would also be gone.

Despite the productivity loss, technology could fill enough gaps that we might not be much less wealthy than we are today. Advancing technology could help take the sting out of some of the losses in education quality, reduced specialisation, and the requirement for online rather than in-person collaboration. We would see remote classrooms for the super-bright, virtual offices and cafes, virtual reality theatre and sports, online gaming, and sex with robots replacing the mix-and-mingle with distant human populations.

While a new order in which countries consist of 50,000-strong communities that seldom exchange members with others seems technically feasible for the developed West, it would take at least a few years to achieve. It probably would allow the control and elimination of even highly infectious diseases inside those communities. Social life inside the communities could be quite pleasant and the productivity losses could be kept low.

However, such a system could not be introduced quickly for the majority of the population in poor countries. After all, if they were capable of rapidly implementing such a sophisticated reorganisation, they would not be poor. Decades could pass before they caught up enough economically and technologically to be able to reorganise in this way. During that time, all the infectious bugs would be lurking in their midst.

There would still be large benefits available for those who mixed more. More fun, more education, more creativity, and more diversity. This is why big cities today are so rich and why ambitious young people from all over the world are drawn to them. It's why about half the private office workers in London in early 2020 were from other countries. People and groups meet in big cities randomly, observe each other, are inspired by them, bring them home and try out wacky ideas on their own patch. No matter the adjustments made to cities of 50,000 so they are reasonably wealthy and pleasant, big cities and international jet-setting between them will remain attractive.

Big city life will remain particularly attractive to the rich. Cities of 50,000 are small potatoes through the eyes of the rich showboaters of the world. The top artistic performers, top sports people, top models and top businessmen want to impress others and learn from each other in close proximity, not from a distance through a webcam. They want to experience the adulation and sexual interest of many others. They want the wealth and excitement that only comes from mingling in large groups.

Whether the bubble economy can be sustained therefore depends on whether or not all countries do it. If an alternative is available to living in a country that outlaws dense office life and face-to-face contact, thereby losing creativity, fun and motivation, then over time people and companies will choose that alternative by voting with their feet. Countries that reopen their offices and business parks will steal the top workers and clients of the countries that don't. Even if 95% of countries were so terrified of viruses and bacteria that they were willing to live in cities of 50,000, the remaining 5% would keep their large cities and their populations would travel far and wide. They would be visibly richer and have more fun than those stuck in the cities of 50,000. Slowly but surely, those 50,000-strong cities would be drained of their best people.

Services requiring close contact like theatres, massage and music festivals also feed into these competitive forces. The region that keeps offering these services will attract tourists and business from the regions that close them down. Services that always involve close proximity, like school teaching and hospital care, are representative of large swathes of the economy that online alternatives cannot replace because it is the close proximity that makes them work. Closing them down in one country simply means the impoverishment of that country and an outflow of young, ambitious, fun-loving people who will look for a better life elsewhere.

For these reasons, basic competition between regions is a huge counterforce against the lockdowns and social distancing measures of the Great Panic. Politically, this force means that some countries will soon be offering opportunities for experiences that are not being offered in countries still under restrictions. Even without any overt political opposition, this competition might cause the Covid crowds to lose their power and disperse. More than the technical issues of how to organise a bubble economy, it is the competitive force between countries and regions that consigns the idea of perpetually isolated cities to the dustbin of history.

The historical experience in Europe, the US and even in Asia is that jealousy of the success of others is a very powerful motivator for change.

Successful formulas are emulated, perhaps not everywhere, perhaps not even by the majority, but by enough to ensure that such formulas are perpetuated. Even within countries today, the same competitive forces will emerge. Big cities that refuse to play along with restrictions will grow in attraction and then in population over time, proclaiming their success loudly and sucking in migrants from everywhere else.

A historical precedent for this is the speed at which life returned to normal after the waves of Bubonic plague in Europe. Plague waves were frequent for centuries, but despite their deadliness never made much difference to the overall fate of a city or region. No city was ever permanently abandoned because half of its inhabitants died of the plague. The lure of city life once the plague subsided was always strong enough to overcome the fear.

Small risks cannot deter the ambitious from being lured out of their bubbles by the promise of life in a big city and the freedom to jet around from place to place. Importantly, fear cannot be so easily maintained either, because that too is part of competition that the big cities will win: they will have greater media firepower with which to extol their advantages and will be able to shout over whatever messages smaller communities send to demonise them.

Massive rural-to-urban migration flows took place prior to the advent of modern plumbing or the germ theory of disease. Evidently then, the perceived advantages of the city were enough for large numbers of people in many professions to migrate there even with the understanding that they would die at far younger ages and be ill far more frequently than if they had stayed on the farm. We live in a gentler age now and people are not so willing to trade health for wealth, but still it would take a sustained higher risk of death in cities relative to small communities to truly undermine the pull of the big-city, jet-set lifestyle.

This wide musing reveals the limits of what can happen when a new virus hits, or what any increased interest in pathogens can lead to. In the absence of a powerful and obvious threat that is around for a very long time, bubble communities cannot outcompete major cities and the jet-set life. The latter can be disrupted temporarily, but the underlying reasons for its appeal have not gone away with the advent of modern technology. Following the path to establishing bubble communities would take many years and involve not only significant social disruption but the disintegration of large offices, universities, technology parks, modern entertainment venues and shopping malls. To sustain humanity's motivation to do this, the pressure would have to be on, strongly and obviously, for many years.

WILL POWER GO BACK TO THE PEOPLE EASILY AFTER THE GREAT PANIC?

Will the centralisation of power in the hands of governments and large companies that increased during the Great Panic be reversed quickly? This final question has an easy answer.

Would medieval barons and kings have quickly given up the gains in power or status that flowed to them as a result of some natural disaster? More generally, do the powerful give up their gains easily? Is humanity 'nice' in this way?

Governments and businesses always profess the nobility of what they are doing. But alas, more mundane human motivations are always present. The Great Panic was a great moment for people close to power to grab more resources for themselves, and we saw this happen in spades over the past 18 months all over the world.

Did similar consolidations of power happen in all previous crises? The answer is 'no'. Changes in power during previous crises depended very much on whose help was really needed in the crisis itself.

The First and Second World Wars are great examples of crises that led ultimately to huge increases in the political power and influence of the general population, rather than of only a few, despite politics becoming very top-down during the war years themselves. The First World War led to the victory of representative democracy in many European countries, with all men and women given the vote. The Second World War gave rise to the welfare state in America and across Europe, and a large increase in universal education and mass political participation.

The reason why these benefits accrued to the great mass of people following the two world wars is extremely simple: the people themselves were needed to win the wars. It was from the combined energy, genius and manpower of the people that armies were built. Mobilisation and running the war-time economy didn't just require people willing to serve as cannon fodder. It also required the enthusiastic efforts of inventors, battlefield commanders, factory designers, farm workers and everyone else. The world wars needed populations to feel as one, and for everyone to take on more responsibility and different tasks than they were used to. After four years of living as equals and giving their countries all they had, people were not going to return quickly to the positions of subservience they had occupied before. They demanded and were given votes for the women who had taken the men's roles while they fought, welfare programs to assist the war veterans, the orphans, the widows and other victims, and other benefits that elevated their political and economic power.

The Great Panic is a different beast. The close-proximity service workers (with the exception of healthcare workers on hand for Covid cases) and many manual labourers have become unwanted and unused in 2020. Their jobs were declared nonessential and their work itself viewed as an express train for spreading the virus. They were seen to have nothing to offer in terms of creativity or useful technology.

What has historically happened to groups that were no longer useful to those in power? Sometimes they have found different things to do to make themselves useful again, such as when surplus farm labourers in China found jobs in factories in the major cities, fuelling the huge Chinese economic expansion after 1980. Sometimes however, large groups have failed to find new things to do from which the powerful could benefit.

When they were no longer needed in the countryside, unwanted farm labourers flooded England's cities in the period 1770-1850, creating a vast urban underclass. They did fuel new industries, but those industries did not grow quickly enough to absorb them all. What resulted was their marginalisation and outshipment to foreign lands to 'decrease the surplus population',[266] as delinquents, prisoners or poor migrants. Excuses were found to strip them of their political rights and to simply get rid of them. Many were sent to Australia on prison ships.

Other European regions similarly 'relieved themselves' of millions of starving poor people by sending them to the Americas and elsewhere throughout the 19th century. This could be seen most spectacularly during the Irish famine when the poor faced the choice between starvation and boarding trans-Atlantic ships. The Irish had no political power and the English did little to help them.

It is now a very dangerous time for the masses of people all over the world whose jobs have been deemed nonessential, or whose work simply earns very little. If they do not quickly assert their political power and somehow become able to earn their keep, their status will diminish and they will be increasingly seen by those in charge as disposable baggage.

A similar dynamic will emerge if the poor do not quickly organise to defend their political power. Their right to vote will come under pressure and their right to exist will eventually become a serious topic for debate among the rich. For this existential reason do we expect the poor in nations around the world to radicalise quickly in the coming months and years towards some ideology in which they matter. The obvious ideology available to them is

---

266 Dickens (1843), p. 12.

nationalism, because it would elevate the importance of the main thing they have left, which is their citizenship.

PHASE III

THE END GAMES

THE EXPERIENCES AND OUTLOOKS FOR JANE, JAMES AND JASMINE DURING THE END GAMES

JANE'S END GAME

Jane was starting to get impatient with the whole Covid business. She had supported lockdowns, track-and-trace, social distancing, masks, school closures, tiered restrictions, working from home, closure of nonessential businesses, quarantines, and all the rest of it. She had told herself the disruptions to her own and her family's lives were necessary, and that the isolation of the elderly and others was for their own benefit. In many other ways for months she had toed the line and blamed the virus for anything that was bad. She had kept faith in the authorities, the state media and science.

And yet, her frustration was mounting. Jane missed human company, festivities, travel and even random meetings with strangers. She needed some sign that the situation was not going to go on indefinitely. New virus waves kept coming back, despite the earlier sacrifices and the many promises of control made by learned people on the news.

During the many months of the Illusion of Control, Jane had grown a little hateful towards anyone having too good a time. She believed students partying were a menace, rich people traveling were importing new versions of the virus and large-scale festivities were super-spreader events. She was increasingly frustrated at the inability of governments to make the many apps and measures introduced against Covid work to eliminate this vile pest.

In the Great Fear phase, they said lockdowns would not prevent infections but would spread them out across time, which Jane figured was better than seeing hospitals get overrun, but still not as good as hearing that she would never get ill. In the Illusion of Control phase, they promised to achieve elimination of the virus, which Jane thought was more clearly the right goal — but now, even after a year of sacrifice and worry, virus waves still kept coming. Also, quite a few of her friends and family had tested positive without having any real problems, which started to make her think. In sum, Jane was a bit over it. She was ready to move on from the promises of prior phases and to be sold the next promise.

Jane was delighted to be told now that all the suffering had been for the purpose of achieving a final victory, soon, with a vaccine. She didn't believe the many official warnings that this would not end the need for eternal vigilance, mask-wearing and social distancing. A final solution was a solution, even if it was gene therapy and came with nasty side effects. She wanted to declare victory, hear that she had done the right thing all along, congratulate herself and the government for a tough job well done, and get back to her regular life again. If that took until mid-2021 she could endure it, though her patience was wearing thin.

Mid-2021, vaccinated and ready to move on, Jane expected and increasingly demanded an opening up. She slowly became more dismayed that she was still seeing stories of new variants and other developments, such as the need for booster shots, that supposedly required her to remain obedient to continued special measures. She was also impatient with those who were hesitant to be vaccinated like her. What was the problem with these 'anti-vaxxers', as she referred to them? The government says the vaccines are safe, the health experts say they're safe and the vaccine manufacturers say they're safe. Three authoritative sources, and that was enough for her.

Slowly though, she began to ignore the rules in her everyday life as much as possible while pretending to follow them. She started having parties, found loopholes so she could travel again, began inputting fake mobile phone numbers on 'CovidSafe'-style technology, and even invented new online identities to bypass the regulations. She stopped following much of the news and what the politicians said, and began quietly to support those around her who were openly pushing for a resumption of a more normal life.

BERND KOHLER'S STORY

It's April 2021 and the German union representing schoolteachers is urging a return to online learning. This is the story of one teacher, taken verbatim from the public comments of a real person whose identity is concealed.

Remote learning cannot replace learning with physical presence. Not even close! But for people to accuse us of not caring about children's education? Wow! Have you any idea how much more difficult it is and how much more time it requires for us to convert our lessons to something engaging and as meaningful as our physical lessons? It is sooo much harder. It would be far easier for us to say, "Nope. Enough remote learning. Everyone in the classroom." But it is not safe. I have two little girls as students whose father is in a medically induced coma as his life hangs in the balance due to Covid. I have students whose parents are undergoing cancer treatment. If you're asking which we care about more — that our kids have parents to go home to or that they master their 9 times table by the end of year 3… I guess I'd have to choose the former.

I've worked every day through the pandemic. I'm paid for 40 hours a week but have worked about 50 since the pandemic started. My contact hours have stayed the same, but the students need way more time and direction outside of lessons whenever we are online. I'm making far more appointments to tutor kids or re-explain things or answer questions. As are my colleagues.

The teachers in NRW [our region] have only been able to get one dose of vaccine so far. Most of us couldn't get scheduled for our second dose until mid-June. So, we're not even technically vaccinated until we have the 2nd dose.

Believe me when I say that we teachers are working harder and longer than ever before. We are converting physical lesson materials into digital; we are engaging with students between classes to address gaps; we are logging in earlier or staying later to have an extra couple minutes to try to cultivate social-emotional relationships with kids who seem lonely or sad; we are making tutorials to visually explain how to use some tools; we are keeping meticulous seating charts; contacting parents more often than ever; uploading worksheets and instructions in about 3 different platforms for the parents' convenience; downloading returned student work, marking, and uploading again. Tomorrow, after getting to school an hour before students so I can self-test, I'll be assisting first graders with their self-tests and super-discretely and gently dealing with those children who test positive (again).

We want so badly for the students to be back 100% full time — when it is safe for them and their families. It's so much better for the students and teachers alike. Their emotional well-being is suffering by not being in school. Hopefully, in addition to the support we offer in school (be it online or in-person), they have a supportive parent who can listen to them and help them make sense of all this stuff that doesn't really make all that much sense.

I hope you never have to comfort a crying child who repeatedly bursts into tears months after losing her father to disease. I've had 3 students under the age of 8 in the past two years alone who've had a parent die.

I have two kids on two separate Zoom conferences sometimes WHILE I'm teaching from a third device. And at 3:15, when my teaching day is over, I have to help my own kids make up the work they didn't get done while I was working. And then I have to do my prep after they go to bed, which is way too late these days. It really, really, really sucks.

BOB PEPPERSTOCK'S STORY (CONTINUED)

We've been having periodic restrictions here in Vietnam and right now there is a bit of a surge in cases, mainly up north, but they have mostly shut down Ho Chi Minh City anyway.

If you book a taxi you have to fill out an online health declaration, which takes as long as the ride. If there are two of you, the government insists that the company send a 7-seater. But when the taxi arrives the couple climbs in and sits next to each other anyway.

If I go to a restaurant with my girlfriend we have to sit two metres apart and yell at each other across the table. The cops do random checks and if the restaurant is breaking the rule then it can be closed down. So they are strict about it.

As yet I have no idea about when vaccinations will be available or which of the vaccinations it will be. They haven't said anything yet. I am now hearing a lot of conflicting information about the effectiveness of different vaccines so maybe it is just as well I haven't been forced to make any kind of decision yet. Anyway, the Vietnam government has done such a good job containing the virus here that I am somewhat relaxed about the situation regarding vaccination, so far at least.

I have been getting into frequent arguments with a friend in a neighboring country who tried to convince me that lockdowns and other restrictions on freedom were the wrong thing to do. The guy is an economist and he kept on sending me so-called 'expert opinion', which was largely in the form of cherry-picked data from people I suspect were charlatans, supposedly showing lockdowns cost more than they were worth, face masks were not helpful and other nonsense that has been completely debunked by the CDC and the information I got from other people I know. Sometimes our discussions got very heated. But now we avoid the subject altogether and our friendship is warm again.

V. HEMSWORTH'S STORY

The following story is based on a letter to the editor of the Stabroek News in Guyana, South America, on May 6, 2021.

I write in response to the multiple letters I've seen recently on Covid-19, primarily as it relates to the curfew hours and the need for a lockdown.

The blame for our plight should not be laid only at the feet of the government. It ought to be shared by the people. It is no surprise that huge numbers of Guyanese simply do not take Covid-19 seriously. The flouting of curfew, social distancing, mask-wearing and other restrictions is absolutely well known and documented in the press. So who is to blame for this? When someone purposely violates the Covid-19 guidelines and regulations is it the government's fault? Did the government tell them to not wear a mask, to not social distance, to break the curfew hours?

Others also note there is a reluctance for persons to take the vaccine. Anyone who looks at the media pages will be bombarded with information on getting vaccinated and the importance of it. Even opposition politicians have joined in to urge persons to get vaccinated. So who is responsible for this vaccine reluctance? If the government and opposition personalities are united in encouraging the population to be vaccinated and people still don't want to, who is to take responsibility for that?

What I say will be uncomfortable for some to hear, but a lot of Guyanese enjoy misery. They enjoy it because it allows them to complain. Our national pastime isn't cricket, it's complaining. We will complain about everything, rather than take responsibility for things that are within our power. Abiding by the Covid-19 regulations, social distancing, mask- wearing, not playing sports, not gathering en masse during curfew hours and getting vaccinated are all within our powers as individuals.

Yet in true fashion we lay the blame somewhere else. I do not believe for one moment that people won't find a way to disregard safety during these times to do what they want regardless of what the guidelines say. Then to defend their actions, they argue about something or some idea they heard about Covid-19, which they don't fully understand, but think they are an authority on due to them possessing their social media PhD.

What should happen, which is the case in our sister CARICOM states, is that the fines for breaking the Covid-19 guidelines and regulations should be clear and steep. This should have been done from the very beginning. In Barbados and Trinidad the fines are clearly stated and promptly assessed. In Guyana, the fine mentioned references a public health ordinance from the days of British Guiana. New guidelines ought to clearly sound the warning and state the fine clearly so people would know exactly what the penalty is for violating Covid-19 guidelines and regulations. People who go about breaking these guidelines and regulations don't hear with their ears, they hear with their pockets.

We can all agree that the Covid-19 situation in Guyana is worrying. With such a large landmass and a small population, our Covid-19 numbers should not be where they are.

The people, yes the people, need to take responsibility for their actions, because nothing the government writes on paper will stop Covid-19 automatically and magically.

JAMES' END GAME

James was feeling the weight of his own success. He had grabbed power and money by pursuing the new opportunities that so unexpectedly came along during the Illusion of Control phase and was now rolling in the fruits of his opportunism. He and his mates were now more regularly in the limelight and surrounded by new contacts and partners who had grown in importance, market share, capacity or profitability — or all of the above — during the Great Panic. Their problem now was how to get out of the trap they had made for themselves.

Political unrest had been bought off by printing lots of money, running up huge debts, and keeping large segments of the economy afloat with subsidies. The attempts by the Jameses in government at shoring up the economy by pumping huge amounts of money into circulation had not prevented a huge loss in output. The mental health of their populations (including their employees) was deteriorating, and the sceptics were increasingly hot on their heels with stories of their corruption, incompetence, and fake science. They had for a while managed to swamp that opposition by wheeling out carefully chosen 'experts' on state media channels, but found themselves increasingly struggling to gloss over the ever-more-obviously collapsing social and economic system that they had created. How to get out of this mess while keeping their winnings?

James saw two means of escape. He could either find a new obsession for the population, or offer them a way to deflate the Great Panic while telling them they had all done the right thing and thus that the many sacrifices, of which new ones were now emerging on a weekly basis, had all been worth it.

New obsessions were not hard to create. Obvious ones were around: James could blame the Chinese, the migrants, the poor, the young, or even private security services for the virus or its return. Yet they were risky targets, as there was no clear path to final victory against them.

The main escape he saw was to sell the notion that a vaccine allowed the declaration of victory and the slow unwinding of the most damaging of the regulations and institutions he had built during these past eight months. Still, to preserve his winnings, he would have to keep his most lucrative new alliances going while pursuing this 'vaccine hero' strategy.

Small inconveniences might arise, such as the high likelihood that vaccines were going to be largely ineffective and that some of the new disease-oriented industries were going to show that ineffectiveness with their tests, but at least the idea of a solution would allow him to switch sides with grace.

So when various companies started to announce that they had prepared vaccines that conferred some degree of protection, James set to work on pushing the idea of vaccinating as many people as possible as quickly as possible, making sure all the while that he would not be personally liable if anything went wrong.

One of the many politicians who quietly gave up the ghost in this way was Spain's Prime Minister, Pedro Sánchez, a fervent lockdown fan who had closed off his country almost continuously since March 2020. 'We are just 100 days away from achieving group immunity, that is, from getting 70% of the Spanish population vaccinated and thus immunized,' he said on May 10, 2021.[267] Shortly after that he announced that Spain was welcoming back vaccinated British and Japanese tourists, desperate for something to reboot an economy made moribund by the multiple 'hibernations' he had foisted upon it.

Sánchez's hand was forced by competition. He had been in a battle of words for months with the conservative government of Madrid, headed by Isabel Díaz Ayuso, who was running for reelection and characterised Sánchez's anti-Covid measures as job-killing. More colourfully and perhaps not inaccurately, she said the prime minister was a constant liar with an unhealthy Madrid obsession who was using the virus in a 'pathetic and disgusting attempt to spread fear due to the elections.'[268]

With the economy in desperate straits and regional governors like Díaz Ayuso becoming increasingly belligerent, Sánchez called time on the national emergency measures that provided the legal underpinning for lockdowns. Under cover of his aggressive vaccination schedule, Sánchez, with fingers undoubtedly crossed, just up and walked away from his previous lockdown strategy before the political and economic damage overwhelmed his administration.

---

267 Mouzo et al. (2021), https://english.elpais.com/society/2021-05-10/coronavirus-spain-is-100-days-away-from-group-immunity-says-pm.html

268 Dombey (2021).

Spain's prime minister was just one of many ardent advocates for a vaccination solution who had hitherto committed themselves zealously to lockdowns but were rolling them back in the End Games using vaccination for cover. This is hardly surprising. They had not succeeded in eliminating the virus through the lockdowns and they were presiding over disastrous economic outcomes. Their working people and small business owners were screaming blue murder.

California's governor Gavin Newsom was also looking for a way out of trouble. He had initially seen his popularity surge during the Great Panic by acting decisively in locking down the state before any other governor had the nerve.[269] As time went on and the economic damage became clearer, the pressure grew to ease up on the restrictions more quickly than Newsom and his health advisors wanted. Many businesses were closed and ordinary people were hurting, as were Newsom's poll numbers. So Newsom let up on the restrictions by early summer 2020.

Predictably, case numbers started giving the governor a serious problem again in the fall and by December, now committed to a repeated lockdown strategy, he felt obliged to put another stay-at-home order in place. But like other Jameses who thought so little of their own restrictions that they didn't personally follow them, Newsom attended the birthday celebration of a lobbyist at a famous Napa Valley restaurant at a time when such gatherings were against his government's rules.[270] This was a reprise of the scandal that had enveloped Neil Ferguson in the UK in May 2020, when he had had to resign his post on the UK government's Covid advisory panel for breaking the rules that he himself had been instrumental in making. Later, in July 2020,

269 https://www.latimes.com/california/story/2021-03-19/one-year-anniversary-newsom-sweeping-covid-19-lockdown-stay-at-home-order

270 https://www.latimes.com/california/story/2020-11-16/gavin-newsom-apology-french-laundry-dinner-covid-19

it was the turn of the New Zealand Health Minister, David Clark, to fall on his sword partly for failing to abide by his own lockdown rules.[271]

By February 2021 things were getting trickier for Governor Newsom. The state's unemployment rate was twice what it was before the pandemic and 2% above the US national rate. To be sure, most of Newsom's friends in Big Tech and Hollywood were thriving, and his own businesses were surviving because he was riding the gravy train of the federal government's Paycheck Protection Program.[272] He was also continuing to dole out PPE contracts to companies like BYD, the Chinese electric vehicle manufacturer, and other sterling contributors to his election campaigns such as UnitedHealth.[273] In Newsom's inner circle then, things could hardly have been better.

But Newsom's enemies were stepping out of the shadows. The Republican National Committee financed a petition to have him recalled, and it quickly got more than the minimum required number of signatures.[274] Newsom's poll numbers were starting to go south. So, again, he simply rolled back the lockdown.[275] Lacking the declining infection numbers to support such a relaxation, Newsom gambled that the vaccine rollout would get traction and take the sting out of the virus. Then spring arrived in California, infections subsided, and millions got vaccinated. Leaving nothing to chance, Newsom even put a 'Vax for the Win' lottery in place which made Californians eligible for prizes if they got vaccinated.[276] Perfect.

---

271 https://www.theguardian.com/world/2020/jul/02/new-zealand-health-minister-david-clark-quits-over-handling-of-covid-19-outbreak

272 https://abc7news.com/plumpjack-management-group-llc-gov-newsom-winery-sba-releases-detailed-ppp-data-what-business-does-gavin-own/8618229/

273 https://www.capradio.org/articles/2021/03/25/another-282m-in-no-bid-pandemic-contracts-to-major-newsom-contributor-unitedhealth/

274 https://www.nytimes.com/2021/02/19/business/newsom-coronavirus-california.html

275 https://www.newsweek.com/gavin-newsom-facing-recall-eases-lockdown-california-hospitals-are-overwhelmed-1564161

276 https://calmatters.org/newsletters/whatmatters/2021/06/california-vaccine-lottery-newsom/

Newsom took credit for everything: for bringing down the number of infections, for moving quickly on vaccinations, and for the economic recovery that began because his lockdown ended.

The governor got the message out to the people of California that the recall was just a power grab by his Republican opponents. He signed a bill providing a US$6 billion tax cut for businesses.[277] His poll numbers went up. The recall election became a media circus with porn stars, pastors, and even Caitlyn Jenner entering the race.

Governor Newsom, despite riding California businesses into the dirt, depriving 40 million people of their liberty for months at a time, and elevating cronyism to a whole new level by throwing billions of dollars at entrepreneurial Jameses, had positioned himself to come out the other side of Covid in a stronger position than ever before.

Beyond California, James naturally took advantage of the new opportunities presented by a vaccination plan which, like lockdowns, involved many new lucrative contracts. For example, he could mandate that international travellers take tests, and could choose which tests he would recognise as valid. He could insist on vaccine passports, allowing him to choose which vaccines were recognised at which point in time. He could allocate places and facilities for storage and transport of the vaccines. He had a say in who would be given the vaccines and what commercial benefits early vaccination would bestow upon businesses. All of these choices, taken wisely, presented great opportunities for James to bag billions of dollars' worth of windfall profits.

---

277 https://www.gov.ca.gov/2021/04/29/governor-newsom-signs-bill-giving-small-business-a-6-2-billion-tax-cut/

James did have a problem though. The beast he had helped create did not want to let go of its control. When the population had been jabbed with one vaccine, another manufacturer and group of medics would talk about how bad that vaccine was and how the population needed another one.

Mask-sellers and test-sellers kept talking up the fearsomeness of new variants. After all, many had made a fortune selling PPE and had ramped up their production capacity to take advantage of the panic that ensued when the virus first broke out. Take for example 3M, a global corporation based in St. Paul, Minnesota, headed by Mike Roman. The company, which is the largest PPE manufacturer in the US, made an operating profit of US$7.2 billion in 2020 on sales of US$32.2 billion. It paid out US$3.4 billion in cash dividends to shareholders. Mr. Roman's own compensation package in 2020 was worth US$21 million, an increase of 13% over 2019.[278]

For Roman's company, Covid created a golden year, a year when it went to town making disposable respirator masks, hand sanitisers, safety glasses and room air purifiers. It manufactured 95 million respirators in the US every month. Globally, it produced 2 billion respirators in 2020, representing a tripling of production from 2019. Roman's factories were humming 24 hours a day, 7 days a week, to keep up with demand.

So what lay in store for 3M now that there was a distinct possibility that the Covid obsession might burn itself out? In the US, mask mandates had already been relaxed in a number of states that reopened their economies in the spring of 2021. The US Centers for Disease Control and Prevention (CDC) announced on May 13 that vaccinated individuals could 'resume activities without wearing a mask or physically distancing'.

Roman was far from despondent. He believed that there had been a permanent cultural shift in attitudes toward the wearing of masks in Western countries. He was confident that masks were going to be part of a new dress code for people all over the world, since a significant subgroup of the population could be scared into continuing to wear them, a practice that public health authorities were already encouraging.

But the CEO of 3M had another trick up his sleeve. He put about the idea that PPE supplies are a national security issue and began lobbying for a national stockpile to insulate the US from future domestic demand

278 https://www.execpay.org/news/3m-co-2020-compensation-934,
https://investors.3m.com/news/news-details/2021/3M-Reports-Fourth-Quarter-and-Full-Year-2020-
Results-Provides-Full-Year-2021-Guidance/

surges, much like the Strategic Petroleum Reserve operates to cushion the country from shocks to the world oil supply. To create and maintain such a stockpile, government and business must work closely together, of course. The stockpile would need to be fully funded and there must also be a flexible inbuilt budgetary mechanism for funding sudden surges in demand, as happened in early 2020.[279]

The chances of 3M getting its way were good, since the company had formidable lobbying resources as well as the ability to leverage the US Chamber of Commerce's lobbying apparatus, where it not only had a Board member but also a conference room named for it.

While companies in the PPE sector concerned themselves with how the rage would be maintained in a Covid-less world, producers of vaccine passports and businesses that tried to pinch customers by being 'more safe' than other businesses also wanted to keep their advantages going. His fellow travellers in the Covid racket started to look to James like a problem, and he to them. With so many hands in the till, all grasping for more, James eventually calculated that there was just too much effort needed to keep trying to milk the continuing madness. He started quietly to shift political allegiances towards any reasonable exit strategy that would allow a dismantling of the fear industry while keeping his own spoils.

JASMINE'S END GAME

The countermovements went mainstream in the End Games, as many institutions started hedging their bets. Newspapers, televised talking heads, governments, scientific journals, international organisations and others who had for almost a year depicted the critics as deluded anti-scientists started to run pieces by prominent sceptics. Jasmine became popular in boardrooms

---

279 https://multimedia.3m.com/mws/media/1954744O/white-paper-covid-19-policy-recommendations.pdf

and at cabinet tables around the world. As a sceptic of Covid vaccines she became useful to the competitors of the leading vaccine-producing bodies, and even to the testing companies and many other industries benefiting from continued restrictions that were still being sold as the only alternative to mass vaccination.

There were also more serious political groups and civil society institutions that took shape in the End Games, with the agenda of a full return to the pre-2020 situation and a rejection of various cultural phenomena that were by then associated with pro-lockdown policies. The new movements could be described as nationalistic and neo-Enlightenment in that they embraced the values and habits of the Enlightenment, but they also reflected how the lockdowns and border closures had created more strongly nationalistic identities and mistrust in international organisations.

Jasmines everywhere became embroiled in new political conflicts. Some Jasmines returned to their previous occupations as scientists, business-people, civil servants, students, journalists and lawyers. Some continued to pursue particular causes they had become involved with during the first two phases of the Panic, such as court cases or scientific investigations. Some joined existing political parties or became involved in prominent inquiries. Others found entirely different paths, spurred there by the sober lessons they had learned.

NEIL'S STORY, CONTINUED

Recovery has been slow but sure. I'm asymptoting to my old self, but like $1/x$ I don't think I'll ever quite get there. I am more cynical about the state of the world and human nature, partially from my experience with my own emotions. But with this newfound dissatisfaction has come a creative drive unlike any I have had before. I am writing a musical, and I am at once a member of 5 different musical groups and ensembles while continuing to practice piano to fulfil one half of my dual degree. I have three jobs and may soon pick up an internship. I will be 22 when I go back to Boston in September, and I have two more years of undergraduate study ahead of me. My future has not gotten lost in the mist of Covid. I am one of the lucky ones.

It has helped that my arguments have been affirmed time and time again by the data. Here I'm not referring to the advice spouted by "experts", but rather to hard statistics on deaths and case numbers. As various countries and states have gravitated towards different levels of severity in their restrictions, it has become increasingly clear that there is no correlation between lockdowns and similar policies, and lives saved. Life satisfaction has gone down while mental health issues continually rise. This does not make me happy, of course, but I am hopeful that validation of the viewpoint for which my family and I have fought will pour ever more rapidly out of the cracks of the standard narrative. More and more people are coming out of the woodwork to protest. Unfortunately, it will probably still be far too few. Even so, the Covid-safe ideology becomes increasingly easy to satire.

Life isn't all peachy. The university has announced that Covid vaccines will be mandatory for the coming semester. This is yet another small step in the worryingly tyrannical direction our leadership and sense-making organizations have been moving in the past year. We must stop sacrificing human liberty for this foolish dream of total safety and protection. It's not realistic, and even if it were, it wouldn't be worth it.

ARI JOFFE'S STORY, CONTINUED

It turns out that lockdowns were the exact opposite of what was needed to manage the pandemic. The devastation they cause at best does not balance potential benefits, and at worst has no potential benefits. The governments, medical officers of health, pandemic advisory groups of healthcare 'experts', and media were inducing unwarranted fear in the population as a strategy to enforce misguided restrictions on individual freedoms. But no one listened to the evidence I presented. Crowd effects prevailed over reason.

A personal story might demonstrate a small part of this drastically out-of-proportion fearful crowd response. This past weekend, our beloved 6-year-old yorkie "Shadow" started vomiting and having difficulty breathing. We rushed her to the veterinary hospital. I knew that she likely had an esophageal foreign body as she previously had an esophageal stricture from a bout of pancreatitis. At the door to the veterinary hospital, I found we could not walk in (even wearing masks) but had to phone. As I phoned, Shadow was turning blue from inadequate breathing. I insisted I needed to come in to explain the problem, but the gowned, masked, gloved, and visor-bearing veterinary assistants (that looked to be about age 20-30 years) told me "hospital COVID restrictions" did not allow that. They took Shadow and she was intubated, and then the young veterinarian phoned me. I gave her history over the phone, and asked for her to have a scope to check for a foreign body, which was done, and the obstruction (a dog-treat) successfully removed.

But Shadow had suffered hypoxic brain damage, and continued to deteriorate over the next 3 days. We could not visit her, we were told, because of "hospital COVID restrictions." Finally, we insisted on her having a 3-hour pass from the hospital so we could spend some time with her in our home. The next day we were told she continued to worsen. We came to visit, but even this end-of-life visit was limited to only two visitors (not even allowing alternating who was visiting). When we decided it was time to let her go, at least we could, all five of us together, hold her outside in the windy rainy cold while the young veterinarian administered euthanasia.

Shadow's last days were apart from her family. Shadow likely only saw gowned masked visor-bearing staff who were at no risk from SARS-CoV-2. Shadow did not get three-times-daily visits from her family (which we did the last time she was in hospital with pancreatitis) because we were considered a risk of transmitting the virus, from us (all vaccinated) to people at no risk.

This cost of lockdowns cannot be calculated. Shadow suffered. Our whole family suffered and continues to suffer having missed sharing in Shadow's last days. But at least the veterinary hospital staff were protected from their unreasonable fear. They certainly were not protected from a virus we did not have, and from which they were not at risk. Similar stories no doubt played out with other families who had their loved ones, human and non-human, in hospitals and long-term-care facilities around the world.

CARMEN'S STORY, CONTINUED

Now that the lockdown restrictions are slowly but surely being lifted, I'm starting to regain some optimism about the future. Since the anti-curfew protests from January onwards, I've noticed the increased amount of scepticism towards the effectiveness of the government and the policies implemented to counter the spread of Covid. I doubt that I will ever forget the level of stupidity and delusion that I've witnessed first-hand by people I thought were critical, but I've slowly stopped associating with them in favour of people who are actually critical (or just don't care).

Being able to go to university again, as well as to bars and house parties, gives some semblance of life getting back to normal. However, the requirement for testing for absolutely everything, the upcoming enforcement of quarantine as well as the necessity of vaccine passports suggests that everything is far from over. Until the world collectively awakens to admit that the policies implemented in 2020 were a colossal mistake for the worse, it seems to only be a matter of time before something similar happens again.

SANJEEV SABHLOK'S STORY, CONTINUED

Around Easter 2021, Peter Harris, the founder of the Family First party, identified the cause of Australia's problems: the failure of representative democracy.

Elected members of the big political parties had become spruikers of vested, global interests and did not care for the opinions of their constituents. This analysis resonated with me since Matthew Guy, my local member of Victorian Parliament from Bulleen, had blocked me on Twitter when I asked him to seek evidence in the Parliament for the CHO's directive on mandatory masks outdoors.

Thousands of Australians have experienced similar unhappy incidents with their elected representatives, who virtually never bother to respond to their concerns.

Peter Harris and I have one political party each under our belt. We know how hard it is to form and run a party. But after a week of discussion and despite innumerable challenges that faced us, we decided to proceed to create a new political party for Australia, to be called Australia's Representatives. The party would embed into its DNA rules and processes to foster debate and make its elected members accountable to their constituents. A core ideology of liberty would underpin the party and a commitment to care for those who can't look after themselves for reasons beyond their control.

At the time of writing this, I am preparing the party's application for registration – a huge administrative chore with many pitfalls. If the party does manage to get registered in time for a possible November 2021 election, I will contest under its banner. If that doesn't materialise, I'll seek other options to contest elections – if for nothing else but to lay down in stone my firm opposition to the policies of the big parties.

The prospect of success of my battle against Australia's totalitarian post-Covid regime is unclear. But my philosophy of life is simple.

There are times when we must fight for basic principles. This is one such time. We need to fight regardless of whether we are successful. The *nishkam karma* principle in the *Bhagwad Gita* (I'm not a religious person but agree with this principle) states that one must do the right thing without having any regard for the consequences.

In the bigger scheme of things, life is at its core a *Mahabharata*, a battle-field between good and evil. Today, evil has dramatically overrun and taken over almost all the institutions of the world. There is no longer an assurance that the good will ever come back from this comprehensive rout.

But the good can't even imagine a comeback without being a perpetual contender in every battle. We need to channel the Churchill that exists within each of us: "We shall fight on the beaches, we shall fight on the landing grounds, we shall fight in the fields and in the streets, we shall fight in the hills; we shall never surrender".

WHAT'S NEXT – AND WHAT
HAVE WE LEARNED?

At the time of writing, the Great Panic is over in some places, unwinding in others and still getting warmed up in a number of countries such as Australia and the nations of Southeast Asia. We sketch here in broad strokes what we expect to happen in the coming years and what can be done to avoid a repeat of the events of this disastrous period.

THREE SCENARIOS

In Western countries, where we live and which we understand best, three possible future scenarios have emerged.

The first scenario, which we think most likely, is a gradual unwinding of the Great Panic and its many restrictions, together with the adoption of social mechanisms to allow people to move on without too much bitterness. We envision no quick restoration of previous power and wealth structures, however, so most groups that have gained power and money will not have to give it all up in one go. Rather, history will restart, in the sense that normal competitive pressures and new events will drive political and economic agendas.

The second scenario is that this period of madness will usher in a new techno-fascist era in which the political elites of many countries ricochet from one control myth to another. In that scenario, of which the 'Great Reset' vision is one manifestation, governments try to hold on to totalitarian authority by finding other causes to justify the same powers.

Increasingly, totalitarian Western governments would then coordinate with other totalitarian governments and with the large international corporations that dominate global flows of information and goods, making it hard for resistance groups to organise. The other causes used to excuse continued control could most obviously be carbon emissions, other diseases including new Covid variants, or the supposed threats posed by other countries.

On balance we think competitive pressures between countries make this second scenario highly unlikely. Ambitious, fun-loving populations will flee from totalitarian places to other countries or states that are open for both business and fun. This type of voting with the feet has been a powerful force historically, and has already been observed in the Covid period, for example in the recent US migration from California and New York to less locked-down states like Texas.[280] Humans can be manipulated by fear for a while, but they do have other emotions and desires that don't go away and that eventually carry the day.

The third scenario is that there will be an enormous backlash against those held responsible for the Great Panic and its abuses. The only force we see as powerful enough to embody that backlash and channel it is nationalism. In this scenario, a violent nationalism would start to emerge in many countries that openly battles 'international elites', 'woke culture', and anything else seen as a threat to the idea of a great nation. We would then witness nationalistic crowds with all their capacity for both renewal and destruction.

This third scenario seems unlikely because life is still too good in rich Western countries to generate the anger and desperation required to make nationalism sufficiently appealing. Also, elites in rich countries already see

---

280 For a lengthy discussion, see Molinski (2021).

nationalism as the main threat to their power and are therefore probably willing to strike a compromise that yields up the worst excesses of their own power and wealth, if this reduces the appeal of nationalism.

While we see the first of these possible futures as the most likely, we do not totally discount the other two, streaks of which have already been seen in different regions across the world. Our best bet is that the rich countries will follow the first scenario, and that this example will then be emulated in most of the remaining world, with some exceptions like China.

TRUTH AND RECONCILIATION, JUSTICE AND COMPENSATION – WHAT ARE THE CHANCES?

Supposing it comes to pass, what will the 'gradual unwinding' scenario mean for politics and society?

In our view, the Prohibition period in the US (1919-1933) offers the best guide from history on what to expect next. Now as then, the many measures implemented to reduce social interactions will gradually be wound back. Protocols that have been mandated in various countries, such as Covid testing for schoolchildren and quarantining for travellers, will start to become more voluntary and then gradually fade away.

In democracies, emergency powers will be challenged and eventually repealed. Populations will become increasingly weary of the propaganda, and tougher questions about corruption and abuses of power will emerge. A new delicate balance will eventually be found. In short, much of what was normal before 2020 will slowly return in most countries.

Just as the instigators of Prohibition were never punished and those who lost their businesses during Prohibition were never compensated, so too do we expect the gains and losses of the Great Panic to remain without recognition or recompense. The gains secured through corruption and abuses of power are likely to remain in the claws of those who grabbed them, a prediction supported by the scarcity in human history of examples in which those who abused their positions have later been punished and stripped of their wealth.

Only when incumbent elites are conquered by an invader, for example Japan in WWII, or pushed aside by an angry population as in the Russian Revolution, has it happened that ill-gotten gains are taken away. What is normal in a restoration period after a time of great folly, like Prohibition, is that those who had played powerful roles during the folly start to lay low. Populations are eager to forget the silliness to which they acquiesced, and the powerful successfully cover their tracks and fade into the background while still clinging to as many of their gains as they can.

Only a very strong backlash, fuelled by vengeful anger channelled through a political movement, could lead to ill-gotten gains being recouped in the democratic West. Only under the third scenario sketched above do we see such a strong backlash emerging. Instead, the victims of the Great Panic, who are mainly the weakest members of society, are unlikely ever to be fully recognised or compensated. We write this with pain in our hearts, but this is how it has gone so many times in history. The victims of the world wars, of famines and of dictatorships have usually been left to dust themselves off in private and carry on fending for themselves.

Still, we do envision a hunger for forgiveness, as families and communities must find a way to move on without permanent bitterness. The Janes, Jameses and Jasmines sharing families, friendship networks, economic ties, and local communities with one another will have to find a way to forgive and move forward together.

In some countries, official mechanisms for forgiveness may emerge. One possible mechanism would take the same form as the 'Truth Commission' used in South Africa after the end of Apartheid to promote some degree of mutual understanding without bloodshed or physical punishment. This type of mechanism allows the most powerful members of the 'old system' to confess their crimes in an open forum in return for future immunity. These confessions allow the country as a whole to hear what happened. In other countries, something similar can be achieved via parliamentary inquiries, Royal Commissions, national debates, and so on. In countries that are well-run, we expect the population to openly reevaluate what has happened and the varying degrees to which different people and groups have been 'right all along' or 'misled all along'.

Alongside this group-level reckoning and forgiveness, we think it likely that the unwinding of the Great Panic will be followed by a short period of more humility, just as the First World War in Europe was followed by a period in which the population lost faith in its leaders and in the promises of authority. The many mistakes of the previous 18 months will force some degree of soul-searching in scientific communities too. We expect this to culminate in a relearning of how easy it is to exaggerate both dangers and the certainty of solutions, and of how damaging the consequences of these exaggerations can be. Unfortunately, we also expect it to take quite a few years for this relearning and limited reckoning to occur.

CONSEQUENCES FOR CIVIL STRUCTURES AND MARKETS: THE GOOD, BAD AND UGLY

It would be naive not to expect some developments that strengthened during the Great Panic to endure. Some evil will survive, and so too will some of the good spawned during this period.

A big 'bad' development — where our moral judgment is informed by what is ultimately desirable for human thriving in aggregate — is the accelerated rise of a new kind of feudalism, featuring a small number of very big companies that have come to dominate our economies.

A significant 'good' development is the array of structures built by Jasmines during this period. These include a massive increase in citizen journalism and new media forums that openly dismiss the narratives of mainstream political parties and media.

Let us consider both the bad and the good.

First, consider the rise in dominance of small groups of companies within large sectors of the economy. These groups are colloquially known as 'Big Tech', 'Big Pharma', 'Big Media', the MIC ('military-industrial complex'), 'Big Oil', and so on. While the world economy shrank during the Great Panic and whole industries like international travel almost vanished, 'Big' became...well, even bigger. Consider the following staggering statistics:

- The revenues of the top 25 pharmaceutical companies increased to US$837 billion in 2020, up US$41 billion from 2019. This is the equivalent of 1% of the world economy and about the size of the economy of the Netherlands. After-tax profits of these companies amounted to a shade under US$100 billion.[281] This represents an enormous concentration of power and money in the hands of a small number of companies and the people who run them.

- The revenues, profits and concentration seen in Big Tech are higher still, with the top 20 technology companies generating revenues of over US$2 trillion in 2020, bigger than the size of the Canadian economy. This represented an increase of US$135 billion in revenues while the world experienced a deep recession.

- The increase in profitability of technology companies in 2020 was also mind-boggling. Big Tech achieved net after-tax profits of US$320.6 billion, an increase of US$50.7 billion on 2019.[282] These 20 companies also directly employ about 4 million

---

281 Sourced by the authors from company reports.

282 All data on the revenues and profits of technology companies has been sourced directly from company reports.

workers and determine the fate of many more if one counts the employees of the many other companies that totally depend on them. Collectively, the value of these companies soared on stock markets. For example, an index of the price of FAANG stocks — Facebook, Amazon, Apple, Netflix and Google — rose by 180% between the beginning of 2020 and mid-2021.[283]

The same kind of story holds for Big Media, the MIC, and other powerful clusters of companies. The hold these oligarchical groups have over the economies of Western countries greatly expanded in 2020, with more people working for them directly or indirectly, and more control by them over information flows.

Similar developments have occurred in sectors not big enough to earn a recognised label of 'Big <Something>'. The coffee shop market has consolidated, with large chains like Starbucks expanding while thousands of small independent cafes have disappeared. The market for second-hand cars has become dominated by a few companies using the internet as the place of sale, replacing thousands of small backyard dealerships that used to sell cars on-site. The markets for garden supplies, toys, pubs, and so on have all become concentrated in the hands of a few large chains, while small independent bricks-and-mortar businesses have suffered huge attrition.

---

283 https://www.tradingview.com/symbols/FX-FAANG/

The control of workers and small businesses over their own lives had been under the cosh for a while, but the pandemic worsened this diminution of power. This is clearer in the US than elsewhere in the West.

During the Great Fear in the US, the groups with the highest education and best prior work experience, which is to say those with the characteristics of the top 25% of income earners in January 2020, were actually more likely to have jobs in June 2021 than they were at the outset of 2020. They have done fine and in fact you could say they've had a good pandemic.[284]

On the other hand, those with the educational and work experience characteristics of the bottom 25% of earners in January 2020 had still not regained about a quarter of their jobs in June 2021. The International Labour Organisation, a long-running statistical organisation that is usually on the side of trade unions, had already documented many aspects of the rapid increase in 'precarious work' before 2020.[285] Scholars in the US had claimed some 15% of the workforce were in 'alternative' (read: insecure and low-paid) work arrangements in 2015, a 50% increase since the 1980s.[286] This all got worse during the Great Fear.

To put it bluntly, the economic losses during Covid in the US were non-existent for the top bracket but glaring for the bottom-feeders. This is why some commentators called the lockdowns a 'ruling class privilege'.[287] Similar developments, though less dramatic, have been documented for Europe and other rich regions.[288]

This illustrates today's feudalism. The vast majority of workers now, in one way or another, are almost completely dependent on a small number of very large companies. Most workers must now sign long contracts forcing them into all kinds of financial and behavioural straitjackets before being able to earn money from their labour. People have gone from being proud small business owners and independent workers to being pawns of large businesses. The 'precariousness' of work has increased, with more workers on temporary contracts, casual contracts, contracts with no or few guaranteed hours, or

---

284 We refer here to the employment graphs at https://tracktherecovery.org/ which aim to track groups of workers in different quartiles. Since they do not follow individuals over time, they essentially track over time the employment outcomes of individuals with characteristics that predict their January 2020 job outcomes, which is something calculable each month.

285 See the discussion in Rudolph et al. (2021).

286 Katz & Krueger (2019).

287 Tucker (2021), https://brownstone.org/articles/lock-down-policies-reflect-ruling-class-privilege/

288 E.g., Major et al. (2021).

insecure lease arrangements.[289] Even workers with permanent jobs are now less autonomous than they were 30 years ago.[290] This disempowerment brings forced compliance with the rules of those companies. Workers must not rock the boat, say anything that embarrasses the company, violate its dress code or do anything else that the company frowns upon, if they want to keep their jobs.

Things were much the same in the feudal society of the European Middle Ages. Although it now seems very strong and will undoubtedly be a dominant force in the coming months and years, we think neo-feudalism is now at its high point and will subside despite the formidable coalition in favour of it. The reason to doubt its ability to become the dominant 'new way' is that neo-feudalism is inefficient and therefore vulnerable to challenge by countries, and coalitions of countries, that oppose it and offer an alternative.

At the individual level, the inherent weakness of the neo-feudal system as it is now, in mid-2021, is seen in the theft of people's confidence and zest for life as they are belittled and told in many ways that they are inferior and worthy of blame.[291] This creates resentment. At the system level, today's neo-feudalism carries a huge overhead of useless regulations, enforcers and ideologues. This 'bullshit industry' of pointless work produces rules and habits that are destructive of both productivity and happiness, while achieving nothing that helps us move forward. Such an encumbered system should be outcompeted by something better.

Another weak point of today's neo-feudal system is its ill-suitedness to the reality that the vast majority of production in Western countries is generated by educated people rather than by unskilled labourers working

---

289 Kalleberg (2018).

290 Lopes et al. (2014).

291 Such messages are seen, for example, in the notion that just by consuming, an individual is bad because he causes climate change; that expressing disagreement with the dominant narrative being offered by the media is categorically wrong-headed; or that failing to follow a nominated procedure around 'Occupational Health and Safety', 'Diversity and Inclusion', or other favoured processes is bad. See Chapter 8 for more discussion.

on the land, as in the Middle Ages. The value generated and captured by Big Tech, Big Pharma, Big Media and other large companies is produced by well-educated workers. Without them, a company would very quickly be replaced by competitors, even today.

This matters because education cannot be taken away from people once they have it, something not true of land, which was the main resource held by medieval workers. Land can be taken away or taxed directly at any time. Educated workers are immune from any threat that the value of their educational investments will be stolen or taxed away: what is in their heads remains there. They want to feel good about themselves and to be bossed around as little as possible. For this reason, when continuously lorded over and belittled they will eventually choose to migrate to other countries or companies, or set up their own businesses, taking their education with them.

This effective market power limits how badly 'Big X' companies can treat their educated workers and more broadly places a natural limit on the dominance of modern neo-feudalism. One might think that the 'solution' for barons is then to advocate a reduction in education, but a nation that stops educating people becomes far less productive and thus less powerful, so this alternative is also not an option for Western countries.

In sum, neo-feudalism cannot dominate Western countries because it will be countered by the education embodied in most Western workers, and the desire and ability of people to move towards more pleasant, more productive societies. The giant overhead of inefficient bullshit that accompanies modern neo-feudalism is also a big long-term burden that limits the degree to which neo-feudalism can become the dominant dynamic in the West.

If we are not heading towards a self-perpetuating neo-feudalist coalition of large companies and sin-shouting political elites, what longer-term structure of Western countries will emerge? Such things are very hard to predict. There are signs though that a more nationalistic constellation of countries featuring much more participatory democracy is taking shape as the superior alternative package.

The last 20 years have seen frequent experimentation in the US and European states with local forms of participatory democracy, such as citizen assemblies that draft new laws to be decided on in local referenda. These trials began to flourish partly in response to the problems with power being concentrated away from the citizenry.[292] The move to greater nationalism because of distrust with 'internationalism' is similarly a feature of the last 20 years, exemplified by the majority of the UK voters supporting Brexit, a move often derogatorily described as 'populism'.[293] We think that more participatory local democracy and burgeoning nationalism are likely to fuse into a powerful package, and that some of the positive lessons of the Great Panic are likely to affect that package.

The Jasmines who opposed the Great Panic included many people with influence and talent who observed during 2020-21, sometimes with horror, how their countries really function. They will not so quickly forget. We suspect that the media structures they have built will increasingly be seen as more truthful and trustworthy than previous ones. Similarly, they have set up coalitions that nurture real debate and advice on health threats, as well as groups campaigning for more representative democracy. These initiatives can feed into a gradual renewal of citizen-oriented media, science, and politics in the coming years.

A related discovery likely to survive beyond the Great Panic is the value of diversity for countries and continents. The Great Panic showed the destructiveness of a single truth insisted upon by an obsessive crowd. Many Jasmines of the Covid period have recognised the strength inherent in a community

---

292 E.g., Sørensen & Torfing (2019).

293 For a similar analysis, see Berman (2019).

where many people radically disagree and try different things, led by their disparate beliefs. The 'radical diversity' delivered to decision-making by the presence in the public space of totally different truths will, in the long run, yield wiser outcomes for humanity. We expect it to outcompete neo-feudalism and monoculturalism, and to be embedded into Western institutions moving forward.

Consider how things played out in the United States. While most states and most highly influential Americans were fully on board with the Covid madness and the Illusion of Control, some states and minority groups disagreed and went their own way. South Dakota, with fewer than 1 million inhabitants, refused to instigate Covid restrictions and thrived. Its first copycats were from states ideologically close to South Dakota, like Florida and Texas. The clear success of those larger states in reviving a zest for life while observing no Covid apocalypse then became an extremely seductive example for others.

American youth flocked to the freer states to party. Businesses boomed in the states that opened earlier. Leaders in the more diehard Illusion of Control states became jealous and fearful of losing their own youth and businesses. In the end, the successful examples were followed not because of deep debates that convinced anyone through masterful argument, but because individuals and businesses flock to obvious success, no matter what nutty narratives are making the rounds.

THE ROLE OF RADICAL DIVERSITY

The diversity that nurtured state-by-state experimentation with Covid policy in the US contains many different truths. In South Dakota for example, the predominant sentiment was tremendous distrust of the mainstream media, with a sprinkling of gun enthusiasm and belief in conspiracies about the Washington elites. Before 2020, many Jasmines would have viewed at least some of these beliefs as crazy.

Yet the intelligence of individuals and that of a whole system can sometimes be at odds. Those parts of the US that many Jasmines would consider to harbour the dumbest individual beliefs hit upon some of the smartest system-wide policies during the Covid period. It is precisely the stubborn adherence to such alternative truths by feisty sub-groups that resulted in the American state-level experiments, and thereby allowed the whole of the US to see the folly of lockdowns earlier than many other countries.

The provocative takeaway is that the intelligence of a whole country is enhanced when it contains communities adhering to truths completely opposed to those of the intellectual elites. That takeaway is, moreover, a deep lesson from history that Western countries have embedded into their institutions over centuries. It has been remarked upon before by historians that competition between radically different systems leads Western countries to learn faster than more centralised places like China.

A famous example is seen in the adventures of Christopher Columbus, who was dismissed from several European courts when he asked them for ships to sail westward. He was convinced that the earth was round — or more accurately, kind of pear-shaped[294] — and that he would find land, but was turned away by courts who bought the mainstream truth that the earth was most definitely flat.

Columbus eventually found sponsors in the king and queen of Spain, who accepted the gamble that the earth might be round after all. They hoped Columbus would prove to be right and that a route to the west and access to rich new lands would increase their power. Ferdinand and Isabella, in their quest to steal a march on the other royal courts of Europe, took a gamble on Columbus' truth that paid off. In other examples too, giving alternative truths the benefit of the doubt led to discoveries that increased the influence of Europe as a whole.

---

294 https://www.sacred-texts.com/earth/boe/boe26.htm

More generally, radical diversity in truth sits at the heart of three pillars of Western civilisation: the market economy, democracy, and science. The rediscovery of the benefits of radical diversity during the Great Panic is perhaps the biggest good to come out of this saga. It is uplifting to rejoice in the value of such a modern re-unveiling.

The market economy at its best contains many companies, each run by leadership totally convinced of its own truths. They think they know the best way to make some product, provide some service or convince others to buy something. Their convictions lead them to invest in particular production processes, marketing strategies, tax strategies, worker compensation schemes and myriad other things. When they then compete with other companies for suppliers, clients and government favours, it is revealed whose beliefs worked best. More radical diversity in a market means a higher chance that someone indeed does have a good idea and that the system as a whole, thanks to the force of competition, will learn what works well.

For society to get the biggest prizes from the spawning of multiple truths, companies should neither adopt the same principles to start with nor even talk much to each other. They should dream in different directions, build different infrastructures, and then only upon entering a marketplace find out who has come up with the best package. The best creations will naturally be copied, followed by progress towards fresh ambitions through finding new truths to believe in.

The market system, at its best, combines extreme individual hubris with systemic humility. The political system governing a healthy market economy is a monument to acceptance of the fact that no one leader can know beforehand which truth works best. It doesn't pick winners, but rather humbly sets the rules of the game that allow space for multiple truths to go head-to-head. The system is not arrogant in itself but it exploits the innate arrogance and self-belief of ambitious individuals and their companies. It lets all the competing truths have a shot and permits most to fail. The benefits of the workable solutions are then shared by the rest. Systemic humility implicitly acknowledges that competition rather than diktat is the best route to discovery and progress for society as a whole.

It is not that particular politicians or groups within the political system in a healthy modern economy need to be humble or wise. It is rather that the implicit knowledge embedded in many different institutions and habits collectively maintains systemic humility.

Bees have almost no individual intelligence, but in their thousands can build beautiful honeycombs with stunning symmetry, showing a kind of collective intelligence. So too do human political systems have a humility and intelligence that is only revealed through interactions between humans. True political leaders reflect on the collective intelligence their systems possess and do their best to add consciously to that collective intelligence through well-considered edits to the habits and institutions of their societies.

What holds for markets also holds for science. Science works best when smart individuals and research groups gallop ahead, fuelled by some truth they have hit upon. Their conviction will make them invest in experiments, machinery and field trips. They will build whole intellectual structures around their convictions, manifested in mathematical theories, books and stories of causation. It is then on the shoulders of society as a whole to gradually judge who has come up with the best package in each field at any given moment, essentially in the same manner as 'the market' judges. Society eventually judges scientists' efforts by their results, which could be whether a rocket lands where it was supposed to, or whether an economic policy has enriched the country adopting it. Society's judgment might take many decades to be passed, and can be postponed by institutional barriers and outright corruption. However, success and failure are always somewhat visible in science, and so there is gradual learning.

In the core of democracy too sits a form of radical diversity. The separation of powers seen in modern democracies, for example, is a trick that European countries hit upon to avoid the recurrent problems that stemmed from power being too concentrated in one position, namely a king. In 18th-century France, where very powerful kings had ruled for a long time, society was becoming unhinged because the king and his court had no idea how to run the emerging economy of merchants and industrialists. Institutional thinkers like Montesquieu, on the basis of their historical research, realised that the system as a whole would be more stable and learn faster if power was not unified. He openly advocated a system of power in which the top would always be systematically distrusted and challenged.

Montesquieu wanted to split the power of the king into at least three pieces: the executive, the legislative and the judiciary. He envisioned those separate powers comprising three different groups of professionals. Each group would largely set its own rules as to how it functioned and recruited new workers, such as when the judiciary sets its own educational standards and rules for promotion. Even within the seats of executive and legislative power, radical diversity was actively sought in the form of constant open competition for places, via elections. Not only did Montesquieu want three totally different 'truths' baked into democracy via the separation of powers into competing groups, but even within those groups he imagined a perennial competition between new truths and old ones.

Montesquieu's advocacy of dispersing power was motivated by a desire not to weaken his country, but to strengthen it. His idea was not in the 'divide and rule' category like the sin stories discussed earlier, but borne of the desire to promote competitive cooperation. The diversity he sought was not mortal combat in which different groups in a country question the right of others to exist. Rather, he was thinking of a society in which truths and material interests were contested under a shared sense of belonging to a single overarching entity, namely the country as a whole. The preservation of systemic humility requires some ideal, such as the well-being of the country, that is shared across the diversity of perspectives housed in the system. Designing such a system is a tricky balancing act, and many thinkers of Montesquieu's time were not at all sure that the separation-of-powers idea struck the needed balance.

European countries did not adopt diversity quickly in the market, or in science, or in democratic institutions. For centuries, those who ruled the roost did their very best to hold on to central power and thereby perpetuate a single truth. The United States adopted Montesquieu-style ideas earlier than most, precisely because the early patriots feared the emergence of a king like the one from whom they had fled.

Competition between countries gradually compelled Europe to adopt the political structures that worked best, because countries that didn't got taken over or left behind by those that did. The route to embracing radical diversity involved all kinds of incremental steps and reversals, but its long march was unstoppable because it worked so well. Along the way, alternative systemic packages were tried, including various forms of totally centralised power, but time and again those alternatives failed.

Totalitarian systems like fascism and communism fail for reasons well reflected in the events of the Great Panic. A system that adopts a single truth and then concentrates power in one like-minded group becomes very stupid very quickly. The countries and regions that turned into Covid cults became stupid in many ways. Not only did they adopt policies that were extremely self-destructive, but their single-mindedness gave them blind spots. The very fact that their truth was not continuously, vigorously, and publicly challenged made them complacent and arrogant. This led to a cessation of true debate and shut down many paths of inquiry that would have helped hugely during this period, such as the reevaluation of alternative medical interventions.

The attention of top politicians and civil servants within the Covid cult countries was not drawn to the negative effects of their actions. Their advisors became too afraid to tell them of the unsustainability of their daily choices, whether those concerned government debt or the disruption of children's education. Worse, the advisors of central governments fell over themselves to lie to government officials and pretend that they had total control over the virus. Without countervailing powers, central governments empowered by 'emergency declarations' became easy targets for flattery and misdirection. Bullshitters were all over them like flies at an Aussie barbecue.

This is exactly how events have unfolded before in totalitarian systems, for example in Nazi Germany, the Soviet Union and the French royal court of the 18th century. Absolute power leads to immense confidence on the part of the powerful in their truth. This confidence blinds them to both opportunity and danger. Without ever-present examples of others around them who think differently and are experimenting with different things, elites with total power become complacent and end up doing stupid things that lead ultimately to their demise. The bullshitters seduce them, but reality ultimately intervenes in their dreams of control, showing them the hard way that our societies are far too complex to understand and direct from a central seat.

The actual span of control of the totalitarian systems of history proved far less vast than the illusions of control that the bullshitters promised. Ironically, the leaders of these regimes would have retained some degree of power for longer had they surrounded themselves with people who totally disagreed with them.

The great gain of the Great Panic is a renewed awareness of the benefits of radical diversity, of complete disagreement about what the truth is, and of strong competition between regions and businesses on the basis of their own truths.

Going forward, the challenge is how to bake more radical diversity into our systems as a whole, which will involve somehow dismantling the excessive centralisation now in place. The countries that manage to adopt this direction of institutional change will likely be copied by others and win out over countries that do not, just as has been the case for the last 500 years.

What is termed 'radical diversity' above has often been referred to by prior thinkers as 'freedom'. The Enlightenment thinkers recognised the advantages of letting individuals and groups have freedom of thought, of ownership, of religion, of expression, and so on. In that sense there is nothing really new about these arguments, which is why we call this a time of rediscovery. We use the term 'radical diversity' rather than 'freedom' to highlight the mechanism through which individual freedom yields group-level benefits — something not immediately obvious, even to those taught for many years about the supposed benefits of freedom.

'Freedom' on its own does not necessarily lead to a system featuring lots of different truths that rub shoulders in competitive coexistence, combining individual hubris and systemic humility. It is quite possible that many free people repeatedly hearing the same things would all freely decide to agree on the same truth. We authors confess to previously having thought that would be a good outcome, educated as we were in the idea of a single truth: an 'optimal way' of doing something, as taught in economics. We did not see that the emergence and establishment of a single truth is dangerous, even if it is our own truth. To maintain a healthy system, not only is innovation required as time progresses, but at any specific point in time a lot of disagreement, even of the crazy variety, is needed.

The institutional changes we advocate in the ensuing pages are designed to help a system as a whole to actively resist total consensus of thought. A healthy system must invent and promote disagreement if there is too much consensus going around. In a market economy that supports a reasonable amount of competition, individual hubris will usually be enough to generate real diversity, but in science and government there are now many mechanisms that produce anti-social consensus.

The challenge we address in the remaining pages is to discover how both science and government can be broken up a bit more, not into chaotic and inefficient free-for-alls, but into healthily competing centres of truth.

LESSONS FOR SCIENCE – HOW WE CAN REFORM IT

The Great Panic taught us that many scientists today are herd animals with a limited commitment to conducting or disseminating actual science. They used their training to rationalise what the public and the powerful want to hear. Academic journals and academic societies have been shown to do the same.

This rationalisation often involves an implicit flipping of the burden of proof, as discussed at length in Chapter 6. For example, so-called scientific appeals for lockdowns on the basis of the 'precautionary principle' during the Covid period implicitly asked others to prove that the risks of Covid were not so extreme as to require dramatic 'precautionary' steps. In this framing, it was simply assumed that lockdowns would help with something. In normal times, taking dramatic steps must be justified by their proponents.

Science also served as an excuse-maker during the Second World War, and at moments in history when whole societies have been in the grip of communist or anti-communist sentiment. In each case, scientists working for one side or the other made themselves available as tools to rationalise the opinions of their side. That this held for social scientists during the Great Panic may surprise few, but the pattern of 'working for the team' proved no different for medical scientists, physicists, and other practitioners of the 'hard' sciences. When their societies and governments centralised around a single truth, then confirmation of that truth is what the sciences of all stripes started to deliver.

We expect the same to happen the next time populations transform into crowds that lose their minds, and history suggests no way to shield society from this dynamic. Indeed, if scientists don't go along with the follies of their societies at such a moment, they will probably be set aside. This is exactly what happened in the Great Panic: many top epidemiologists, virologists, and other scientists were set aside when they did not parrot the story that populations wanted to believe.

Yet the end of the Great Panic does allow the opportunity for a rejuvenation of science. Long lists of alleged scientists have revealed themselves during this period to be non-scientists. There are also lists of scientists who were willing to defy the Covid crowds and argue their case in the presence of censorship and abuse, embodying the ideals of science. Those lists can now be used by academic journals, academic societies, hiring boards and government enquiries interested in reforming their education and practices. Reforms will not prevent the next emotional wave from infecting scientists as a group, but as is normal for the end of a conflict, the system updates with new knowledge about the mistakes that were made.

In particular, the Covid period has shown the huge value of cost-benefit analysis based on well-being. This approach proved able to deliver quick, roughly correct judgments about the losses involved in social distancing measures, lockdowns, school closures and reductions in future government services.

We have written about ways to institutionalise this approach and the rules of thumb it delivered that proved so useful during the Great Panic.[295] The suffering that was invisible in the media was made visible, and therefore potentially actionable, in the well-being data produced during this period. Using these data and the cost-benefit approach, we predicted on the record the losses of the Panic in March 2020.[296] Those predictions have proven to be far more accurate than the predictions of most of the models of Covid's trajectory.

The rediscovery of the importance of radical diversity could also be applied in science more generally. Like politics, science in Western countries has

---

295 Frijters et al. (2020).

296 Frijters (2020A), https://clubtroppo.com.au/2020/03/18/has-the-coronavirus-panic-cost-us-at-least-10-million-lives-already/

become a monoculture. The same research ethics rules apply for everyone, undergraduate students everywhere use more or less the same first-year textbooks, a small group of top journals dominates every discipline, the same language is used by all within a discipline, and on and on.

This monoculture has emerged for understandable competitive reasons. Students wanted degrees recognised everywhere in the world, which necessitated that cohorts in different universities and countries received a roughly equivalent education. Scientists increasingly participated in a global job market, which meant that their PhD education had to become similar the world over. League tables based on publications and impact were increasingly based on a narrow range of journals and judges, pushing the system further towards a monoculture in jargon and in what was considered 'top science'.

The Great Panic has uncovered the staleness and intellectual weakness of modern science's monoculture. The monoculture made it harder for individual groups of scientists to escape the groupthink of their discipline, which slowed down the discovery process. The policy disasters that fuelled the Global Financial Crisis of 2008-2010 also related to a monoculture — that time in economics — but the pressures coming out of the GFC were still not strong enough to lead to institutional changes in economics or other disciplines. Sure, there was some hand wringing and finger pointing, but soon the forces gravitating towards monoculturalism simply overwhelmed the small alternative schools of thought that had briefly blossomed post-GFC.

BREAKING UP THE MONOCULTURE

One remedy for the present monoculture of science that suggests itself is to set up and directly subsidise alternative schools of thought in every discipline.

Imagine that the European Science Foundation every year allocated €100 million to one team of mid-career scientists who want to establish a school of thought in direct competition with the orthodoxy in their disciplines. That €100 million would be distributed in yearly instalments of €5 million — enough to guarantee about 20 full-time academic jobs plus support staff for 20 years, a sufficient base on which to set up a genuinely new line of thinking. The selected team would need to have a supporting university, or set up their own, with a reasonable number of students for whom a new curriculum would be developed.

With its 20 years' worth of secure funding, this team would have the chance to develop its own jargon, research culture and ethics rules, bound only by the laws of land.

Each year, the European Science Foundation would start a new school of thought in a different discipline, so that over a cycle of 10 years a radically different philosophy would emerge in 10 different disciplines. After 20 years the subsidy would stop, so only those new schools of thought that had proven themselves in terms of attracting students, scholars and sponsors would live on. Just as with business start-ups, the vast majority of sponsored teams would fail to establish themselves and simply fade away once the subsidy — essentially a government-funded venture capital investment — ceased.

How would deserving teams be selected? In the current environment, the European Science Foundation, for whom the authors have done a few jobs, would undoubtedly select an insider team whose decisions would accentuate the monoculture within disciplines rather than challenging it. Unsurprisingly, the Foundation is entirely monocultural itself. It engages insiders as reviewers and deciders, it judges scientists on how well they have done inside the institutions that traditionally confer academic status, and it has uniform rules on research ethics, grant writing and so on. It is 100% part of the problem and would undoubtedly make things worse if it were given the job of allocating €100 million each year to a 'new school of thought'.

The only thing that can break the hold of insiders, or indeed any powerful individual with an agenda, is to build in an element of randomness. An appealing means of doing this would be to involve complete outsiders as key decision makers. The goal would be to take the allocation decision out of the hands of insiders and place it in the hands of the one group that stands to benefit from increased diversity, which is to say the population as a whole.

Of course, some expertise from within the existing discipline would still be required because a jury of Joe and Josephine Sixpacks cannot do it all by themselves. Our suggestion is a two-chambered jury, both randomly selected: one somewhat expert and the other not.[297]

Consider how this might work in economics. Thirty citizens are randomly selected each year from the European Union to occupy seats on the 'citizen jury' of the European Science Foundation. Thirty people are also randomly selected from amongst those who studied economics in the past but no longer work as economists. These people sit on the 'economic jury' of the European Science Foundation, a body formed only in a year in which economics is the discipline scheduled to receive the new-truth subsidy.

The object is to find and appoint a team of ambitious, promising young economic scientists interested in setting up a new school of thought. The 'economic jury' is tasked with finding, say, 10 candidate teams in different European countries. The 'citizen jury' then selects the one it most prefers from that group of 10. Both juries decide entirely independently how they go about their search and their deliberations.

At the core of this proposal is trust that the population, not academics or government, is best placed to recognise reasonable independent groups of scientists. It uses a form of inclusive democracy in the service of bringing more radical diversity to science, for the ultimate benefit of society as a whole. Like radical experimentation in markets and democracy, such a system should

---

297 The notion of involving juries of citizens in the awards of prizes is widespread. When looking in the literature for prior thinkers with similar ideas to ours, we found that Simon Threlkeld already 25 years ago suggested using juries for appointments of many Canadian public officials (Threlkeld 1997). Here we take that idea further still.

not be expected to select 'the best' people, which is a monocultural idea as it supposes that there is a single truth that can be used as a reference point for judging what is 'best'. Rather, our proposal is designed to generate the diversity in truth required to lead to a better system as a whole.

HOW DO WE FORTIFY SOCIETY AGAINST THE NEXT GREAT PANIC?

The lesson that many alert politicians have so far taken from the Great Panic is that it is possible to make the public obsess over a disease to the exclusion of all else, and then amass huge personal power and wealth for as long as they can keep the obsession going. As things stand, that is a rather ominous sign. Future politicians will take note and want in by creating new public fixations. The very minimum that must happen to prevent the next Great Panic, then, is to change the incentives of politicians.

The next generation of politicians is more likely to choose a more proportionate response to a new threat if they know that something bad happened to the previous generation that betrayed their people. The best solution in this space would be to uphold the Nuremberg Code against the politicians who presided over Covid. The Nuremberg Code crucially demands that public policy be oriented towards public health as a whole.[298] When it comes to mass public health experiments, like lockdowns or vaccines, the 6th Nuremberg Code demands that the decision maker must have the reasonable view that the benefits of the intervention will be higher than the costs. Failure to abide by this code is a crime against humanity, recognised as such since the 1950s.

Western politicians in early 2020 did not try to ascertain whether their policies would do more good than harm, nor were their advisors bound by that condition. They simply went along with the mania and the loud calls of much of the population to do something. In going along with the Panic, it

---

298 See https://en.wikipedia.org/wiki/Nuremberg_Code or Katz (1996).

can be argued that they broke the Nuremberg Code and the basic public health laws that are based on that code. The politicians and their advisors could therefore be arraigned as criminals and taken to face an independent court to be tried for their crimes against humanity. Many court cases started by human rights lawyers are now underway in Western countries following exactly this reasoning.[299]

Criminal convictions for the politicians who violated the Nuremberg Code during the Great Panic would serve as a warning to future politicians who find themselves in similar circumstances, where in the face of overwhelming demands from their populations they could become criminals. It would give them an incentive to more vigorously combat the wave of fear in their populations, and to act within the boundaries of the law.

If courts convicted top Covid-era politicians, it is also likely that many of the top civil servants and company directors who betrayed their duties would also be punished. This would help create better incentives for future generations of civil servants and company directors too.

But let's not indulge ourselves in fantasies here. We see almost no chance that justice will be served in this way. The reality in much of history is that top politicians who become criminals get away with their crimes. We don't even need to go far back in history to illustrate this. Which US general or politician went to jail for killing a million innocent Cambodians in the bombing raids of the 1970s? Which UK politician went to jail because of the clearly illegal Iraq war of 2003 that killed hundreds of thousands of civilians? Which European politician faced justice for the help they gave the American military in organising the torture of Islamic radicals by flying suspects to countries that would do the dirty deed? The answer is 'none'.

In other countries and at other critical moments in history, the story has

---

299 See https://www.fuellmich.com/ for regular updates by Reiner Fuellmich and companions.

been the same. The only occasion when politicians face real justice is when a powerful opponent overthrows them and proceeds to make an example out of them. That happened when the surviving German Nazi politicians were hauled in front of the Nuremberg tribunals by the Americans who occupied Germany after the Second World War. A more recent example was the trials of the Khmer Rouge leaders in Cambodia.

While they almost surely will not be held to account for their actions in court, the politicians of the Great Panic will still suffer some negative consequences. We suspect that their lives will be tough in the coming years as they are dragged from one inquiry to the next, and from one court case by victims to the next. The gradual return of common sense will mean a reevaluation of the actions of politicians during the Great Panic, which will be unpleasant for them. Particularly glaring examples of greedy politicians helping themselves to many millions during the Great Panic might well be punished. Political parties that were in hindsight seen to get it totally wrong might also face a reckoning in elections.

We think that in a few years' time, Western politics will be genuinely interested in the question of how to avoid a repeat. But truly going after the crimes of former politicians is not something their successors will have much of an appetite for. Our current crop of politicians will know a lot of nasty secrets that future politicians will not want to come out. And understandably, future politicians will not want the idea of taking their predecessors to criminal courts to become too popular. Usually, such considerations win out against calls for justice.

If we leave the fantasy world in which justice can be done, the question is what lesser actions can be taken that might be palatable politically in a few years' time.

One idea we have seen advocated by Sanjeev Sabhlok in Australia is for governments to instigate a 'Black Hat' commissioner whose job it would be to play devil's advocate against all proposed policies, in an attempt to embed real disagreement at the heart of government.[300] The hope is that such a commissioner would articulate a loud dissenting opinion on all policies that channels the interests of the wider public and future generations. We agree on the objective of a Black Hat commissioner, namely to inject genuine diversity into politics even in times of crisis, but we think that politicians will very quickly sabotage a Black Hat Commissioner.

Consider that in early 2020 Western countries had no shortage of supposedly independent advisory bodies. Places like France and the UK had many of them, ranging from planning bureaus to scientific councils, to independent statistical agencies, to Ombudsmen, to 'What Works Centres', and so on. They variously kept mum, joined in with the madness, failed to broadcast via the media, or only very quietly raised some tentative objections when talking to governments. They thus failed spectacularly, and we would expect no better from an official Black Hat Commissioner.

INDEPENDENT HEALTH AUTHORITIES

A different idea is to learn from what seems a good existing example, namely Sweden. For several years pre-Covid, Sweden had an independent health authority. Its chief scientist was Anders Tegnell, in turn supported by like-minded Swedish academics such as Johan Giesecke. This independent authority had 600 workers. The role of this body was to set health policy around viruses and similar biological threats in a manner independent of politics. When Covid erupted, its leaders had the authority to enact the blueprints that it had prepared for such an eventuality. No lockdowns, no coercion, full information and open debate became the order of the day.

Other countries could also organise their health systems along these

---

300 The 'tenth man' initiative within Israeli decision-making, adopted after the Yom Kippur war and discussed in Kaplan (2017), is a similar attempt to embed disagreement into institutional deliberations for the good of the group as a whole.

lines, establishing an independent state agency with full authority to decide on major health policies. After a few years, those agencies would become the normal custodians of such things as pandemic contingency plans, which while abruptly scrapped in many countries in March 2020 were in fact perfectly fine. The hope is that in a future Panic, those health agencies would act as the Swedish one did during Covid.

Would the Swedish health model work well in other countries? We admit that we doubt it. Sweden is far less corrupt than an awful lot of countries. As a result, Anders Tegnell truly was independent of politics and truly did feel that his role was to do his best for the Swedish population at large. The broad-based support in Swedish society for that kind of role and that kind of tenacity prevented Tegnell from being overruled by Swedish politicians for a long time, though they did eventually start to get to him at the end of 2020 when they sniffed an opportunity to increase their popularity by going along with the general global hysteria.

In many other countries, an independent health authority would probably be politically captured or totally ignored in a crisis. Independent institutions were sidelined *en masse* in most countries during the Great Panic when their message did not fit the hysteria. The UN did not cut through with its warnings on the impacts of lockdowns. Whole groups of doctors, lawyers and social scientists talking about the costs of policies were simply ignored, shouted over, and locked down along with the rest.

The reality in countries more corrupt than Sweden is that the heads of supposedly independent state agencies are not independent at all. Appointments to such posts are used as rewards for political loyalties and past political choices. A political animal who owes his position to having previously followed the party line will not change much when he spends a few years heading an 'independent' agency.

As a rule, in times of crisis governments very quickly surround themselves with others who agree, benching all the rest and offering a stark 'are you with us or against us?' choice for civil servants and leaders of 'independent' institutions. Once politicians are in panic mode, little that is within the government machinery can stop the political snowball. Help has to come from outside. Knowing that the snowballing is inevitable, the better challenge to tackle is how to stop governments entering panic mode in the first place when a threat emerges. The memory of criminal convictions for the previous mob who were panicked into becoming criminals, suggested above, may help.

The Swedish model is perhaps worth a try in less-corrupt countries with well-functioning institutions, like the Northern European nations and places like New Zealand and Singapore. In very corrupt countries, independent health agencies are simply another avenue for corruption, with their leadership likely only to further fan the next fear in the hopes of gaining wealth and power.

CITIZEN JURIES FOR OFFICIAL APPOINTMENTS

Another idea is to directly confront the entrenched monoculture of Western politics with more independent thinking and alternative truths, so as to weaken the tether between policy settings and wealthy special interests. How to do this?

Just as they can assist in deciding which schools of new thought to subsidise, thereby helping to break the monoculture in science, citizen juries could also be used successfully to create more diversity in Western politics. Citizen juries made up of, say, 20 random citizens could be given the role of deciding who will run important institutions. One jury, one top position.

We do not envision that citizen juries would appoint senior politicians, but rather that they would appoint the key people within the government bureaucracies who work with the senior politicians — the Sir Humphrey Applebys of the world.[301] Democratic processes would still elect politicians,

---

[301]Sir Humphrey Appleby is the British policy 'mandarin' in the British sit-com series 'Yes, Minister' and 'Yes, Prime Minister'. He is the career civil servant running the country behind the scenes.

but citizen juries would appoint the heads of government departments, the central bank, the planning bureaus, the ombudsman, the statistical agency, the public universities, the public media, and so on.

The usual objection by political insiders is that one cannot trust the citizens to appoint someone like the head of the central bank or the planning bureau because they don't have the required 'expertise'. Yet these are the same power brokers and politicians who also like to say that you have to trust the voter.

Giving random citizens the power to appoint important people is an old idea in democracy. It was popular in Athens and Rome two thousand years ago, and also worked well for centuries in Florence and Venice until around 1800. Citizen juries were pivotal in appointing the leaders of those cities.[302]

The historical experience is that citizens are apt to behave quite reasonably when they are given actual power to decide something important. This is why the jury system is relied upon in courts of law, where achieving 'justice' is the core objective. Lack of expertise is simply not that relevant. We think citizens should be trusted to decide for themselves how important they think expertise is for a given role, and they should also be trusted to find and then use any relevant expertise in making their decision. If politicians can find experts and use their advice, then so can citizen juries.

A great advantage of having heads of government ministries and state institutions elected by citizen juries is that those leaders will then be far more diverse. They will be independent both of the current politicians and of the huge state machinery. Citizens do not want their country led by buffoons, careerists or destructive mavericks. They want to live in a well-run country, so they have every incentive to pick people who will do a decent job and not pick fights with politicians or with the departments they lead.

Just as the citizens of Venice ended up with pretty good leaders for

302Dowlen (2008).

centuries because their citizens wanted good leaders, so too should we expect the use of citizen juries today to lead to reasonably good picks. It would be a powerful way to combat both the corruption and the monoculture of current politics. For this reason, we firmly expect current politicians to hate the idea, just as the elites in Europe resisted the ideas of true science, market economics, and democracy for centuries.

Why not instead hold elections for leadership positions in ministries and independent agencies? The big problem with elections is that because there are many voters, each individual citizen has so negligible an effect on the overall outcome that there is little incentive for her to pay close attention. That makes voters as a group easy prey for those who dominate the information flows, which is to say those with the most money. Another disadvantage of elections for dozens of posts every year is that they would become a nuisance to the citizens themselves. In the jury system, by contrast, an individual citizen would serve maybe once in her whole lifetime. Citizens' efforts would be concentrated and independent, rather than diffuse and for sale.

Another drawback of elections is that they do not involve real deliberation, by which we mean reasonable people sitting together to figure out complex things. In the lead-up to elections, people listen to soundbites in the media. They hear different messages but they don't usually work through issues with others, or see things from different angles using different knowledge. The alternative of real deliberation is very powerful. It happens in teams, cabinets and boardrooms, essentially because the members then openly listen and share, and better outcomes result.

Each member of a citizen jury tasked with deciding something really important feels truly consulted and valued. All members then pay far more attention than voters would in an election. Also, deliberations between random people about something very specific, such as whom to appoint to a post or whether to convict someone, have a community-creating dynamic to them.

History and our own experience in courtroom juries reveal that people do their best in such situations and become cooperative rather than competitive. Juries bring out the best in citizens, while elections can often bring out their worst.

There are many key questions on how citizen juries could be organised. At the risk of overwhelming the reader with detailed practical advice, we sketch below in just over 600 words our best suggestion on how to set up a whole system of appointments by citizen juries. For this we draw on various elements initially suggested by Terry Boudicious and Simon Threlkeld (but not necessarily endorsed by them).[303]

- A purely administrative organisation would organise the citizen jury elections, their communication systems, their expenses, and so on. That administrative function could sit within a current electoral organisation, like an electoral commission that organises a country's democratic elections.

- Relevant laws would be changed to read that all top positions in organisations with some minimal number of workers (e.g., 100) that also receive some minimal fraction of their income from the government (e.g., 20%) are decided upon by a citizen jury. The politicians and organisations familiar with the position to be filled would set the powers and amenities (such as salaries) of that position but filling the vacancy would be up to the citizen jury.

- Jury members would be chosen randomly from the whole population, with jury duty compulsory and with hefty fines for refusal to serve. The jury itself would decide how to search for candidates, how to proceed in evaluating them, and whom

303 See the discussion at https://equalitybylot.com/2021/07/01/guest-post-from-paul-frijters/

to appoint. The jury would deliver an appointee decided by majority vote, a report on its decision, and a justification for its expenses. The jury could call on any help, with the backing of the administering organisation of all the citizen juries.

- Until its decision is made, the composition of a jury would be secret. Potentially interested applicants for the top position being filled would know of the job opening and its minimal description, but jury membership would be strictly confidential.

- Accompanying the citizen jury structure, an independent 'sortition commission' would be established, made up of a limited number of fixed-term commissioners (say, 7 members each serving 4-year terms) that are themselves appointed by a jury. This commission would function like the executive of the citizen jury system, helping to smooth out hiccups. It would organise stand-ins (found by juries tasked with finding people for a stand-in list) for top positions in the event that one of the incumbents in a top position falls extremely ill. It would quickly set up new juries if there are suddenly more positions to fill or some other emergency arises. The commission would also be the champion of the system, in charge of coming up with new ideas on how to improve the jury system, to find more uses for juries, to organise those who served on juries previously and want to help ('jury alumni'), and so on. Ideally, major changes suggested by the sortition commission would need to pass the occasional 'sortition parliament', a short-lived rule-making body with randomly chosen members. The sortition parliament could then decide whether to take up the commission's suggestions, such as changing the number of jury members or how to find them.

- Together, the jury administration, citizen juries, sortition commission, and sortition parliament would constitute a parallel democratic system with the narrow duty of appointing the top layer of the public sector. It would not decide on government policies or budgets, and those appointed by it would still be bound by laws and directions coming from the existing political system.

We offer the blueprint above as a conversation starter on how to do this. It is deliberately much more minimalistic than many other suggested democratic reforms, so as to keep it totally focussed on the role of juries in making appointments.

This is not some big utopian project. It is a pragmatic suggestion for putting within reach the obvious big gain of breaking the hold of politicians and barons over top appointments in the public sector. Once the power of the current barons over the public sector is broken and the latter is once more independent and less afflicted by the bullshit that now drags it down, new ideas are sure to come to many parts of the citizenry. This is why it makes sense to have a standing sortition commission that can channel those ideas.

As with courtroom juries, there are many smaller details involved in how they would operate in reality. How would they be shielded from media propaganda during their deliberations? Where would they be housed? What if the appointed person resigns quickly? Who would fund them? What if the jury feels it cannot make a decision? What list of citizens is the basis for being on a jury? These questions will need to be answered according to local habits and practical constraints, with adjustments made as problems arise or good examples emerge. This is no different to the case of courtroom juries, where such details also differ from place to place.

INSTITUTIONALISED SERENITY

Our final suggestion recognises that the Great Covid Panic started as an international emotional wave, much like a hurricane building up over the oceans before it crashes over the land of a particular country at full strength. Even citizen jury-appointed leaders might well be swept along in such waves of emotion, just as much of the population of the Western world was swept along. Our final idea is to confront this dynamic head-on by creating an international institution whose role it is to fight global waves of panic.

We have an extensive blueprint for how this can be done[304] but at heart it is simple. This international organisation would have the job of reading the world media landscape as if it were a weather system, picking up gathering panics when they first emerge, tracking them as they migrate across borders and languages, and organising the defences of the countries that are in their paths and that have a good chance of weathering the storm.

The basic hope in setting up such an organisation, which we call the World Anti-Hysteria Organisation (WAHO), is that it could alert like-minded governments early that a large panic is building with significant policy implications, just as the Great Covid Panic was building in January 2020 and headed in the direction of lockdowns.

The WAHO would make policy direction judgments as early as possible, requiring the use of on-call scientists, but its primary role would be as an early-warning system for well-run governments. Alerted governments would then know what might be coming and have enough time to organise a countermovement in the media and in science against the approaching panic. They might even choose to temporarily shut down the social media system, much like stock markets altruistically freeze trading in the midst of selling frenzies. In general terms, the WAHO would alert and then help like-minded

---

304 Frijters (2021C), https://clubtroppo.com.au/2021/03/17/a-world-anti-hysteria-organisation/

governments organise fast against an incipient panic on the basis of what helped nip in the bud or extinguish previous panics.

The task of watching and then acting appropriately on the enormous flows of information on the world's social and mainstream media channels is formidable. It would first require the development of artificial intelligence systems that can spot an emerging panic. Then it would need the ability to analyse the panic, understand its policy trajectory and judge whether that trajectory is or isn't leading towards dangerous waters. Years and thousands of workers would be needed to develop the expertise to discharge this role.

Supposing the technical challenges could be met, the main remaining challenge in the design of the WAHO is to make sure it does not become part of the problem. Clearly it should not have direct policy-setting power. Even with the limited mandate to warn of impending panics, however, the WAHO could easily start impending panics, much like the boy who cried wolf too many times. It could easily be in the interests of a WAHO staffed by increasingly corrupted leaders to exaggerate some threats, like those of political opponents, and downplay other threats that were started by friendly governments.

A key question is who would run the WAHO. Would tasking a citizen jury with appointing the leadership work to prevent political capture? Perhaps, but only if the WAHO were clearly tied to a specific large population that shared some broad interest. Perhaps Europe as a whole could set up such an institution with a leadership appointed by a jury of European citizens.

An alternative means of establishing an independent WAHO is for a coalition of interested parties to simply ask some Scandinavian government to set one up. The Americans, or NATO, or Europe, or the UN, or a billionaire could provide the funds and ask, say, the Swedish government to house and organise the WAHO in Sweden. If this were to happen, we feel Anders Tegnell would be a great hire.

MORE TAKEAWAYS

Above are our main ideas about how our societies' institutions can be strengthened. These ideas are in areas we have worked in for decades, and therefore in which we think we have something sensible to say. Yet the Great Panic threw up many problems in realms that are much less clearly within our purview as economists. We want to mention briefly the lessons that we perceive in those realms.

One issue is the relationship our societies have with death. A 'healthy' relationship is one in which death is seen as a normal part of life, an inevitable end that is only marginally different from the many ways in which we fade over time anyway. In a relaxed view of death, no one remains the same person over time, so we all die a little each moment just as a slightly new person is born within us each moment. Our final deaths should be moments we say goodbye to our loved ones and take pride and joy in the quality of the life we spent.

During the Great Panic, fear of death by Covid was whipped up to absurd levels, making the issue of death more generally problematic for years to come. Every other possible cause of death can now be further milked by those who profit from it, something that takes away from the quality of life and even the length of life. Staring blindly at one risk, as we have seen over the past 18 months, is to the detriment of dealing sensibly with all risks.

Many observers have already said this, but we find it hard to see how better conversations around death can break through anytime soon. Instead of a spiritual maturation in how our societies view death, we have witnessed an infantilisation. The relationship with death that has been encouraged is that of a mindless teenager who believes she will live forever if only Covid is dealt with.

This is a total absurdity, but one that matches the shallowness of interactions in social media and fits a society increasingly obsessed with image. It fits, more broadly, many developments over the past 20 years in how people interact with others and present themselves to partners, employers and social groups. The infantilisation of death has coincided with the infantilisation of much of morality, personal interactions, and political life.

While it is tempting to blame this or that group in the West for this infantilisation, we think it is not specific to the West, or to any group within it. After all, we saw most of the world give in to the Great Panic, including the East Asian countries with very different cultures.

What is signalled by the infantilisation of death is to our minds deeper than the 'simpler' problem of Panics, political abuses, or crowd behaviour. What is signalled is the infantilisation of wide swathes of our lives that have become hostage to an obsession with image and influence. The constant connection to the promises and projections of others through the relentless presence of what the rest of the world shows us on our mobile phones, email and social media makes for shallow interactions and thus shallow minds. We all start to fall in line with the habit of 'looking good', projecting a false image to others of how we manage effortlessly to do the impossible.

To reverse this trend requires a radical break with the continuous digital connection to the rest of the world. Whole communities could for example disable distance communication, having mobile phone and internet-free periods of the day. Living a life with fewer constant distractions and images from others would allow growing depth of thought and private self-development. But how can this come about? Constant connection is totally built into people's modern economic and social lives, so it seems unthinkable that individuals would willingly divorce from it. Moving away from constant connection will require experimentation by individuals, companies and countries.

One approach that is intuitively appealing is to treat compulsive attention to mobile phones as substance abuse, or an addiction like to drugs, alcohol or tobacco. Treatments would then include a mix of counselling, group and individual therapy, retreats, rehab clinics, substitution therapy and so on. We could even see the treatment of phone addiction becoming a niche in psychotherapy and spawning a whole new line of wellness businesses.

Another issue lying outside our direct expertise is how to embed remembrance of the folly of the Great Panic. The Europeans tried to remember the folly of the First World War by erecting monuments and staging remembrance days. The attempt to remember the madness of the First World War didn't do Europe much good though, as it failed to prevent the next one from erupting in the same generation. Remembering the Great Panic in a way that is useful will be similarly difficult. This is the kind of question that artists are better at answering than economists. More creative emotional types may be able to better capture the spirit of our times, and to do so in images and rituals that have a chance of making populations remember the lessons of the folly.

Next, how to make a dent in the huge bullshit industry that thrives on exaggeration and gratuitous virtue signalling? Our argument is that an increasingly neo-feudal society will naturally beget new forms of bullshit, produced by artists who belittle the weak while flattering and weaving a protective layer of myths around the powerful. The bullshit then is the symptom, not the cause, meaning the challenge is to counter the neo-feudalist tendencies of our era. For example, we might target reducing inequality, and more generally taking the uber-rich and their organisations down a peg. How to do this?

As the historian Scheidel said,[305] the inequality of bygone civilisations has only been observed to ease after disasters like wars, floods and social collapse. Disasters did not merely directly destroy physical and financial assets such as buildings and currencies, but just as importantly they created fanatics who wanted to change society. Those fanatics were willing to defy the wealthy people in charge, which led to quite a few of them being offed before success arrived.

We agree with Scheidel. The implication is that we need to look around for

---

305 Scheidel (2018).

possible sources of fanaticism that are less deadly than wars or total societal collapse, yet still carry an ideology that is pro-change and anti-inequality.

One suggestion we have raised elsewhere[306] is a peculiar kind of religious fanaticism involving a harmless obsession with constructing our own gods. The basic idea is that if whole populations became involved in building divine artificial intelligence machines, then the fanaticism involved in that project would make currently powerful humans seem rather mundane by comparison and thus easier to challenge. We are not very convinced of this idea ourselves and it carries many possible risks. We see it merely as one reasonably peaceful solution to the extremely difficult question of how to generate the fanaticism needed to successfully challenge the people in charge. A more realistic route to reducing inequality is the more violent one to which we have become accustomed throughout history: angry crowds charging over the ramparts of the castles of the rich.

Many other pressing problems confront us today, including a changing climate, degradation of much of the environment, the growing ranks of parasitic professions (think of divorce lawyers or tax advisors), the rivalry between superpowers, and religious tensions. Yet, these problems were not central to the emergence or strength of the Covid panic. The wave of panic and the subsequent abuse that occurred was a worldwide phenomenon, independent of any other pressing issue. We leave those other problems to be the focus of further commentary elsewhere.

---

306 https://www.themintmagazine.com/good-god

CONCLUSIONS

The Great Covid Panic started with fear and a primitive call for human sacrifices in the form of nonsensical lockdowns. Over time the Panic transformed into a big push by a new coalition of politicians and big companies towards a neo-feudal society wherein the vast majority has little freedom in either their personal or their work lives. The development towards neo-feudalism preceded the pandemic but many additional elements were put in place during the Panic, such as mass surveillance, mass censorship, travel restrictions for the vast majority, and the idea that freedom is something governments can give or withhold, rather than a fundamental right.

What should have happened early in 2020, what should ideally happen now, and what can we realistically do now?

Early in 2020, Western populations should have mobilised against the fear. Governments should have organised media campaigns warning of the folly of lockdowns, quarantines and other measures, pointing out how damaging and futile they would be. Panels of scientists should have convened to openly discuss the damage that various options would inflict. Honest discussions by medics should have made clear the small benefits that could be expected from hospital treatments of Covid, and the immense damage to population health of disrupting normal care and normal social life. In sum, vibrant communities should have been laughing at proposals for lockdowns and at the very idea that one could control diseases in such a way.

Unfortunately, the opposite happened. Many scientific journals and academic communities betrayed their missions. Many governments quickly folded to public pressure. Many opportunists poured into the halls of power to gorge themselves at the troughs full of easy money.

WHAT SHOULD HAPPEN NOW?

Ideally, there should now be justice and renewal. Politicians and medical advisors should be held to account, offending scientific journals (like *The Lancet*) should be abolished, and the halls of science should see soul-searching and a recognition that the core scientific mission was betrayed *en masse*. Parents should apologise to their children for disrupting their education and their childhood. Truth commissions should nurture open discussion of the stupidity of the last 18 months so that populations can come to terms with what they have been subjected to and often participated in.

To achieve renewal, the structures of institutionalised medical advice should be broken down and so too the whole zero-risk industry. The Big Tech companies and other 'Big' contributors to the madness should be broken up into smaller companies and taxed at reasonable rates. Citizen juries should make nearly all the top appointments that are currently decided by politicians. The royal courts of state, national and international governments should be cleansed of the bullshitters that now dominate, retaining only skeleton crews and skeleton regulation. In sum, the window of opportunity should be seized upon to clean up all the elements of our institutions that have proven corrupt, incompetent, or weak.

WHAT CAN WE REALISTICALLY DO NOW?

What should happen now is unfortunately not what can happen now. The reality is that the Jameses have gotten away with their theft and their increased control over others' lives, and this is not likely to be undone in a single 'big bang'. So what should we, the Jasmines of this world, now do? What realistically can we do to improve our societies and aim for a future in which the stupidity of the Great Covid Panic will not be repeated?

One thing to do is to paint and cherish a vision of a better future, while sharing hope and conviction that this vision can be achieved. In places where the Panic continues, this means continued resistance. In places where the Panic is now over and societies are starting to look for answers and lessons, the task is to convince others of a better way, and to rebuild.

The authors' vision for a better future is best described as a renewed Enlightenment. Just as the first feudal period came to end with Enlightenment, so must the second, more recent one, end with Enlightenment — involving a renewed appreciation of radical diversity, freedom of speech and thought, and the benefits of open-minded deliberation. Each person and institution can be arrogant and convinced of one truth, but the system as a whole must be ever agnostic and humble.

How can this come to pass? Those Western countries that are currently freer and more sensible than others should seize the opportunity to attract the many smart and ambitious individuals presently being devalued in their own countries. Countries that open for business and travel will motor ahead of others, but it is not only their own interests that will be served by their actions. Examples of successful countries ignoring the continuing madness of others will do more for the return of sanity everywhere than libraries full of wise words. Jealousy of others is a much stronger motivator than reams of statistics.

In countries still stuck in the Illusion of Control, Jasmines should consider building alternative structures to ensure their loved ones can live reasonably good lives. They could organise their own media, their own childcare, their own education and their own workplaces in a manner that celebrates reason and warm social contact. They should openly take the role of visionaries, thinking out loud about how their societies can be improved once the madness is over.

The abuse meted out by politicians, medical advisors and commercial interests during the Panic has held up a mirror to our societies. Now we know how bad it really is. We see how acutely politics has become a mono-culture, how captive our institutions are, how influential big companies have become, how gullible and state-led the media have become, and more. The severity of these problems varies by country, but the picture doesn't look great anywhere. Neo-feudalism is with us and we expect it to unwind only slowly. The reflection in the mirror forces us to ask what should happen next, both to avoid another Panic and to improve our societies in general.

One of the silver linings to have emerged from the Great Panic is that a lot of smart people have suddenly found themselves confronted with ugly truths about their own countries. People who used to be on the inside of powerful structures and favoured groups suddenly found themselves on the outside, and horrified at what they saw that they hadn't previously been aware of. Pre-Covid, they had never needed to acknowledge who was being left behind, or to understand why many of those protesting against the system were upset. Suddenly, problems became crystal clear to a whole layer of smart people who had previously been blind, happy members of the winning groups.

It is exactly these Jasmines, who know how the institutions of their societies work and have now suddenly seen how rotten various parts of them have become, who can become great visionaries. We eagerly invite them to spend time thinking about how to reform the hundreds of institutions we have — the legal system, the school system, the internet, the universities, the security services, the whole works. The authors are only able to analyse part of the whole picture, which limits our suggestions as to the way forward. The task of rebuilding is far too great for three thinkers to imagine. This task needs tens of thousands of thinkers in their own niches across many countries to analyse the problems and offer their suggestions on the optimal way forward.

This is just how it went with the first Enlightenment. In every country, many thinkers started to reimagine their societies. They started wondering what the roles of the barons and kings really were. They started contemplating seemingly impossible futures, like those with universal primary schooling and welfare states — things that are now reality in many countries. Some thinkers, like Montesquieu, wrote practical blueprints for how to reorganise society. The ideas of these thought leaders eventually led to constitutions and new forms of government and bureaucracy.

Before the Great Panic, meaningful debates about what our societies should look like were nearly impossible because the airwaves were so dominated by bullshitters and grandstanding politicians. Any attempt at open deliberations would be swamped by the bullshitters who insisted on the agendas of their masters. Now, however, there is a chance.

The Great Panic has delivered to the authors lists of people who appear uncorrupted by money or bullshit. We might not like them or agree with them on all things, but we do trust that they are not an immovable part of the problem. We now know personally whom to ask to organise conferences, systems of citizen juries and other institutions. The kernel of renewal is there. For a while it can help engender much broader discussion, inspire new generations and set up new institutions that help safeguard our species against the lure of power and money.

The key innovation we advocate as the spearhead of renewal is the widespread use of citizen juries in the selection of heads of government departments, the funding of truly new schools of scientific thought, and the leadership of independent organisations. The stronger the voice of citizens throughout all public entities in society, the more diversity of thought will be maintained in the system as a whole and the less any small groups can control institutions and the media. That diversity is our best bet next time for discovering the truth quickly and holding on to its lessons. Citizen juries also help to strengthen societies against the power of the new barons who now own much of the world and whose desires dictate so much of our culture.

A major insight from the Great Panic is that a group of people looking in different directions better serves their own collective good than a group in which all are looking the same way. The cliché that everyone should be pulling together, like a rowboat with eight oarsmen, does not apply when big policy decisions have to be made.

In the long run, there are reasons for hope. Humanity as a whole was wealthier and longer-lived than ever before in 2019. Yes, many aspects of our societies and institutions had accumulated rotten elements that were largely unseen in 2019, but a lot of good was happening too. Moreover, the coevolution of institutions and politics has always followed a dialectical dynamic wherein problems brew underneath for a time until a wave of reform sorts them out. The current set of problems is just the set our generation has to deal with. They may seem daunting, but we are comforted by the fact that in the long arc of history, humanity has shown itself to recognise what works well and what does not, and has reliably continued its march forward.

EPILOGUE AND ACKNOWLEDGEMENTS

The three authors had fun writing this book. Each brought a different perspective to the whole, much as it takes different skills to prepare a meal. Paul imagined the recipe, Gigi assembled the ingredients, and Michael did the cooking. Writing the book was our way of engaging with the Jasmines in every country, who were struggling to turn their despair at what was happening into resistance and a search for positive lessons for the future. The whole project and period has given us a community of like-minded thinkers from all over the world. There have been songs and dance, tears and laughter.

Throughout, our hearts have been with those whose lives have been destroyed in the stampede of the Great Panic. While the media, the politicians, and the powerful inside our countries looked away, their policies created hundreds of millions of neglected children, lonely people, and stranded businesses. The gains of the few have caused losses among many. Anger and despair about the enormous costs paid by millions during this time due to decisions made by thousands of powerful people around the world were what motivated us to write this book.

We fear that the pain of the many victims will remain buried from public sight as long as the powerful can manage, but we ourselves at least want to openly recognise the unfairness of what has been done to them. Their schools should not have been closed. Hospitals should not have rejected them. They should not have been locked into their homes. Their businesses should not have been destroyed. They should not have faced the incessant propaganda pouring through media channels. Their rights and freedoms should not have been taken away. They should not have been treated like imbeciles. Our societies should apologise to them for these monumental stupidities. We honour the victims of Covid mania by offering this book about why it all happened, and what is needed to avoid a repeat.

We thank the direct contributors to the various Jasmine stories who were prepared to write their personal experiences in their own words: Carmen, Neil, Ari, and Sanjeev.

We also thank the many in-depth reviewers who gave their time and skills to improve the manuscript by weeding out our mistakes and adding what was missing. Robert Bezimienny, Archie Maclean, Jorg Probst, Anthony Samson (retired scientist extraordinaire) — we owe each of you, at the very least, an excellent bottle of wine.

We are very grateful to Jeffrey Tucker and the nascent Brownstone Institute, our visionary publisher, for taking on this project with amazing drive, speed, and dedication.

We gratefully acknowledge the very useful contributions of research assistants Tom Houlden and Jason Baena-Tan. We also congratulate and thank our illustrator Corrine Edwards for the communicative and uplifting illustrations.

Finally, we thank family and friends for putting up with our book-production obsession for a little while and for their steadfast support over the past 18 months when we have faced public defamation, ridicule, bullying, and calls to be censored. Thanks to Erika, Andrew, Neil, Robert, Sienna, Jasmine, and Carmen.

In spite of what we have witnessed during this period, we remain hopeful for humanity in the long run, and encourage our readers to be hopeful too. Life is wonderful, far too short, and best enjoyed with ample helpings of closeness, freedom, and experimentation.

BIBLIOGRAPHY

ABC. (2020, December 17). Lockdown of Victoria's public housing towers during COVID crisis breached human rights, ombudsman finds. https://www.abc.net.au/news/2020-12-17/lockdown-public-housing-towers-breached-human-rights-ombudsman/12991162

ABC News. (2021, July 23). Lorna Jane fined $5m by Federal Court for false COVID-19 prevention claims about its clothing. https://www.abc.net.au/news/2021-07-23/qld-lorna-jane-fined-5m-false-covid-claims/100318840

Acemoglu, D., Chernozhukov, V., Werning, I., & Whinston, M. D. (2020). A Multi-Risk SIR Model with Optimally Targeted Lockdown. National Bureau of Economic Research, Working Paper 27102. 10.3386/w27102

Alain, C. (2021, June 4). The Lab Leak Theory: Who Suppressed It? Who Uncovered It? And What Should We Do About It? The Daily Sceptic. https://dailysceptic.org/the-lab-leak-theory-who-suppressed-it-who-uncovered-it-and-what-should-we-do-about-it/

Albendín-Iglesias, H., Mira-Bleda, E., Roura-Piloto, A. E., Hernández-Torres, A., Moral-Escudero, E., Fuente-Mora, C., Iborra-Bendicho, A., Moreno-Docón, A., Galera-Peñaranda, C., & García-Vázquez, E. (2020). Usefulness of the epidemiological survey and RT–PCR test in pre-surgical patients for assessing the risk of COVID-19. The Journal of Hospital Infection, 105(4), 773–775. 10.1016/j.jhin.2020.06.009

Aldhous, P. (2014, May 29). We are killing species at 1000 times the natural rate https://www.newscientist.com/article/

dn25645-we-are-killing-species-at-1000-times-the-natural-
rate/#ixzz6x9OYGWjQ. New Scientist.

Alexander, D. (n.d.). How Old is the Average Cruise Passenger?
Cruise 1st. https://www.cruise1st.co.uk/blog/cruise-holidays/
how-old-is-the-average-cruise-passenger/

Alexander, P. (2021, July 23). Covidanity: Australia's new state
religion. The Spectator. https://spectator.com.au/2021/07/
covidanity-australias-new-state-religion/

Almonte, A. M., & Bates, G. (2020, September 8). Corruption
and Coronavirus in Latin America. Corporate Compliance
Insights. https://www.corporatecomplianceinsights.com/
corruption-coronavirus-latin-america-covid/

Alstadsæter, A., Johannesen, N., & Zucman, G. (2019). Tax Evasion and
Inequality. American Economic Review, 109(6), 2073-2103. 10.1257/
aer.20172043

Alvaredo, F., Atkinson, A. B., Piketty, T., & Saez, E. (2013). The top 1 percent in
international and historical perspective. Journal of Economic Perspectives,
27(3), 3-20. 10.1257/jep.27.3.3

Alvaredo, F., Chancel, L., Piketty, T., & Saez, E. (2018). World inequality report
2018 (G. Zucman, Ed.). Belknap Press.

Anderson, P. (2013). Lineages of the Absolutist State (Verso World History
Series). Verso Books.

Anonymous. (2021, March 9). Public sector porkies – 10 years of lying up the
hierarchy. Center for Public Impact. https://www.centreforpublicimpact.org/
insights/public-sector-porkies-10-years-of-lying-up-the-hierarchy

Ariely, G. (2012). Globalisation and the decline of national identity? An
exploration across sixty-three countries. Nations and Nationalism, 18(3),
461-482. 10.1111/j.1469-8129.2011.00532.x

Associated Press. (2020, February 9). Where Did They Go?

Millions Left Wuhan Before Quarantine. VOA News. https://www.voanews.com/science-health/coronavirus-outbreak/where-did-they-go-millions-left-wuhan-quarantine

Associated Press. (2020, May 13). U.S. regulators won't approve Chinese firm's N95 masks, potentially scuttling $1 billion California deal. Market Watch. https://www.marketwatch.com/story/us-regulators-wont-approve-chinese-firms-n95-masks-potentially-scuttling-1-billion-california-deal-2020-05-13

Aum, S., & Shin, Y. (2020, October 22). Why Is the Labor Share Declining? Federal Reserve Bank of St. Louis. https://research.stlouisfed.org/publications/review/2020/10/22/why-is-the-labor-share-declining

Autor, D., Dorn, D., Katz, L. F., Patterson, C., & Van Reenen, J. (2020). The fall of the labor share and the rise of superstar firms. The Quarterly Journal of Economics, 135(2), 645-709. 10.1093/qje/qjaa004

Bangham, G. (2019, June). Game of Homes. Resolution Foundation. https://www.resolutionfoundation.org/app/uploads/2019/06/Game-of-Homes.pdf

Baron, S., Fons, M., & Albrecht, T. (1999). Viral Pathogenesis. In S. Baron (Ed.), Medical Microbiology (4th ed., Chapter 45). Galveston: University of Texas Medical Branch at Galveston.

Bartik, A. W., Bertrand, M., Cullen, Z., Glaeser, E. L., Luca, M., & Stanton, C. (2020). The impact of COVID-19 on small business outcomes and expectations. Proceedings of the National Academy of Sciences, 117(30), 17656-17666. 10.1073/pnas.2006991117

Bar-Yosef, O. (2001). From Sedentary Foragers to Village Hierarchies: The Emergence of Social Institutions. In W. G. Runciman (Ed.), The Origin of Human Social Institutions (Vol. 110, pp. 1-38). Proceedings of the British Academy.

Baxendale, R., Peel, C., & Lunn, S. (2020, April 24). Coronavirus Australia: Health boss changes his tune on return to schoolyards.

The Australian. https://www.theaustralian.com.au/nation/coronavirus-
   health-boss-changes-his-tune-on-return-to-schoolyards/news-story/
   c15c7398c3ab31617c07f2737c752a8a

BBC. (2020, February 17). Coronavirus: Armed robbers steal
   hundreds of toilet rolls in Hong Kong.. https://www.bbc.com/news/
   world-asia-china-51527043

BBC. (2020, February 24). Coronavirus: UK 'well prepared' to deal
   with cases, says government. https://www.bbc.com/news/
   uk-51612039#:~:text=The%20UK%20is%20%22well%20prepared,UK%20
   had%20come%20back%20negative

BBC. (2020, April 20). Timeline: Covid contracts and accusations of
   'chumocracy'. https://www.bbc.com/news/uk-56319927

BBC. (2020, May 6). Coronavirus: Prof Neil Ferguson quits government
   role after 'undermining' lockdown. https://www.bbc.com/news/
   uk-politics-52553229

BBC. (2021, May 4). Covid: Disposable masks pose pollutants risk, study finds.
   https://www.bbc.com/news/uk-wales-56972074

Begley, S. (2020, April 8). With ventilators running out, doctors say the
   machines are overused for Covid-19. Stat. https://www.statnews.
   com/2020/04/08/doctors-say-ventilators-overused-for-covid-19/

Berman, S. (2019). Populism is a symptom rather than a cause: democratic
   disconnect, the decline of the center-left, and the rise of populism in
   Western Europe. Polity, 51(4), 654--667. 10.1086/705378

Biddle, N., Edwards, B., Gray, M., & Sollis, K. (2020, May 7). Hardship,
   distress, and resilience: The initial impacts of COVID-19 in Australia. ANU
   Centre for Social Research and Methods. 10.26193/HLMZNW

Birrel, I. (2021, June 8). Beijing's useful idiots. Unherd. https://unherd.
   com/2021/06/beijings-useful-idiots/

Bishop, M. (2001). The Middle Ages. Mariner Books, Houghton Mifflin.

Blanco-Perez, C., & Brodeur, A. (2020). Publication Bias and Editorial
    Statement on Negative Findings. The Economic Journal, 130(629),
    1226–1247. 10.1093/ej/ueaa011

Bloom, N., Fletcher, R. S., & Yeh, E. (2021). The Impact of COVID-19 on US
    Firms. National Bureau of Economic Research Working Paper, 28314.
    10.3386/w28314

Brumfiel, G., & Wilburn, T. (2020, May 15). Countries Slammed Their Borders
    Shut To Stop Coronavirus. But Is It Doing Any Good? NPR. https://
    www.npr.org/sections/goatsandsoda/2020/05/15/855669867/countries-
    slammed-their-borders-shut-to-stop-coronavirus-but-is-it-doing-any-goo

Bursztynsky, J. (2020, April 29). Zuckerberg warns against reopening public
    spaces too soon. CNBC. https://www.cnbc.com/2020/04/29/facebook-ceo-
    zuckerberg-warns-against-reopening-public-spaces-too-soon.html

Burton, T., & Wootton, H. (2020, July 2). Victoria's COVID-19 infection
    spreads interstate. Financial Review. https://www.afr.com/politics/federal/
    victoria-s-covid-19-infection-spreads-interstate-20200702-p558c4

Butler, B. (2020, March 3). Coronavirus recession? Expert modelling shows
    Australian economy could take huge hit. The Guardian. https://www.
    theguardian.com/world/2020/mar/03/coronavirus-recession-expert-
    modelling-shows-australian-economy-could-take-huge-hit

The Carer. (2021, May 28). Covid Death Rate In Scottish Care
    Homes Higher In Larger Homes. https://thecareruk.com/
    covid-death-rate-in-scottish-care-homes-higher-in-larger-homes/

Carey, A., & Preiss, B. (2020, March 16). Facing 'uncharted waters',
    independent schools close to ward off virus. The Melbourne Age. https://
    www.theage.com.au/national/victoria/independent-schools-close-to-ward-
    off-virus-20200316-p54ai9.html

Centre for Public Impact. (2021, March 9). Public sector porkies – 10 years
    of lying up the hierarchy. https://www.centreforpublicimpact.org/insights/

public-sector-porkies-10-years-of-lying-up-the-hierarchy

Cesur, R., Güneş, P. M., Tekin, E., & Ulker, A. (2017). The value of socialized medicine: The impact of universal primary healthcare provision on mortality rates in Turkey. Journal of Public Economics, 150, 75-93. j.jpubeco.2017.03.007

Chan Kim, Y., Dema, B., & Reyes-Sandoval, A. (2020, April 30). COVID-19 vaccines: breaking record times to first-in-human trials. npj Vaccines, 5, #34. 10.1038/s41541-020-0188-3

Chicago Booth Initiative on Global Markets. (2020, March 27). Policy for the COVID-19 Crisis. Chicago Booth Initiative on Global Markets. https://www. igmchicago.org/surveys/policy-for-the-covid-19-crisis/

Cirera, X., Cruz, M., Davies, E., Grover, A., Iacovone, L., Lopez Cordova, J. E., Medvedev, D., Maduko, F. k., Nayyar, G., Ortega, S. R., & Torres, J. (2021). Policies to Support Businesses through the COVID-19 Shock: A Firm Level Perspective. The World Bank Research Observer, 36(1), 41-66. https://doi.org/10.1093/wbro/lkab001

Clemens, J., & Veuger, S. (2021). Politics and the Distribution of Federal Funds: Evidence from Federal Legislation in Response to COVID-19. NBER Working Paper Series, Working Paper 28875.

Coatsworth, N. (2020, June 21). Deputy Chief Medical Officer press conference about COVID-19 on 21 June 2020. health.gov. https://www. health.gov.au/news/deputy-chief-medical-officer-press-conference-about-covid-19-on-21-june-2020

Collins, D., Gregory, A., Pogrund, G., & Calver, T. (2020, August 9). Tory backers net £180m PPE deals. The Times. https://www.thetimes.co.uk/ article/tory-backers-net-180m-ppe-deals-xwd5kmnqr

Collins, D., Gregory, A., Pogrund, G., & Calver, T. (2020, August 9). Tory backers net £180m PPE deals. The Times. https://www.thetimes.co.uk/ article/tory-backers-net-180m-ppe-deals-xwd5kmnqr

Comptroller and Auditor General. (2020, November 13). Investigation into government procurement during the COVID-19 pandemic. National Audit Office. https://www.nao.org.uk/wp-content/uploads/2020/11/Investigation-into-government-procurement-during-the-COVID-19-pandemic.pdf

Cook, S. (2020, January). Beijing's Global Megaphone. Freedom House. https://freedomhouse.org/report/special-report/2020/beijings-global-megaphone

Darwin, J. (2013). Nationalism and Imperialism, c.1880–1940. In J. Breuilly (Ed.), The Oxford Handbook of the History of Nationalism (Chapter 17). Oxford University Press.

Davey, M., & Hurst, D. (2020, October 19). Daniel Andrews lashes Josh Frydenberg over attack on Victoria's Covid strategy. The Guardian. https://www.theguardian.com/australia-news/2020/oct/19/daniel-andrews-lashes-josh-frydenberg-over-attack-on-victorias-covid-strategy

de Best, R. (2021, 21 May). Coronavirus (COVID-19) deaths worldwide per one million population as of May 21, 2021, by country. Statista. https://www.statista.com/statistics/1104709/coronavirus-deaths-worldwide-per-million-inhabitants/

Delić, A. (2020, May 14). Where a media crisis and a health crisis collide. The Ballot. https://www.theballot.world/articles/where-a-media-crisis-and-a-health-crisis-collide

Delić, A., & Zwitter, M. (2020, April 3). Opaque Coronavirus Procurement Deal Hands Millions to Slovenian Gambling Mogul. Organized Crime and Corruption Reporting Project. https://www.occrp.org/en/coronavirus/opaque-coronavirus-procurement-deal-hands-millions-to-slovenian-gambling-mogul

Department of Health and Social Care, Office for National Statistics, Government Actuary's Department, & Home Office. (2020, December 17). Direct and Indirect Impacts of COVID-19 on Excess Deaths and Morbidity:

November 2020 Update. Gov.uk. https://www.gov.uk/government/
        publications/dhsconsgadho-direct-and-indirect-impacts-of-covid-19-on-
        excess-deaths-and-morbidity-december-2020-update-17-december-2020

Dickens, C. (1843). A Christmas Carol. London: Chapman & Hall.

Doctors for Covid Ethics. (2021, February 28). Urgent Open Letter from
        Doctors and Scientists to the European Medicines Agency regarding
        COVID-19 Vaccine Safety Concerns. Doctors for Covid Ethics. https://
        doctors4covidethics.medium.com/urgent-open-letter-from-doctors-
        and-scientists-to-the-european-medicines-agency-regarding-covid-19-
        f6e17c311595

Dodsworth, L. (2021). A State of Fear: How the UK government weaponised
        fear during the Covid-19 pandemic. Pinter & Martin Ltd.

Dolan, K. A., Wang, J., & Peterson-Withorn, C. (Eds.). (2021). World's
        Billionaire List. Forbes. https://www.forbes.com/billionaires/

Dombey, D. (2021, April 14). Political Polarisation Hampers Spain's
        Pandemic Response. The Financial Times. https://www.ft.com/
        content/8dc8850a-c912-4c0b-bd03-3758fb528698

Dombey, D. (2021, April 14). Political polarisation hampers Spain's pandemic
        response. The Financial Times.

Dong, E., Du, H., & Gardner, L. (2020, February 19). An interactive web-
        based dashboard to track COVID-19 in real time. The Lancet Infectious
        Diseases, 20(5), 533-534. 10.1016/S1473-3099(20)30120-1

Douglas, Y. (2020, April 29). The Costs of Social Isolation: Loneliness and
        COVID-19. Psychiatry Advisor. https://www.psychiatryadvisor.com/home/
        topics/general-psychiatry/costs-of-social-isolation-loneliness-covid19/

Dowlen, O. (2008). The Political Potential of Sortition: A study of the random
        selection of citizens for public office. Exeter: Imprint Academic.

Dreger, C., & Gros, D. (2021). Lockdowns and the US Unemployment Crisis
        [IZA Policy Paper No. 170]. IZA Institute of Labor Economics. http://ftp.iza.

org/pp170.pdf

Duncan, J. M. (2019, October 30). Oppressive Wokeism Needs
to Stop. Joe Dunan (Blog). https://joemduncan.medium.com/
oppressive-wokeism-needs-to-stop-3e0c1283e4f6

The Economist. (2021A, February 2). Global democracy has a very
bad year. https://www.economist.com/graphic-detail/2021/02/02/
global-democracy-has-a-very-bad-year

The Economist. (2021B, May 15). There have been 7m-13m
excess deaths worldwide during the pandemic.
https://www.economist.com/briefing/2021/05/15/
there-have-been-7m-13m-excess-deaths-worldwide-during-the-pandemic

Edgecliffe-Johnson, A., & Gray, A. (2020, December 9). Starbucks chief bullish
as crisis engulfs smaller coffee shops. The Financial Times. https://www.
ft.com/content/ab959c91-7ef2-44d7-bf8c-d03718ae5393

Estcourt, D. (2021, April 15). Watchdog cancels licence of lawyer leading tower
lockdown lawsuit. The Age. https://www.theage.com.au/national/victoria/
legal-watchdog-cancels-licence-of-lawyer-leading-tower-lockdown-lawsuit-
20210415-p57jfo.html

Evening Standard. (2020, September 2). The Londoner: Let children be
exposed to viruses, says Professor Gupta. https://www.standard.co.uk/
news/londoners-diary/the-londoner-let-children-be-exposed-to-viruses-
says-professor-gupta-a4538386.html

ExecPay News. (2021, March 25). 3M Company CEO Michael
Roman's 2020 pay rises 13% to $21M. https://www.execpay.org/
news/3m-co-2020-compensation-934

FDA. (2021, March 24). Letter to Manufacturers of Imported, Non-NIOSH-
Approved Disposable Filtering Facepiece Respirators; Health Care
Personnel; Hospital Purchasing Departments and Distributors; Importers
and Commercial Wholesalers; and Any Other Applicable Stakeholders.

https://www.fda.gov/media/136403/download

FDA. (2021, April 29). Removal Lists of Tests that Should No
    Longer Be Used and/or Distributed for COVID-19: FAQs on
    Testing for SARS-CoV-2. https://www.fda.gov/medical-devices/
    coronavirus-covid-19-and-medical-devices/removal-lists-tests-should-no-
    longer-be-used-andor-distributed-covid-19-faqs-testing-sars-cov-2

Ferguson, J. (2020, August 2). Freedom the first casualty in an anxious
    city. The Australian. https://www.theaustralian.com.au/nation/
    coronavirus-freedom-the-first-casualty-in-an-anxious-city/news-story/
    c7dfd4568e9ebdc3d96123cc6dfadb5c

Ferguson, N., & Al-Khalili, J. (2020, September 22). Neil Ferguson on
    modelling Covid-19. BBC 4. https://www.bbc.co.uk/programmes/
    m000mt0h

Field, M. (2020, April 16). Facebook to warn users who 'liked' fake coronavirus
    claims. The Telegraph. https://www.telegraph.co.uk/technology/2020/04/16/
    facebook-warn-users-exposed-fake-coronavirus-claims/

Field, T. (2010). Touch for socioemotional and physical well-being: A review.
    Developmental Review, 30(4), 367-383. j.dr.2011.01.001

Finley, A. (2021, March 5). Vindication for Ron DeSantis. Wall Street Journal.
    https://www.wsj.com/articles/vindication-for-ron-desantis-11614986751

Flynn, C. F. (2005). An Operational Approach to Long-Duration Mission
    Behavioral Health and Performance Factors. Aviation, space, and
    environmental medicine, 76(6), B42-B51.

Food and Agriculture Organization of The United. (2021, March 23). Acute
    hunger set to soar in over 20 countries, warn FAO and WFP. Food and
    Agriculture Organization of The United States. http://www.fao.org/news/
    story/en/item/1382490/icode/

Food and Agriculture Organization of the United States. (2021, May 6).
    FAO Food Price Index. World Food Situation. http://www.fao.org/

worldfoodsituation/foodpricesindex/en/

Foster, G. (2021, June 28). Stop this Human Sacrifice: The case against
    lockdowns. The Sydney Morning Herald. https://www.smh.com.au/national/stop-
    this-human-sacrifice-the-case-against-lockdowns-20210627-p584o7.html

Foster, G., & Reinhart, C. (2020, March 26). The Economists
    [As the coronavirus marches on, can wartime measures
    save us from a depression?] [Podcast]. ABC. https://
    www.abc.net.au/radionational/programs/the-economists/
    covid-19:can-wartime-measures-save-us-from-depression/12093478

Frijters, P. (2020A, March 18). Has the coronavirus panic cost us at least 10
    million lives already? Club Troppo. https://clubtroppo.com.au/2020/03/18/
    has-the-coronavirus-panic-cost-us-at-least-10-million-lives-already/

Frijters, P. (2020B, March 21). The Corona Dilemma. Club Troppo. https://
    clubtroppo.com.au/2020/03/21/the-corona-dilemma/

Frijters, P. (2020C, June 29). From being to seeming:
    why empirical scientists failed in times of Covid.
    Club Troppo. https://clubtroppo.com.au/2020/06/29/
    from-being-to-seeming-why-empirical-scientists-failed-in-times-of-covid/

Frijters, P. (2020D, December 10). What stock markets tell us about the
    covid-mania. Club Troppo. https://clubtroppo.com.au/2020/12/10/
    what-stock-markets-tell-us-about-the-covid-mania/

Frijters, P. (2021A, January 8). Historical Analogies for the Covid
    Mania. Club Troppo. https://clubtroppo.com.au/2021/01/08/
    historical-analogies-for-the-covid-mania/

Frijters, P. (2021B, February 3). Covid-congestion effects: why are lockdowns
    so deadly? Club Troppo. https://clubtroppo.com.au/2021/02/03/
    covid-congestion-effects-why-are-lockdowns-so-deadly/

Frijters, P. (2021C, March 17). A World Anti-Hysteria
    Organisation? Club Troppo. https://clubtroppo.com.

au/2021/03/17/a-world-anti-hysteria-organisation/

Frijters, P., Clark, A. E., Krekel, C., & Layard, R. (2020). A happy choice:
wellbeing as the goal of government. Behavioural Public Policy, 4(2),
126-165. 10.1017/bpp.2019.39

Frijters, P., & Foster, G. (2013). An Economic Theory of Greed, Love, Groups,
and Networks. Cambridge University Press. 10.1017/CBO9781139207041

Frijters, P., & Krekel, C. (2021). A Handbook for Wellbeing Policy-Making.
Oxford University Press, Oxford.

Gabbat, A. (2021, June 9). Richest 25 Americans reportedly paid 'true tax rate'
of 3.4% as wealth rocketed. The Guardian. https://www.theguardian.com/
business/2021/jun/08/richest-25-americans-jeff-bezos-elon-musk-tax

Gallego, J., Prem, M., & Vargas, J. F. (2020). Corruption in the Times of
Pandemia. Available at SSRN 3600572.

Gallego, J. A., Prem, M., & Vargas, J. F. (2020). Corruption in the Times of
Pandemia. Documentos de Trabajo LACEA 018164, The Latin American
and Caribbean Economic Association - LACEA.

Grafton, Q., Kompas, T., Parslow, J., Glass, K., Banks, E., & Lokuge, K.
(2020). Health and economic effects of COVID-19 control in Australia:
Modelling and quantifying the payoffs of hard versus soft lockdown.
medRxiv. 10.1101/2020.08.31.20185587

Graham, B. S. (2020). Rapid COVID-19 vaccine development. Science,
368(6494), 945-946. 10.1126/science.abb8923

Griffiths, J. (2020, February 17). The coronavirus crisis is raising questions over
China's relationship with the World Health Organization. CNN. https://edition.
cnn.com/2020/02/14/asia/coronavirus-who-china-intl-hnk/index.html

Grimes, K. (2020, May 28). Exclusive: Gov. Newsom's
BYD Mask Deal Profitable for Insider Dealmakers.
California Globe. https://californiaglobe.com/section-2/
exclusive-gov-newsoms-byd-mask-deal-profitable-for-insider-dealmakers/

Guterres, A. (2020, April 23). Secretary-General's remarks to the ECOSOC Forum on Financing Sustainable Development in the Context of COVID-19 [as delivered]. United Nations Secretary General. https://www.un.org/sg/en/content/sg/statement/2020-04-23/secretary-generals-remarks-the-ecosoc-forum-financing-sustainable-development-the-context-of-covid-19-delivered

Hamburger, T., & Eilperin, J. (2020, March 6). Justice Department investigates Blue Flame Medical after claims that it failed to provide masks to Maryland. The Washington Post. https://www.washingtonpost.com/politics/justice-department-investigates-blue-flame-medical-after-claims-it-failed-to-provide-masks-ventilators-to-maryland-california/2020/05/06/e30b5224-8fa1-11ea-9e23-6914ee410a5f_story.html

Hammond, G. P. (2018, December 14). Nationalism and Anti-Nationalism: A Matter of Perception. Political Animal. https://www.politicalanimalmagazine.com/2018/12/14/nationalism-and-anti-nationalism-a-matter-of-perception/

Harding-Smith, R. (2011, August). Media Ownership and Regulation in Australia. Centre for Policy Development Issue Brief. https://cpd.org.au/wp-content/uploads/2011/11/Centre_for_Policy_Development_Issue_Brief.pdf

Haslam, C., & Haslam, A. S. (2012). The social cure: Identity, health and well-being. (J. Jetton, Ed.). Psychology Press.

Haw, D., Forchini, G., Christen, P., Bajaj, S., Hogan, A. B., Winskill, P., Miraldo, M., White, P. J., Ghani, A. C., Ferguson, N. M., Smith, P. C., & Hauck, K. (2020, November 16). Report 35 - COVID-19 How can we keep schools and universities open? Differentiating closures by economic sector to optimize social and economic activity while containing SARS-CoV-2 transmission. Imperial College London. https://www.imperial.ac.uk/mrc-global-infectious-disease-analysis/covid-19/report-35-schools/

Hazan, S., Dave, S., Gunaratne, A. W., Dolai, S., Clancy, R. L., McCullough, P. A., & Borody, T. J. (2021). Effectiveness of Ivermectin-Based Multidrug

Therapy in Severe Hypoxic Ambulatory COVID-19 Patients. medRxiv.
https://doi.org/10.1101/2021.07.06.21259924

Health and Youth Care Inspectorate. (2021, March 25). Fine for doctors
who prescribe hydroxychloroquine or ivermectin for corona. Inspectie
Gezondheidszorg en Jeugd (IGJ). https://www.igj.nl/actueel/
nieuws/2021/03/25/boete-voor-artsen-die-hydroxychloroquine-of-
ivermectine-voorschrijven-tegen-corona

The Health Protection (Coronavirus) Regulations 2020 No. 129. (2020,
February 10). Retrieved April 28, 2020, from https://www.legislation.gov.
uk/uksi/2020/129/contents/made

Heneghan, C., Brassey, J., & Jefferson, T. (2020, April 6). COVID-
19: What proportion are asymptomatic? The Centre for
Evidence-Based Medicine. https://www.cebm.net/covid-19/
covid-19-what-proportion-are-asymptomatic/

History.com Editors. (2019, July 30). The Puritans. https://www.history.com/
topics/colonial-america/puritanismerica/puritanism

Human Rights Watch. (2021, February 11). Covid-19 Triggers Wave of
Free Speech Abuse. Human Rights Watch. https://www.hrw.org/
news/2021/02/11/covid-19-triggers-wave-free-speech-abuse

Human Rights Watch. (2021, May 20). Bangladesh: Arrest of Journalist
Investigating Corruption. https://www.hrw.org/news/2021/05/20/
bangladesh-arrest-journalist-investigating-corruption

Imperial College COVID-19 Response Team. (2020B, October 29). COVID-19
Infection Fatality Ratio Estimates from Seroprevalence. Report 34, 1-18.
10.25561/83545

Imperial College London. (2020A, March 16). Impact of non-pharmaceutical
interventions (NPIs) to reduce COVID-19 mortality and healthcare
demand. Report 9, 1-20. 10.25561/77482

Ingram, D. (1755). An Historical Account of the Several Plagues That Have

Appeared in the World Since the Year 1346. London: printed for R. Baldwin and J. Clark.

Ives, M., & Mandavilli, A. (2020, November 8). The Coronavirus Is Airborne Indoors. Why Are We Still Scrubbing Surfaces? The New York Times. https://www.nytimes.com/2020/11/18/world/asia/covid-cleaning. html?referringSource=articleShare

Jay, J. W. (2019). Inside the World of the Eunuch: A Social History of the Emperor's Servants in Qing China, written by Melissa S. Dale, 2018. NAN NÜ, 21(2), 341-344. https://doi.org/10.1163/15685268-00212P13

Joffe, A. (2021). COVID-19: Rethinking the Lockdown Groupthink. Frontiers in Public Health, 9, 98. fpubh.2021.625778

Johannesen, N., & Zucman, G. (2014). The End of Bank Secrecy? An Evaluation of the G20 Tax Haven Crackdown. American Economic Journal: Economic Policy, 6(1), 65-91. 10.1257/pol.6.1.65

Johns, S. (2020, June 10). Neil Ferguson talks modelling, lockdown and scientific advice with MPs. Imperial College London News. https://www.imperial.ac.uk/news/198155/ neil-ferguson-talks-modelling-lockdown-scientific/

Kaiser, C. F., & Vendrik, M. C.M. (2019). Different versions of the Easterlin Paradox: New evidence for European countries. In M. Rojas (Ed.), The Economics of Happiness (pp. 27-55). Springer, Cham.

Kalleberg, A. L. (2018). Precarious lives: Job insecurity and well-being in rich democracies. John Wiley & Sons.

Kaplan, W. (2017). Why Dissent Matters: Because Some People See Things the Rest of Us Miss. McGill-Queen's University Press. https://www.mqup. ca/why-dissent-matters-products-9780773550704.php

Katz, J. (1996). The Nuremberg Code and the Nuremberg Trial: A Reappraisal. Journal of the American Medical Association, 267(20), 1662-1666. 10.1001/jama.1996.03540200048030

Katz, L. F., & Krueger, A. B. (2019). The rise and nature of alternative work
    arrangements in the United States, 1995-2015. Industrial and Labor
    Relations Review, 72(2), 382-416.

Katz, R. S., & Mair, P. (2018). Democracy and the cartelization of political
    parties. Oxford: Oxford University Press.

Kehoe, J. (2020, March 3). Virus could kill up to 100,000 Australians.
    Australian Financial Review. https://www.afr.com/policy/economy/
    virus-could-kill-up-to-100-000-australians-20200303-p546a0

Kelleberg, A. L. (2018). Precarious Lives: Job Insecurity and Well-Being in Rich
    Democracies. John Wiley & Sons.

Kirsch, S. (2021, May 16). Do the NIH and WHO
    COVID treatment recommendations need to be
    fixed? Trial Site News. https://trialsitenews.com/
    do-the-nih-and-who-covid-treatment-recommendations-need-to-be-fixed/

Knapton, S. (2020, July 19). Lockdown may cost 200,000
    lives, government report shows. The Telegraph.
    https://www.telegraph.co.uk/news/2020/07/19/
    lockdown-may-cost-200k-lives-government-report-shows/

Knoll, C. (2020, March 13). Panicked Shoppers Empty Shelves as Coronavirus
    Anxiety Rises. The New York Times. https://www.nytimes.com/2020/03/13/
    nyregion/coronavirus-panic-buying.html

Kory, P., Meduri, G. u., Varon, J., Iglesias, J., & Marik, P. E. (2021). Review
    of the Emerging Evidence Demonstrating the Efficacy of Ivermectin
    in the Prophylaxis and Treatment of COVID-19. American Journal of
    Therapeutics, 28(3), e299-e318. 10.1097/MJT.0000000000001377

Kotwal, A. A., Holt-Lunstad, J., Newmark, R. L., Cenzer, I., Smith, A. K., &
    Covinsky, K. E. (2021). Social Isolation and Loneliness Among San Francisco
    Bay Area Older Adults During the COVID-19 Shelter-in-Place Orders. Journal
    of the American Geriatrics Society, 69(1), 20-29. 10.1111/jgs.16865

Kucharski, A. J., Russell, T. W., Diamond, C., Liu, Y., Edmunds, J., Funk, S., & Eggo, R. M. (2020). Early dynamics of transmission and control of COVID-19: a mathematical modelling study. The Lancet Infectious Diseases, 20(5), 553-558. 10.1016/S1473-3099(20)30144-4

Laguipo, A. B. (2020, October 9). 86 percent of the UK's COVID-19 patients have no symptoms. News Medical. https://www.news-medical.net/medical/authors/angela-betsaida-laguipo

Lally, M. T. (2021, July 27). The Costs and Benefits of Covid-19 Lockdowns in New Zealand. MedRxiv: The preprint server for health sciences. https://doi.org/10.1101/2021.07.15.21260606

The Lancet. (2020). COVID-19: too little, too late? Mar 7, 2020, 395(10226), 755. 10.1016/S0140-6736(20)30522-5. https://www.thelancet.com/article/S0140-6736(20)30522-5/fulltext

Landis-Hanley, J. (2020, June 29). Victorians may now be told to wear face masks to halt Covid-19 – what's changed? The Guardian. https://www.theguardian.com/australia-news/2020/jun/29/victorians-may-now-be-told-to-wear-face-masks-to-halt-covid-19-whats-changed

Lasch, C. (1996). The Revolt of the Elites and the Betrayal of Democracy. New York: W. W. Norton Company.

Ledeneva, A. V. (Ed.). (2018). Global Encyclopaedia of Informality, Volume 1: Towards Understanding of Social and Cultural Complexity. London: UCL Press.

Lee, J. (2020). Mental health effects of school closures during COVID-19. The Lancet Child & Adolescent Health, 4(6), P421. 10.1016/S2352-4642(20)30109-7

Leung, B., Hargreaves, A. L., Greenberg, D. A., McGill, B., Dornelas, M., & Freeman, R. (2020). Clustered versus catastrophic global vertebrate declines. Nature, 588, 267–271. 10.1038/s41586-020-2920-6

Liang, W., Gu, X., Li, X., Zhang, K., Wu, K., Pang, M., Dong, J., Merrill, H. R., Hu, T., Liu, K., Shao, Z., & Yang, H. (2018). Mapping the epidemic

changes and risks of hemorrhagic fever with renal syndrome in
Shaanxi Province, China, 2005–2016. Scientific Reports, 8(1). 10.1038/
s41598-017-18819-4

Lind, M. (2020). The New Class War: Saving Democracy from the Managerial
Elite. Portfolio.

Lopes, H., Lagoa, S., & Calapez, T. (2014). Declining autonomy at work in the
EU and its effect on civic behavior. Economic and Industrial Democracy,
35(2), 341-366. 10.1177/0143831X13484606

Machiavelli, N. (1995). The Prince (1513). In S. J. Milner (Ed.), The Prince and
other Political Writings. London: J. M. Dent.

Mackay, C. (1841). Extraordinary Popular Delusions and the Madness of
Crowds. London: George Routledge & Sons.

Magness, P. W. (20120, October 15). The Fake Signature Canard.
American Institute for Economic Research. https://www.aier.org/article/
the-fake-signature-canard/

Major, L. E., Eyles, A., & Machin, S. (2021, February). Unequal learning and
labour market losses in the crisis: consequences for social mobility. Centre
for Economic Performance, CEP Discussion Paper No. 1748, 1-36.

Mansfield, K. E., Mathur, R., Tazare, J., Henderson, A. D., Mulick, A. R.,
Carreira, H., Matthews, A. A., Bidulka, P., Gayle, A., Forbes, H., Cook,
S., Wong, A. Y. S., Strongman, H., Wing, K., Warren-Gash, C., Cadogan,
S. L., Smeeth, L., Hayes, J. F., Quint, J. K., … Langan, S. M. (2021).
Indirect acute effects of the COVID-19 pandemic on physical and mental
health in the UK: a population-based study. The Lancet, 3(4), E217-E230.
S2589-7500(21)00017-0

Martin, W. F., & Mentel, M. (2010). The Origin of Mitochondria. Nature
Education, 3(9), 58. https://www.nature.com/scitable/topicpage/
the-origin-of-mitochondria-14232356/

Mazumdaru, S. (2020, April 14). What influence does China

have over the WHO? DW. https://www.dw.com/en/
what-influence-does-china-have-over-the-who/a-53161220

McGreevy, R. (2021, April 5). Outdoor transmission accounts for 0.1% of
State's Covid-19 cases. Irish Times. https://www.irishtimes.com/news/
ireland/irish-news/outdoor-transmission-accounts-for-0-1-of-state-s-covid-
19-cases-1.4529036

McSwane, J. D. (2020, June 1). The Secret, Absurd World of
Coronavirus Mask Traders and Middlemen Trying To Get Rich Off
Government Money. ProPublica. https://www.propublica.org/article/
the-secret-absurd-world-of-coronavirus-mask-traders-and-middlemen-
trying-to-get-rich-off-government-money

Mehta, P. (2021, July 5). Big Tech's Censors Come for
Science. Jacobin. https://www.jacobinmag.com/2021/05/
big-tech-censorship-science-covid-19-debate

Merck. (2021, February 4). Merck Statement on Ivermectin use
During the COVID-19 Pandemic. https://www.merck.com/news/
merck-statement-on-ivermectin-use-during-the-covid-19-pandemic/

Migration Data Portal. (2021, March 10). Migration data relevant for
the COVID-19 pandemic. https://migrationdataportal.org/themes/
migration-data-relevant-covid-19-pandemic

Molinski, M. (2021, 8 January). Coronavirus May Be The Tipping Point In New
York And California Exodus. Investors. https://www.investors.com/news/
california-exodus-new-york-flight-coronavirus-may-be-tipping-point/

Moloney, W. (2020, April 13). Coronavirus is accelerating the advance of
nationalism over globalization. The Hill. https://thehill.com/opinion/
international/492253-coronavirus-is-accelerating-the-advance-of-
nationalism-over

Montenegro Almonte, A., & Bates, G. (2020, September 8). Corruption
and Coronavirus in Latin America. Corporate Compliance

Insights. https://www.corporatecomplianceinsights.com/
corruption-coronavirus-latin-america-covid/

Motoh, H. (2020, May 6). Slovenia social briefing: Purchases of
medical equipment, related corruption suspicions and the public
response. China-CEE Institute. https://china-cee.eu/2020/05/06/
slovenia-social-briefing-purchases-of-medical-equipment-related-
corruption-suspicions-and-the-public-response/

Mouzo, J., Estaire, Ó., De Blase, E. G., & Urra, S. (2021, May 11).
Coronavirus: Spain is '100 days away from group immunity,' says PM. El
Pais. https://english.elpais.com/society/2021-05-10/coronavirus-spain-is-
100-days-away-from-group-immunity-says-pm.html

Muller, C. P. (2021). Do asymptomatic carriers of SARS-COV-2 transmit the
virus? The Lancet, 4. j.lanepe.2021.100082

Muller, S. M. (2021). The dangers of performative scientism as the alternative
to anti-scientific policymaking: A critical, preliminary assessment of South
Africa's Covid-19 response and its consequences. World Development,
140, 105290. j.worlddev.2020.105290

Multiple Authors. (2017, October 25). 230 Law and Economics Professors
Urge President Trump to Remove Investor-State Dispute Settlement
(ISDS) From NAFTA and Other Pacts. https://www.citizen.org/wp-content/
uploads/migration/case_documents/isds-law-economics-professors-letter-
oct-2017_2.pdf

Murray, A. (2020, February 22). Covid Has Been Contained in Australia - No
Evidence of Any Possibility of Contagion in the Community. News.com.
au. https://www.news.com.au/national/covid-19-has-been-contained-in-
australia-no-evidence-of-any-possibility-of-contagion-in-the-community/
video/381b5022a4f35bfa02f36d62b353d161

National Institute of Allergy and Infectious Diseases. (2014, December 11).
Smallpox. National Institute of Allergy and Infectious Diseases. https://

www.niaid.nih.gov/diseases-conditions/smallpox

Niemiec, E. (2020, November 5). COVID-19 and misinformation. EMBO reports, 21(11), e51420. 10.15252/embr.202051420

9News. (2020, July 13). Coronavirus: Victoria crisis threatens to derail economic recovery, warns treasurer. https://www.9news.com.au/national/coronavirus-economic-recovery-threatened-by-victoria-surge-in-cases-josh-frydenberg-warns/fa80f8de-22fa-4ddb-8e87-533ef12aa0cf

Norman, J., Bar-Yam, Y., & Nicholas Taleb, N. (2020). Systemic Risk of Pandemic via Novel Pathogens – Coronavirus: A Note. New England Complex Systems Institute. https://jwnorman.com/wp-content/uploads/2020/03/Systemic_Risk_of_Pandemic_via_Novel_Path.pdf

Nuwer, R. (2020, June 18). Why the world needs viruses to function. BBC. https://www.bbc.com/future/article/20200617-what-if-all-viruses-disappeared

Nyakarahuka, L., Kankya, C., Krontveit, R., Mayer, B., Mwiine, F. N., Lutwama, J., & Skjerve, E. (2016). How severe and prevalent are Ebola and Marburg viruses? A systematic review and meta-analysis of the case fatality rates and seroprevalence. BMC Infectious Diseases, 16(1). https://doi.org/10.1186/s12879-016-2045-6

Office for National Statistics. (2021, February 4). Data collection changes due to the pandemic and their impact on estimating personal well-being. https://www.ons.gov.uk/peoplepopulationandcommunity/wellbeing/methodologies/datacollectionchangesduetothepandemicandtheirimpacton-estimatingpersonalwellbeing

Orwell, G. (1949). Nineteen Eighty-Four. Secker & Warburg.

Oxfam. (2019, January). Public Good or Private Wealth? Oxfam. https://indepth.oxfam.org.uk/public-good-private-wealth/

Palaszczuk, A. (2020, March 24). Border Control Slows Virus Spread.

Queensland Government. https://statements.qld.gov.au/statements/89585

Panovska-Griffiths, J. (2020, April 4). Coronavirus: we've had 'Imperial', 'Oxford' and many more models – but none can have all the answers. The Conversation. https://theconversation.com/coronavirus-weve-had-imperial-oxford-and-many-more-models-but-none-can-have-all-the-answers-135137/

Pavlov, I. P. (1927). Conditioned reflexes: an investigation of the physiological activity of the cerebral cortex. Oxford University Press: Oxford.

Pearce, F. (2015, August 17). Global Extinction Rates: Why Do Estimates Vary So Wildly? Yale Environment 360. https://e360.yale.edu/features/global_extinction_rates_why_do_estimates_vary_so_wildly

Perper, R. (2020, April 24). China is injecting millions into WHO as the US cuts funds. Experts say Beijing is trying to boost its influence over the agency and its 'deeply compromised' chief. Business Insider Australia. https://www.businessinsider.com.au/china-who-multimillion-dollar-contribution-political-power-move-2020-4?r=US&IR=T

Petherick, A., Kira, B., Cameron-Blake, E., Tatlow, H., Hallas, L., Hale, T., Phillips, T., Zhang, Y., Webster, S., Anania, J., Ellen, L., Majumdar, S., Goldszmidt, R., Boby, T., Angrist, N., Luciano, M., Nagesh, R., & Wood, A. (2021, June 11). Variation in Government Responses to COVID-19. Blavatnik School Working Paper, (WP-2020/032).

Pistor, K. (2019). The Code of Capital: How the Law Creates Wealth and Inequality. Princeton: Princeton University Press.

Porter Wright. (2020, April 29). Importing masks and respirators from overseas during COVID-19 under FDA's relaxed rules. Porter Wright. https://www.porterwright.com/media/importing-masks-and-respirators-from-overseas-during-covid-19-under-fdas-relaxed-rules/

PWC. (2020). Australia Rebooted. https://www.pwc.com.au/important-problems/australia-rebooted.pdf

Qiu, L., & Bouchard, M. (2020, March 5). Tracking Trump's Claims on the
      Threat From Coronavirus. The New York Times. https://www.nytimes.
      com/2020/03/05/us/politics/trump-coronavirus-fact-check.html

Rajgor, D. D., Har Lee, M., Archuleta, S., Bagdasarian, N., & Chye
      Quek, S. (2020). The many estimates of the COVID-19 case fatality
      rate. The Lancet Infectious Diseases, 20(7), 776-777. 10.1016/
      S1473-3099(20)30244-9

Raynor, G. (2021, May 14). Use of fear to control behaviour
      in Covid crisis was 'totalitarian', admit scientists. The
      Telegraph. https://www.telegraph.co.uk/news/2021/05/14/
      scientists-admit-totalitarian-use-fear-control-behaviour-covid/

Read, S. (2020, November 18). Covid spending: Watchdog finds MPs' contacts
      were given priority. BBC. https://www.bbc.com/news/business-54978460

Reporters Without Borders. (2020). 2020 World Press Freedom Rankings.
      https://rsf.org/en/ranking/2020

Richie, H., & Roser, M. (2019, February). Causes of Death. Our World in Data.
      https://ourworldindata.org/causes-of-death

Richie, H., & Roser, M. (2019, September). Age Structure. Our World in Data.
      https://ourworldindata.org/age-structure

Rocha, R. (2020, June 22). What countries did right and wrong in
      responding to the pandemic. CBC. https://www.cbc.ca/news/canada/
      covid-19-coronavirus-pandemic-countries-response-1.5617898

Rodini, E. (n.d.). The sultan's true face? Gentile Bellini, Mehmet II, and the
      values of verisimilitude. The Turk and Islam in the Western Eye, 1450–
      1750: Visual Imagery before Orientalism, 21-40.

Roper, M. (2020, April 2). Governor of the Cayman Islands encourages
      residents to stay home to save lives. Gov.uk. https://www.gov.uk/
      government/news/governor-of-the-cayman-islands-encourages-residents-
      to-stay-home-to-save-lives

Rose-Ackerman, S. (2021). Corruption and COVID-19. EUNOMÍA. Revista en Cultura de la Legalidad, 20, 16-36.

Rosenhall, L. (2020, May 5). Exclusive: California wires mask dealer half a billion dollars, then claws it back. Cal Matters. https://calmatters.org/health/coronavirus/2020/05/california-mask-deal-blue-flame-collapsed-republican-vendor-maryland-porter-gula-thomas/

Rosenhall, L., & Morain, D. (2020, April 13). Amid pandemic, Newsom faces scrutiny over $1B face-mask deal. Cal Matters. https://calmatters.org/health/coronavirus/2020/04/california-coronavirus-face-masks-gavin-newsom-byd/

Rossen, L. M., Branum, A. M., Ahmad, F. B., Sutton, P., & Anderson, R. N. (2020, October 20). Excess Deaths Associated with COVID-19, by Age and Race and Ethnicity — United States, January 26–October 3, 2020. Center for Disease Control and Prevention. https://www.cdc.gov/mmwr/volumes/69/wr/mm6942e2.htm

Rowthorn, R., & Maciejowski, J. (2020). A cost–benefit analysis of the COVID-19 disease. Oxford Review of Economic Policy, graa030. 10.1093/oxrep/graa030

Rudolph, C. W., Allan, B., Clark, M., Hertel, G., Hirschi, A., Kunze, F., Shockley, K., Shoss, M., Sonnentag, S., & Zacher, H. (2021). Pandemics: Implications for research and practice in industrial and organizational psychology. Industrial and Organizational Psychology, 14(1-2), 1-35. 10.1017/iop.2020.48

Ryan, A. (2021, June 16). A Cost–Benefit Analysis of the COVID-19 Lockdown in Ireland. 10.2139/ssrn.3872861

Sagar, M. (2020, March 11). How Drones are Assisting Government in China Fight COVID-19. Open Gov. https://opengovasia.com/how-drones-are-assisting-government-in-china-fight-covid-19/

Sakkal, P., & Fowler, M. (2020, February 4). Hand sanitiser price doubles, face

mask shortage amid coronavirus panic. The Age. https://www.theage.com.
au/national/victoria/hand-sanitiser-price-doubles-face-mask-shortage-
amid-coronavirus-panic-20200203-p53xfm.html

Salman, J., Penzenstadler, N., & Le, D. (2020, July 23). Rookie middlemen
muddle the government's effort to buy coronavirus supplies. USA Today.
https://www.usatoday.com/in-depth/news/investigations/2020/07/23/covid-
ppe-face-mask-shortage-draws-new-companies-us-contracts/5459884002/

Sample, I. (2018, January 15). What is gene editing and how
can it be used to rewrite the code of life? The Guardian.
https://www.theguardian.com/science/2018/jan/15/
gene-editing-and-what-it-really-means-to-rewrite-the-code-of-life

Sandbu, M. (2020, April 7). Economists are united in support of the
coronavirus lockdown. The Financial Times. https://www.ft.com/content/
e593e7d4-b82a-4bf9-8497-426eee43bcbc

Scheidel, W. (2018). The great leveler: Violence and the history of inequality
from the stone age to the twenty-first century. Princeton University Press.

Schnirring, L. (2021, January 11). China releases genetic data on new
coronavirus, now deadly. Center for Infectious Disease Research
and Policy. https://www.cidrap.umn.edu/news-perspective/2020/01/
china-releases-genetic-data-new-coronavirus-now-deadly

Sharma, R. (2021, May 14). The billionaire boom: how the super-rich
soaked up Covid cash. The Financial Times. https://www.ft.com/
content/747a76dd-f018-4d0d-a9f3-4069bf2f5a93

Shi Lee, W., Wheatley, A. K., Kent, S. J., & DeKosky, B. J. (2020). Antibody-
dependent enhancement and SARS-CoV-2 vaccines and therapies.
Nature Microbiology, 5, 1185–1191. s41564-020-00789-5

Sibieta, L. (2021, February 1). The crisis in lost learning calls for a massive
national policy response. Institute for Fiscal Studies. https://www.ifs.org.
uk/publications/15291

Sidley, G. (2021, March 8). Masks – do benefits outweigh the harms? HART.
   https://www.hartgroup.org/masks/

Singer, P. (2021, May 10). Keeping Discussion Free. Project Syndicate. https://
   www.project-syndicate.org/commentary/pseudonyms-to-uphold-open-
   intellectual-discourse-by-peter-singer-2021-05

Sky News. (2020, May 4). Coronavirus: Tanzania testing kits questioned
   after goat and papaya test positive. https://news.sky.com/story/
   coronavirus-tanzania-testing-kits-questioned-after-goat-and-papaya-test-
   positive-11982864

Smaldone, W. (2020). European socialism: a concise history with documents.
   Rowman & Littlefield: London.

Smith, T. (2020, March 24). Health bosses warn THOUSANDS of Australians
   could die in one state alone in a worst-case coronavirus scenario. Daily Mail.
   https://www.dailymail.co.uk/news/article-8145453/Health-bosses-warn-
   THOUSANDS-Australians-die-worst-case-scenario-amid-coronavirus.html

Sørensen, E., & Torfing, J. (2019). Towards robust hybrid democracy in
   Scandinavian municipalities? Scandinavian Political Studies, 42(1), 25-49.
   10.1111/1467-9477.12134

Souris, M., Tshilolo, L., Parzy, D., Kamgaing, R., Mbongi, D., Phoba, B.,
   Tshilolo, M.-A., Mbungu, R., Morand, P., & Gonzalez, J.-P. (n.d.). Pre-
   pandemic SARS-CoV-2 potential natural immunity among population
   of the Democratic Republic of Congo. medRxiv 2021.04.28.21256243.
   10.1101/2021.04.28.21256243

STA. (2020, May 5). Ministry Cancels Controversial Ventilator Delivery Contract
   with Geneplanet. Total Slovenia News. https://www.total-slovenia-news.
   com/politics/6171-ministry-cancels-controversial-ventilator-delivery-
   contract-with-geneplanet

Statistica. (2020, September 4). Cumulative number of coronavirus-positive
   (COVID-19) patients confirmed on Diamond Princess cruise ship docked

in Japan as of April 16, 2020. Statistica. https://www.statista.com/ statistics/1099517/japan-coronavirus-patients-diamond-princess/

Stroup, J. S. (2020, December 26). The 1920s Consensus on Prohibition . . . How Wilson Persecuted the Hutterites . . . American Indian Warriors. Jane Takes on History. https://janetakesonhistory.org/2020/12/26/ the-1920s-consensus-on-prohibition-how-wilson-persecuted-the-hutterites-american-indian-warriors/#more-2331

Sutton, B. (2020, March 16). How you can stay safe. Herald Sun.

Swiss Policy Research. (2021A, May). On the Treatment of Covid-19. https:// swprs.org/on-the-treatment-of-covid-19/

Swiss Policy Research. (2021C, June). Post covid syndrome: Frequency, causes and treatment options. https://swprs.org/ post-acute-covid-long-covid/

Swiss Policy Research. (2021B, June). The Trouble with PCR Tests. https:// swprs.org/the-trouble-with-pcr-tests/

Swiss Policy Research. (2021D, July 25). The Ivermectin Debate. https:// swprs.org/the-ivermectin-debate/

Swiss Policy Research. (2021E, August). Are Face Masks Effective? The Evidence. https://swprs.org/face-masks-evidence/

Táíwò, O. O. (2020, April 3). Corporations Are Salivating Over the Coronavirus Pandemic. The New Republic. https://newrepublic.com/article/157159/ corporations-salivating-coronavirus-pandemic

Taleb, N. N., & Bar-Yam, Y. (2020, March 25). The UK's coronavirus policy may sound scientific. It isn't. The Guardian. https:// www.theguardian.com/commentisfree/2020/mar/25/ uk-coronavirus-policy-scientific-dominic-cummings

Tanfani, J., & Horwitz, J. (2020, April 1). Special Report: The Mask Middlemen - How pop-up brokers seek big paydays in a frenzied market. Reuters. https://www.reuters.com/article/

us-health-coronavirus-masks-specialrepor-idUSKBN21I32E

Taubenberger, J. K., & Morens, D. M. (2006). 1918 Influenza: the mother of
all pandemics. Emerging Infectious Diseases, 12(1), 15-22. 10.3201/
eid1201.050979

Thacker, P. D. (2021). Covid-19: How independent were the US and British
vaccine advisory committees? BMJ, 373, n1283. 10.1136/bmj.n1283

Thompson, D. (2020, July 27). Hygiene Theater Is a Huge Waste of Time.
The Atlantic. https://www.theatlantic.com/ideas/archive/2020/07/
scourge-hygiene-theater/614599/

3M Government Affairs. (2021, January 27). Helping Protect Lives, Save
Global Economies by Applying 3M's Lessons Learned During the
COVID-19 Pandemic. https://multimedia.3m.com/mws/media/1954744O/
white-paper-covid-19-policy-recommendations.pdf

Threlkeld, S. (1997). Democratizing public institutions: juries for the selection
of public officials. Humanist in Canada, 120, 24-25.

Tiku, N., & Greene, J. (2021, March 12). The billionaire boom. The Washington
Post. https://www.washingtonpost.com/technology/2021/03/12/
musk-bezos-zuckerberg-gates-pandemic-profits/

Time For Recovery. (2020). Fear. https://timeforrecovery.org/fear/

Tindale, L. C., Stockdale, J. E., Coombe, M., Garlock, E. S., Lau, W. Y. V., Saraswat,
M., Zhang, L., Chen, D., & Wallinga, J. (2020). Evidence for transmission of
COVID-19 prior to symptom onset. eLife, 9, e57149. 10.7554/eLife.57149

Tørsløv, T., Wier, L., & Zucman, G. (2020, April 22). The Missing Profits of
Nations. Missing Profits. https://missingprofits.world/

Transparency International. (2020, September 24). COVID-19: Documented
corruption and malfeasance cases. https://images.transparencycdn.org/
images/COVID-19-Documented-corruption-and-malfeasance-cases.pdf

Tucker, J. A. (2020). Liberty or Lockdown. American Institute for Economic Research.

Tucker, J. A. (2020A, January 27). Must Government Save Us from the

Coronavirus? American Institute for Economic Research. https://www.aier.
org/article/must-government-save-us-from-the-coronavirus/

Tucker, J. A. (2020B, December 11). The "Expert Consensus" Also Favored
Alcohol Prohibition. American institute for Economic Research. https://
www.aier.org/article/the-expert-consensus-also-favored-alcohol-prohibition/

Tucker, J. A. (2021, June 16). Lock Down Policies Reflect Ruling-Class
Privilege. Brownstone Institute. https://brownstone.org/articles/
lock-down-policies-reflect-ruling-class-privilege/

Tufekci, Z. (2021, May 7). Why Did It Take So Long to Accept the Facts About
Covid? The New York Times. https://www.nytimes.com/2021/05/07/
opinion/coronavirus-airborne-transmission.html

UK Behavioural Scientists. (n.d.). Open letter to the UK Government regarding
COVID-19. https://sites.google.com/view/covidopenletter/home

UN General Assembly. (2020, December 4). Amid Threat of Catastrophic
Global Famine, COVID-19 Response Must Prioritize Food Security,
Humanitarian Needs, Experts Tell General Assembly. United Nations.
https://www.un.org/press/en/2020/ga12294.doc.htm

UNICEF. (2020, November 19). UNICEF calls for averting a lost generation
as COVID-19 threatens to cause irreversible harm to children's
education, nutrition and well-being. UNICEF. https://www.unicef.
org/press-releases/unicef-calls-averting-lost-generation-covid-19-
threatens-cause-irreversible-harm

United Nations. (2021, April 16). Soaring food prices, conflicts driving hunger,
rise across West and Central Africa: WFP. UN News. https://news.un.org/
en/story/2021/04/1089982

Vaitilingam, R. (2020, April 6). European economic policy for the
COVID-19 crisis: Views of leading economists on lockdowns,
Coronabonds and the ECB's role. Vox. https://voxeu.org/article/
european-economic-policy-covid-19-crisis-igm-forum-survey

Vizard, T., Sadler, K., Ford, T., Newlove-Delgado, T., McManus, S., Marcheselli, F., Davis, J., Williams, T., Leach, C., Mandalia, D., & Cartwright, C. (2020, October 22). Mental Health of Children and Young People in England, 2020. NHS. https://files.digital.nhs.uk/AF/AECD6B/mhcyp_2020_rep_v2.pdf

Walker, W. A. (2017). The importance of appropriate initial bacterial colonization of the intestine in newborn, child, and adult health. Pediatric Research, 82, 387-395. pr.2017.111

Ward, H. (2020, April 15). We scientists said lock down. But UK politicians refused to listen. The Guardian. https://www.theguardian.com/commentisfree/2020/apr/15/uk-government-coronavirus-science-who-advice

webfact. (2021, 25 May). Amazing Thailand: Drones spraying alcohol deployed to help fight COVID-19. Asean Now. https://aseannow.com/topic/1218262-amazing-thailand-drones-spraying-alcohol-deployed-to-help-fight-covid-19/

WebFX. (n.d.). The 6 Companies That Own (Almost) All Media. https://www.webfx.com/blog/internet/the-6-companies-that-own-almost-all-media-infographic/

Wheeler, M. (2013). Celebrity Politics. Cambridge: Polity Press.

The World Bank. (2021, May 21). Food Security and COVID-19.. https://www.worldbank.org/en/topic/agriculture/brief/food-security-and-covid-19

World Health Organization. (2019). Non-pharmaceutical public health measures for mitigating the risk and impact of epidemic and pandemic influenza. https://apps.who.int/iris/bitstream/handle/10665/329438/9789241516839-eng.pdf?ua=1

World Health Organization. (2020D, October 5). The impact of COVID-19 on mental, neurological and substance use services.. https://www.who.int/publications/i/item/978924012455

World Health Organization. (2020A, October 12). Coronavirus disease

(COVID-19). World Health Organization Newsroom. https://www.who.int/
news-room/q-a-detail/coronavirus-disease-covid-19

World Health Organization. (2020B, October 14). Tuberculosis. World Health
Organization Newsroom. https://www.who.int/news-room/fact-sheets/
detail/tuberculosis

World Health Organization. (2020C, December 3). SARS-CoV-2 mink-
associated variant strain – Denmark.. https://www.who.int/csr/
don/03-december-2020-mink-associated-sars-cov2-denmark/en/

World Health Organization. (2021, February 5). Cholera. World Health
Organization Newsroom. https://www.who.int/news-room/fact-sheets/detail/
cholera

Wright, R. E. (2021, May 27). Dismisinfoganda. American Institute for Economic
Research. https://www.aier.org/article/dismisinfoganda/

Wu, J. T., Leung, K., & Leung, G. M. (2020). Nowcasting and forecasting the
potential domestic and international spread of the 2019-nCoV outbreak
originating in Wuhan, China: a modelling study. The Lancet, 395(10225),
689-697. 10.1016/S0140-6736(20)30260-9

Wuth, R. (2020, February 22). Virus has been contained in Australia. The
Australian.

WWF. (n.d.). How Many Species are We Losing? https://wwf.panda.org/
discover/our_focus/biodiversity/biodiversity/

Yong, E. (2013, May 20). Viruses in the gut protect from
infection. Nature. https://www.nature.com/news/
viruses-in-the-gut-protect-from-infection-1.13023

Zhou, H. (2012). Dragon Totem in Chinese Culture and Traditions. China and
the World Cultural Exchange.

Zimmer, C. (2017, October 4). Ancient Viruses Are Buried in Your DNA. The
New York Times. https://www.nytimes.com/2017/10/04/science/ancient-
viruses-dna-genome.html

ABOUT THE AUTHORS

Paul Frijters is a Professor of Wellbeing Economics at the London School of Economics: from 2016 through November 2019 at the Center for Economic Performance, thereafter at the Department of Social Policy. He completed his Masters in Econometrics at the University of Groningen, including a seven-month stay in Durban, South Africa, before completing a PhD through the University of Amsterdam. He has also engaged in teaching and research at the University of Melbourne, the Australian National University, Queensland University of Technology, the University of Queensland, and now the LSE. Professor Fritjers specializes in applied microeconometrics, including labor, happiness, and health economics, though he has also worked on pure theoretical topics in macro and micro fields. His main area of interest is in analyzing how socio-economic variables affect the human life experience and the "unanswerable" economic mysteries in life. Professor Frijters is a prominent research economist and has published over 150 papers in fields including unemployment policy, discrimination and economic development.

pfrijtersecon@gmail.com

Gigi Foster is a Professor with the School of Economics at the University of New South Wales, having joined UNSW in 2009 after six years at the University of South Australia. Formally educated at Yale University (BA in Ethics, Politics, and Economics) and the University of Maryland (PhD in Economics), she works in diverse fields including education, social influence, corruption, lab experiments, time use, behavioural economics, and Australian policy. Her research regularly informs public debates and appears in both specialized and cross-disciplinary outlets (e.g., *Quantitative Economics, Journal of Economic Behavior and Organization, Human Relations)*. Her teaching, featuring strategic innovation and integration with research, was awarded a 2017 Australian Awards for University Teaching (AAUT) Citation for Outstanding Contributions to Student Learning. Named 2019 Young Economist of the Year by the Economic Society of Australia, Professor Foster has filled numerous roles of service to the profession and engages heavily on economic matters with the Australian community. Her regular media appearances include co-hosting The Economists, a national economics talk-radio program and podcast series now in its fifth season, with Peter Martin AM on the Australian Broadcasting Corporation's Radio National.

gigi.foster@unsw.edu.au

Michael Baker has a BA (Economics) from the University of Western Australia. He is an independent economic consultant and freelance journalist with a background in policy research. He worked in the 1990s as a policy analyst with the Committee for Economic Development, a New York-based think tank that researched environmental policy, the federal budget and the retirement funding system, among other issues. After moving back to his native Australia in the early 2000s he launched his own consulting business specialising in commercial property economics, consumer demographics and retail. His clients spread across the globe, including Australia, the US, UAE, China and India. In addition to advisory work, he has written frequently for business and trade publications in Australia, the US and Asia. One of his specialties is translating academic research into language comprehensible to the layperson.

mbakerconsult@gmail.com

ABOUT BROWNSTONE INSTITUTE

The Brownstone Institute, established May 2021, is a publisher and research institute that places the highest value on the voluntary interaction of individuals and groups while minimizing the use of violence and force including that which is exercised by public authority.

INDEX

Made in the USA
Columbia, SC
03 November 2021

48193873R00245